Teaching music

The Open University Postgraduate Certificate of Education

The readers in the PGCE series are:

Thinking Through Primary Practice

Teaching and Learning in the Primary School

Teaching and Learning in the Secondary School

Teaching English

Teaching Mathematics

Teaching Science

Teaching Technology

Teaching Modern Languages

Teaching History

Teaching Music

All of these readers are part of an integrated teaching system; the selection is therefore related to other material available to students and is designed to evoke critical understanding. Opinions expressed are not necessarily those of the course team or of the University.

If you would like to study this course and receive a PGCE prospectus and other information about programmes of professional development in education, please write to the Central Enquiry Service, PO Box 200, The Open University, Walton Hall, Milton Keynes, MK7 6YZ. A copy of *Studying with the Open University* is available from the same address.

Teaching music

Edited by Gary Spruce
at The Open University

ROUTLEDGE

London and New York
in association with
The Open University

First published 1996
by Routledge
11 New Fetter Lane, London EC4P 4EE

Simultaneously published in the USA and Canada
by Routledge
29 West 35th Street, New York 10001

Selection and editorial matter: © 1996 The Open University

Typeset in Garamond by J&L Composition Ltd, Filey, North Yorkshire
Printed and bound in Great Britain by Biddles Ltd, Guildford and King's Lynn.

British Library Cataloguing in Publication Data
A catalogue record for this book is available from the British Library

Library of Congress Cataloguing in Publication Data
A catalogue record for this book has been requested

ISBN 0-415-13367-X

Contents

Foreword

The form of teacher education is one of the most debated educational issues of the day. How is the curriculum of teacher education, particularly initial, pre-service education to be defined? What is the appropriate balance between practical school experience and the academic study to support such practice? What skills and competence can be expected of a newly qualified teacher? How are these skills formulated and assessed and in what ways are they integrated into an ongoing programme of professional development?

These issues have been at the heart of the development and planning of the Open University's programme of initial teacher training and education – the Postgraduate Certificate of Education (PGCE). Each course within the programme uses a combination of technologies, some of which are well tried and tested, while others, on information technology for example, may represent new and innovatory approaches to teaching. All, however, contribute in an integrated way towards fulfilling the aims and purposes of the course and programme.

All of the PGCE courses have readers which bring together a range of articles, extracts from books, and reports that discuss key ideas and issues, including specially commissioned chapters. The readers also provide a resource that can be used to support a range of teaching and learning in other types and structures of course.

This series from Routledge, in supporting the Open University PGCE programme, provides a contemporary view of developments in primary and secondary education and across a range of specialist subject areas. Its primary aim is to provide insights and analysis for those participating in initial education and training. Much of its content, however, will also be relevant to ongoing programmes of personal and institutional professional development. Each book is designed to provide an integral part of that basis of knowledge that we would expect of both new and experienced teachers.

Bob Moon
Professor of Education, The Open University

Introduction
Ways of thinking about music

Gary Spruce

Music education has undergone a remarkable transformation in recent years. Lessons which were once dominated by passive listening and the didactic imparting of information, are now characterized by the involvement of children in performing, composing and *related* listening and appraising. Children now learn about music through actively engaging with it.

It would be wrong, however, to suggest that these changes were effected easily or that they were at once universally accepted. Despite various curriculum initiatives – particularly *Music in the Secondary School Curriculum* (Paynter 1982) and the HMI report *Music from 5–16* (DES 1985) – there was resistance to change. This resistance tended to emanate from those teachers who felt uneasy with the new practical approach to music teaching and who were unwilling to compromise on what they perceived as the 'academic' content of the subject. They believed that the academic aspect of music was what gave it comparable status with the core elements of the curriculum and thus its *raison d'être*. Writing in 1986, Hargreaves (Chapter 3 in this volume) bemoaned the fact that 'many teachers still emphasize the academic formal aspects of music rather than its intuitive creative aspects, and may thus be putting the cart before the horse'. Also, the practical, creative approach to music education required teachers to adopt radically new teaching methods which some were unwilling to do. Examination boards, which could have led the way towards the bright new dawn, opted instead to try to be all things to all men, by offering, until recently, two distinct GCSE syllabuses: one that emphasized a practical, creative approach and another that reflected the old 'O' level. Therefore, although many music teachers immediately adopted the curriculum initiatives of *Music from 5–16* and *Music in the Secondary School Curriculum*, it was only with the implementation of the National Curriculum that children gained an *entitlement* to experiencing music through practical and creative involvement with it.

Part I of this book – 'Music education in context' – therefore considers the changes that have taken place in music education over the last fifty years. Bernarr Rainbow considers developments in music education from the Butler Act of 1944 through to the mid-1980s, while Keith Swanwick looks at the state of British music education immediately prior to the introduction of the National Curriculum and discusses the implications of the National Curriculum for music teaching. Both chapters are invaluable not only for what they have to say about the nature of music education but also as contemporary records of some of the more crucial developments in music education during the second half of the twentieth century.

Central to the role of music educators is an understanding of how children learn. Therefore, Part II – 'Teaching and learning in music' – looks at the process of learning in music from a number of perspectives. In Chapter 3 David Hargreaves begins by discussing the increasingly important role of music psychology in understanding the processes of musical learning. He considers the various aspects of psychology – cognitive, developmental and behavioural – and relates them specifically to music education.

Following on from this, in Chapter 4 Margaret Barrett discusses a recurring theme in this book: the somewhat contentious issue as to whether – either on a semiotic level or as a learning model – parallels can be drawn between music and language. In proposing a model for music learning based upon an analysis of language acquisition, she defines six stages in the learning process – immersion, demonstration, engagement, expectations, responsibility, approximation, use and response – and relates them specifically to music education.

Irrespective of the learning model adopted, one of the main aims of music teaching must be the fostering of children's imagination. However, a number of issues proceed from this: 'How do we recognize musical imagination in children?'; 'Why do we frequently fail to encourage and celebrate musical imagination in children the same way as we do their creativity in art and writing?'; 'How do we react as individuals and society to manifestations of creative imagination in children and adults?'; 'Do we agree what imagination and creativity actually are?'. These questions are addressed by Robert Walker in Chapter 5. Drawing on musical examples from many different styles and cultures, he questions accepted ideas about the nature of musical creativity – particularly as it applies to children's compositions – and argues against the language acquisition model put forward in Chapter 4 as a basis for music education.

Having sought a definition of what is meant by creativity, in Chapter 6 Peter Webster discusses the characteristics of creativity by concentrating upon creative thinking as a *process*. In doing so he offers a potential teaching model for the development of creative thinking as well as suggesting what one of the main aims of music education might be.

Conceptual understanding, craftsmanship and aesthetic sensitivity obviously grow with age and experience, but transfer of these abilities into the mosaic of creative thinking does not often occur naturally. This transfer might well be an important goal of formal music education.

Until recently, an unevenness of music provision in the primary sector made the creation of a coherent 5–16 music curriculum problematical. The requirements of the National Curriculum now provide for a basic minimum musical entitlement for all children at Key Stages 1 and 2. A report by OFSTED into the first year of the National Curriculum (Music) indicates that many secondary school music teachers need to be more aware of the music curriculum in the primary phase and of the standards being achieved. This has led to an 'underestimation of the pupil's abilities and skills' during the first part of the autumn term of Year 7 and the setting of 'tasks lacking in challenge so that the pupils could not show the same standard of achievement . . . as in the primary schools from which they were drawn'. In Chapter 8, Janet Mills, a music HMI, discusses the musical development of children during the primary phase describing what many experience and the level of attainment that might be expected of them.

Part III of this book – 'Issues in music education' – is concerned with those things which, while not being specific to music education, particularly impact upon it. In Chapter 9 Lucy Green demonstrates that the preconceived notions that pupils and teachers have concerning the relationship between gender and musical tastes and practices are not an inherent part of music itself, but are the result of historical tradition and social expectations which are 're-enacted daily in the life of the music classroom as a microcosm of a wider society'. She argues that such gender stereotyping must be challenged, first by direct, musical confrontation and second, by an awareness 'of the complexity and depth-embeddedness of gendered music meanings, not only of our educational structures but also in our musical experience'.

Chapter 10 deals with aspects of music and special needs. Yvonne Packer:

> highlights the difficulties relating to the provision of music education in schools for the emotionally and behaviourally disturbed – formerly labelled maladjusted. Often considered unteachable within junior and secondary schools, such children are assigned to EBD schools or units where they seem to fall between two stools of mainstream and special education, unable to reap the benefits of either. The case is argued for the inclusion of music within a programme of therapeutic education based on the writer's research within these schools, and recommendations are made as to how the music may be made more accessible within this context.
>
> (Packer, 1989)

Teachers' professional lives are so controlled by the national condition of education that they frequently fail to consider the possibility of an international perspective on what they do. In Chapter 11, Janet Hoskyns looks at the nature of music education and relates it to the notion of a European dimension. She discusses the difficulties implicit in such a model and proposes strategies for overcoming them, concluding that: 'it is our duty to ensure that music education remains on the agenda and that the European dimension includes wider access to music for all Europeans'.

It is also of great importance that pupils experience music which goes beyond their own cultural perspective – that they are able to engage with music 'from different times and places, applying knowledge to their own work' (National Curriculum 1995 para. 4e). It is therefore crucial that music educators are able to relate confidently to music that is not from the western cultural tradition. It is also important that the teaching of such music should not be merely symbolic, tokenist or compartmentalized as part of 'multi-cultural' education, but should be part of what Robert Kwami (1993) describes as an inter-cultural music curriculum. In Chapter 12, Jonathan Stock argues that commonly accepted definitions of what music is are often unsatisfactory in a consideration of world music. In a discussion which again draws parallels between music and language, he shows that those musical characteristics that we associate with certain emotions are not universally held. Furthermore, he challenges the notion of valuing music in terms of western ideas of development and complexity (i.e. the kind of view which describes folk music as 'primitive' and considers all music in the context of a stage in music's development towards a pinnacle represented by Western 'high art'). Turning for a second time to the relationship between music and language, he analyses those things which he sees as being common to most musical cultures and which could provide a starting point for the teaching of world music. Throughout the chapter he provides examples of classroom activities which support the concepts under discussion.

Assessment lies at the heart of teaching. As Keith Swanwick (1979) says, 'to teach is to assess'. It is therefore of critical importance that the role of assessment is clearly defined and issues relating to assessment are clarified. In Chapter 13, Gary Spruce considers assessment in the arts from the perspective of the nature and function of objectivity. He looks at the relationship between the arts and the sciences and concludes with a discussion of the principles that might underpin the formulation of an effective assessment model for the arts.

Accountability is one of the key words in education. Teachers are accountable to parents, politicians, governing bodies, head teachers and to a number of outside agencies. It is therefore perhaps easy to forget that we are also accountable to the children whom we teach concerning the nature of the education that they receive. Ironically, it is often their opinion which is least often sought. Part IV – 'Music education and the classroom' – therefore begins with a record of an interview with an upper sixth student about his experience of twelve years of music education (Chapter 14).

Classroom management is one of the foremost concerns of any new teacher, and rightly so. It is particularly vital in a subject like music that basic classroom management skills are developed as quickly and as effectively as possible. Much has been written from a generalist point of view on this aspect of teaching (for example, McMannus (1994) and Wragg (1994)) and these are highly recommended. Nevertheless, music teaching makes classroom management demands of a unique and high order, and therefore I have included an article by Margaret Merrion (Chapter 15) which deals specifically with this aspect of music teaching.

Although many teachers are eager to develop their understanding of technology there are fears concerning its implications for their role as music teachers and its impact on classroom management. For an inexperienced teacher, unfamiliar technology can seem to be simply one more variable in an already tense situation. Furthermore, technology is something that students are often at greater ease with than is the teacher. It is, however, a vital part of the music educator's armoury, often reaching those members of the class that other aspects of the music curriculum fail to reach. It opens up new vistas of creativity for music teachers and students alike and cannot be ignored. Kirk Kassner (Chapter 16) recognizes the fears that music educators have about technology and discusses them in a sympathetic and positive way. This is then followed in Chapter 17 by an illustration by Sam Reese of the potential applications of technology to the classroom situation, looking at how MIDI (Musical Instrument Digital Interface) can be used to support the teaching of composition.

The increase in composing and performing as classroom activities has inevitably marginalized the acquisition of listening skills. This is a pity. For, as Philip Priest argues in Chapter 18, developed aural skills are basic to any fostering of musical experiences and understanding. He considers that the ability to have an aural vision of an intended musical outcome is essential to composition, performance and, particularly, improvisation and he is critical of the fact that an undue concentration on music literacy by music teachers has militated against the development of such skills.

Developed aural skills are frequently found in exponents of those musics which attach more importance to constant reinterpretation through performer intervention than to the manufacture of a definitive version: jazz, pop, folk music and many non-western musics fall into this category. In Chapter 19 Peter Dunbar-Hall demonstrates two different ways of considering the nature of music and then applies these to the processes involved in designing a teaching model for pop music.

Chapters 18 and 19 both touch upon the role of improvisation in the classroom. Improvisation can be perceived as something of a soft option:

as an activity not governed by the criteria usually applied to the evaluation of musical skills, a kind of anarchic free-for-all. Yet, as John Stevens, a practising improviser says (Chapter 20), improvising is a skill and the starting point for improvisation in the classroom is the personal development by the teacher of this skill. He argues that the way to learn improvisation is as 'exemplified by the Indian method' through interaction with an already skilled exponent of the art.

The final two chapters of this book are by Keith Swanwick. In the first he looks at instrumental teaching and in the second – 'Music education and research' – he compares different research methodologies, discusses research evaluation and relates both to music education and the music teacher. He demonstrates that the best research has beneficial effects not only for the researcher's own professional performance, but also allows the wider professional community to plan for the demands of the future.

REFERENCES

DES (1985) *Music from 5–16*, London: HMSO.

Kwami, R. (1993) 'Music Education in Britain and the School Curriculum: A Point of View', *International Journal of Music Education* 21: 25–39.

McManus, M. (1994) 'Managing Classes', in B. Moon and A. Shelton Mayes (eds) *Teaching and Learning in the Secondary School*, London: Routledge.

Ofsted (1993) *Music Key Stages 1, 2 and 3. First Year*, 1992–93, London: HMSO.

Packer, Y. (1989) 'Abstract from *Music with Emotionally Disturbed Children*' *British Journal of Music Education* 6(1):

Paynter, J. (1982) *Music in the Secondary School Curriculum*, Cambridge: Cambridge University Press.

Swanwick, K. (1979) *A Basis for Music Education*, Windsor: NFER.

Wragg, E. (1994) *An Introduction to Classroom Observation*, London: Routledge.

Part I

Music education in context

Chapter 1

Onward from Butler
School music 1945–1985

Bernarr Rainbow

The present tripartite system of education in this country with its stages of Primary, Secondary and Further Education was brought about by the Butler Act of 1944 which implemented the findings of the McNair Report and thus incidentally strengthened the place of music in general education. Music teaching in schools was quickly expanded as a result and has since undergone a further series of revolutions often influenced by social and political circumstances rather than purely musical considerations. The concurrent and similarly prompted shift of values which took place in young people's ideals, sense of independence and general behaviour during the 1960s further sharpened the atmosphere of change. This year's anniversary of the passing of the Butler Act presents a symbolic occasion for reviewing some of the events which have so radically altered the pattern of school music teaching during the past forty years.

THE EDUCATION AND TRAINING OF TEACHERS

Anticipating the need for additional teachers due to the introduction of tripartite education, the McNair Report made careful recommendations with different disciplines in mind. The shortage of music teachers would at first be most pronounced in the secondary schools for boys, where the subject had traditionally been neglected. As a first step, headmasters were advised to recruit new staff from among local private teachers and church organists; thereafter, in addition to the universities and music colleges, new or expanded music departments in teacher training colleges would eventually supply a generation of specialist teachers. At the same time the whole question of 'educating' rather than 'training' non-graduate teachers was placed under review. Earlier attitudes toward teacher training were criticized as doing little more than offering 'tips for teachers' without continuing the student's education appreciably beyond the elementary stage.

To remedy that deficiency students in training colleges were required in future to select a 'main study', followed for their own personal advancement, and not necessarily as the subject which they chose to teach. On the pedagogical side the general policy was to encourage teaching skill by the systematic study of 'Principles of Education' and supervised teaching practice, rather than by a demonstration of teaching methods in the lecture room.

As far as the majority of subjects in the school curriculum are concerned, grasp of subject matter coupled with reasonable competence in planned verbal exposition enables the young teacher to survive in the classroom: but however adequate that equipment may prove for teaching English, history, mathematics or geography, for example, additional resources are essential to teachers of music – practical experience and understanding of how to develop such basic techniques as singing and aural perception must precede success in teaching them to children.

Yet in the struggle to attain academic respectability prompted by the new concept of 'teacher education', music syllabuses during the post-war era commonly imitated the theoretical content characteristic of earlier university courses. As a result, would-be teachers who lacked the levels of musicianship to earn a university place received a watered-down version of a university course rather than one designed to develop the practical skills essential to successful work in schools. Instead of being taught choral techniques students learned to analyse fugues; before learning to hear a melody from the page they were asked to harmonize it; and though largely unfamiliar with classroom repertoire their attention was first drawn to Haydn's string quartets. Ideally, of course, both aspects of musical experience should have been made theirs but limitations of lecture time and the reaction against 'tips for teachers' saw to it that priority was given to 'academic' music, consideration of classroom needs coming a very poor second and being seen as an inferior appendix rather than an integral part of the course. This attitude was further hardened with the eventual introduction of graduate courses for the B.Ed.

Entrants to teaching from the universities and colleges of music were not at first required to undergo training for teaching. The possession of a degree or a 'recognized' diploma was accepted as an adequate initial qualification. An attempt on the part of the colleges of music to introduce a graduate diploma incorporating methodology was found not to produce satisfactory teachers and soon abandoned. It was replaced by a voluntary scheme which took diploma-holders to one of the few training colleges selected by the Ministry of Education's inspectors to run a special one-year course in Education, Teaching Preparation and Practice, leading to the award of a teaching certificate. This procedure was later made compulsory for entrants from the music colleges.

University graduates in music were not obliged to undergo professional training for teaching until very recently. Those who chose to might enrol for training at one of the selected training colleges – though some opted to attend a general postgraduate course in a university department. Only when the patent disadvantage of allowing music teachers to be trained in general courses which made no provision for their special needs was later realized were postgraduate courses exclusively designed for music teachers established at the Universities of Reading and London. Even so, many music graduates continued to enrol for general postgraduate training which left them ill-equipped for the realities of the classroom.

Fortunately, the naturally talented among those entering the teaching profession soon overcame such limitations, and whether from training college, music college, or university, most elected to teach in secondary schools. In the wider range of schools for boys and girls over the age of eleven, opportunities now arose to pursue higher levels of musical achievement. Existing Grammar Schools for boys or High Schools for girls which were fortunate enough to have a capable musician on their staff were soon undertaking ambitious performances with choirs and orchestras, backed by soundly organized sixth-form music courses. And although academic standards were necessarily lower in the new Secondary Modern Schools, experience soon showed that under inspiring teaching very satisfactory (and rewarding) levels of musical performance were attainable by children not otherwise much given to shine. Yet in both types of secondary school it was in the classroom that the limitations of the existing system of music in general education were frequently revealed.

It proved virtually impossible in secondary schools generally for teachers to avoid starting music lessons from scratch if they meant to tackle the subject seriously. With each new intake of children the disparity between those who came from primary schools where music was taught competently and those from others where it was neglected or taught badly was regularly emphasized. It seemed difficult to avoid the conclusion that since there was no commonly accepted standard as to what could or should be achieved in the primary school, continuity of teaching throughout the child's school career was simply unattainable. Discussion always revealed the general conviction that it was during the formative years in the primary school that basic musical skills and perceptions were best cultivated. But circumstances in primary schools, staffed as they were by general class teachers rather than specialists, presented problems of organization and teacher training to which answers had not been found – and which remain unresolved to this day.

In the early days of teacher training in this country (midway through the nineteenth century) it was taken for granted that every elementary school teacher should teach singing, and initial training consequently included instruction in approved methods of learning to read music and sing from notes. In spite of changes in the choice of methods approved for the purpose this remained the state of affairs until the 1920s, by which time our elementary schools had gained an international reputation for the ability of their pupils to sing at sight.

Disregarding, for the time being, the question as to whether learning to sing at sight is a desirable pursuit or not, but acknowledging that standards of teaching it varied considerably among elementary teachers depending upon ability and enthusiasm, it seems evident that the state of music in the elementary schools of the 1920s demonstrated what can be achieved in spite of individual limitations, when modest aims are set and those aims are made clear to the teachers concerned. The same might be said, after all, about most of the subjects in the junior school curriculum.

But this argument was not allowed to influence policy when the pattern of post-war training for general class teachers was decided. It was argued instead that the potential content of the junior school curriculum had grown to such an extent that teachers should not be called upon to teach in all areas; and that since music was a subject best taught by those with a liking for it, it should be made an optional choice in the training college syllabus. One unforeseen result of this decision was that most of the students choosing to engage in an optional music course were those who had already learned to play an instrument from childhood and who consequently entertained certain misconceptions about the learning process in music. Almost more unfortunate was the impression created in the child's mind that since music was not taught (like other junior school subjects) by every class teacher there was something 'peculiar' about it; and that if a favourite teacher didn't seem to care for music there was no reason for her pupils to do so either.

A further complication, which particularly affected secondary teaching but also impinged on the primary school, was the amazing growth of the music curriculum during the post-war decades. What had been an exclusively song-based activity in the nineteenth century now offered a multiplicity of possible opportunities involving instrumental music-making, guided listening, interpretational movement and creative work. This development, which demands closer examination, made the choice of classroom musical activities much more dependent upon the teachers' own individual enthusiasms, and the adoption of an authorized core curriculum for the primary school less than congenial in the liberalized atmosphere of the post-war era.

THE BROADENING MUSIC CURRICULUM

Innovations which widened the scope of music teaching in our schools began to appear quite early in the present century, but since they were confined to independent schools and spread only slowly even there, the Musical Appreciation movement, Dalcroze Eurhythmics, the use of the gramophone in the classroom and infants' percussion bands made little impact in state schools before the 1930s. By then, however, listening to music had become a domestic pastime through the advent of gramophone and radio. Although in many households the music broadcast received little conscious attention, the 'Foundations of Music' talks given by Walford Davies became a surprisingly popular feature among middle-class listeners. The climate of public response to music was gradually changing, and with it attitudes to music in schools began to change, too.

Emphasis began to shift from vocally-based activity to instrumental work with the introduction of the bamboo pipe followed by the recorder during the 1930s. The move was hailed, and with some justification, as adding purpose to music lessons by providing an end product for theory. Elsewhere attention turned from singing to listening to recorded music. This innovation in turn was applauded as a realistic preparation for future enjoyment. In both cases older children whose early music lessons had been adequate and whose grasp of basic musical essentials was sound were able to benefit from the new element of variety in their later lessons. But without that foundation, at the hands of less competent teachers, both types of activity invited misuse of limited lesson time. The Board of Education found it advisable to warn teachers not to regard the new activities as *alternatives* but as *adjuncts* to former methods. That warning was in a sense prophetic – for the immense variety of alternative musical activities introduced in schools since the Butler Act has led to a situation in which hardly any two secondary schools have a concordant policy, while such basic skills as singing and aural training are quite neglected in a very high proportion of our primary schools.

Although the outbreak of war in 1939 seriously affected the day-to-day running of schools, planning for post-war development continued, and contrary to what might be supposed, the war years were to see further growth in popular response to music – a circumstance aided by the creation of a national Council for the Encouragement of Music and the Arts, later to become the present Arts Council. The first post-war decade was dominated by austerity, but special resources were made available for building houses and schools. To begin with only the bare essentials of the Butler Act were implemented, but during the 1950s the number of pupils remaining at school until the age of seventeen rose to double that of the pre-war total. Most of the schools which they attended were now better equipped to teach music and had begun to introduce wider activities with resources hitherto found only in independent schools.

At the same time social and technological advances were boosting average weekly incomes which rose by 34 per cent between 1955 and 1960. Ten years later they had risen by 130 per cent. The 'Affluent Society' symbolized by a car, a washing machine and a television set to every household had arrived. With it came the creation of a new consumer society from within the formerly underprivileged (and their children), whose unprecedented purchasing power now made them a tempting target for predatory commercialism. This development helps to explain the rise of the 'pop' music phenomenon, supported as it was by the prodigious growth of recording sales among young people in the 1960s. Calculated populism encouraged triviality, and following the pattern of teenagers in the United States their counterparts on this side of the Atlantic soon adopted the deliberately non-intellectual repertoire provided for them, as a badge of identity.

To begin with, the attitude of the bulk of teachers toward their pupils' odd musical preferences was no different from that of their predecessors. Although not dignified as is now the case by such pretentious labels as 'youth culture' or 'popular culture' a type of popular song formerly regarded as merely vulgar had always existed. Under the influence of Arthur Somervell, HM Inspector of Music at the beginning of the century, and Cecil Sharp, the folk-song revivalist, teachers had accepted that an important part of their task was to wean their pupils away from 'the raucous notes of coarse music-hall songs'. The same attitude had been adopted following the advent of the 'crooner'. The pop-singer seemed to present an identical problem and to merit the same treatment. But then experience with growing numbers of secondary pupils revealed that young people were able to compartmentalize their musical response – finding satisfaction from both 'pop' and 'serious' music. Only with the birth of the 'generation gap' and the adoption of leaders of the pop scene as cult figures, did the true scale of the problem confronting music teachers in schools reveal itself.

Meanwhile attention turned to new opportunities of extending classroom musical activity. Rumour had it that the German composer, Carl Orff, had revolutionized music lessons in his homeland simply by introducing new pitched percussion instruments with detachable tone-bars to suit different levels of ability. Cheaper versions of his glockenspiels and xylophones were promptly marketed in this country together with simple performing scores imitating his originals. Classrooms everywhere began to echo with the clink and bong of metal and wood. Many teachers felt they had found a simpler and more enjoyable way of developing musical literacy. But when authentic English versions of Orff 's *Schulwerk* were later published they revealed that instrumental work provided only a part of his programme, and was designed to complement carefully developed basic aural and vocal skills. Yet for every teacher who examined Orff 's instructions books there were hundreds with only secondhand acquaintance with his methods. By this time, however, the vogue for pseudo-Orff was too well established, backed by wide commercial support, to halt the decline which had taken place in the development of aural skills and class singing.

The teachers who joined the rush to adopt classroom instruments were not simpletons; an instrumental stance appealed to them particularly because most were themselves instrumentalists – mainly pianists – and their own mental approach to the interpretation of musical notation was instrumentally based. During their early lessons they had learnt to 'find' a note on a keyboard rather than to 'hear' it in their heads after identifying the symbol concerned on the page. Even those of them who could play at sight confidently, commonly lacked the ability to sing quite a simple tune from the page. More to the point, as we have seen, during their training as teachers the deficiency had not been corrected and the paradox which explained it had not been thoroughly exposed.

This was a time, too, when instrumental activity had begun to dominate school music exclusively. As developing secondary schools flexed their muscles, the creation of a school orchestra became a common goal and the employment of peripatetic instrumental teachers the essential means to that end. The appointment (which now seems unconventional) of a former leading orchestral player to the post of HM Inspector of Music in Schools served to strengthen what was a growing trend. With the creation of the first three comprehensive schools by the Labour-controlled London County Council in 1955, the large number of pupils enrolled increased both the range of choice for membership of an orchestra and the *per capita* financial grant to provide the necessary instruments and tuition. As more comprehensive schools were created during the 1960s, each school often catering for more than a thousand pupils of mixed ability, music blossomed in them as an extra-curricular activity just as evidently as it declined in effectiveness and popularity as a classroom discipline.

The truth of this situation failed to secure public attention. Scarce references to school music in the press largely consisted of self-congratulatory accounts of performances by school orchestras or the often admittedly excellent youth orchestras which they fed. But the children concerned had been selected for their talent and given special coaching to reach such standards; far from typifying the wellbeing of music in schools these exceptional pupils served rather to emphasize the poverty of the rest – whose unenthusiastic response to their music lessons in the secondary school can readily be traced to an awareness of their own musical incompetence. Lacking the basic skills best taught at an early age but all too often neglected in our primary schools, the musically untalented pupil quickly lost interest in a teacher's efforts to build upon foundations that were simply not there. Also, given the special place that music of a particular sort occupied in the adolescent's lifestyle, active rebellion of a vigour spared to teachers of other subjects was regularly aroused during and after the 1960s.

As a result of this stalemate music's renown as an all-embracing educational force seemed subject to direct challenge in secondary schools. Some thought it should survive there only as an optional subject. Others suggested that radical revision of the music curriculum itself was necessary to meet changed circumstances. There were, needless to say, many rival theories as to the desirable content of future music lessons – ranging from egalitarian pressures in support of populism to equally extreme avant garde calls to outlaw the diatonic scale. Each school of thought had its followers and the current assumption was that salvation lay only in novelty; but partisan interest and support centred particularly around three policies.

The first was based on the argument that it was a mistake to try to educate children to respond to music which, it was claimed, had been written for the edification of an upper-class audience – a 'cultural elite'. Instead, teachers should aim at strengthening the sub-culture presently enjoyed by their pupils, first entering and then coming to terms with it themselves. Efforts to bring the cultural heritage of the past to the children of the present were unlikely to succeed and were, it was said, of doubtful educational value. The 'broad mass of people' did not respond to the heritage of the past, according to radical opinion.

Where this policy was implemented – (notably in inner-city areas) – musical appreciation lessons were dropped, and the song repertoire shifted away from former tradition by introducing songs of the very type that Somervell and Sharp had condemned. To identify the stratum of sub-culture common to all pupils in the wide range of a comprehensive school obviously meant selecting the lowest. And so the process of 'levelling-down', already familiar in other schemes of social engineering, began its debasing progress in the unlikely field of music teaching.

The second proposal was an off-shoot of the first. The requisite sub-culture selected here for investigation and development was the 'pop' music so favoured among young people of school age. The declared aim was to heighten discrimination within the sub-culture itself, as well as to develop a wider response to music generally. Supporters of this policy included many young teachers whose limited knowledge of the background of pop found them poorly placed to teach its devotees – who in turn resented this incompetent invasion of their preserve. Hence the aims of this revisionist policy were seldom realized. Then, otherwise capable and enthusiastic teachers became disenchanted as pop's obvious associations with drug abuse and youthful revolt became inescapable, making serious attempts at criticism and assessment less than realistic. Few teachers were equipped to deal with problems of this magnitude and complexity.

A third alternative syllabus sought to apply the currently favoured technique of 'creativity' to the music lesson. Even if confident that a child was as able to experiment with sound in the music lesson as with design and colour in the art lesson, teachers had hitherto been brought to a halt by their pupil's inability to record in standard notation the sound patterns he could easily invent. With the adoption of graphic musical notation by avant garde composers a way of overcoming this handicap presented itself; and through their spontaneous use of sound without trying to ape the formal structures of earlier music, children's efforts even acquired a 'contemporary' quality. After George Self 's pioneering work in this vein at a London school, other influential teachers adopted what came to be known as 'Experimental Music in Schools.'

The new technique, so adventurous in concept compared with traditional methods, attracted many young teachers who started creative work with their classes. However, an element essential to success in this activity was an ability on the teacher's part to guide and sustain positive criticism of children's efforts in performance and this attribute, owing to a combination of immaturity and limited acquaintance with contemporary music, proved to be sadly beyond the reach of many of the teachers concerned. Moreover, since the new activity made a virtue of musical illiteracy, an already strong movement to abandon teaching the use of standard notation received further impetus.

In pursuit of spontaneity a generation of schoolchildren had already grown up without skills which had previously been regarded as essential in elementary education. Theories that children should not be pestered to learn to spell, write grammatically or learn multiplication tables later found a musical counterpart in arguments against teaching the use of notation. Its opponents reinforced their position by remarking that sight-singing had first been added to the school curriculum largely in order to improve congregational singing in churches. That policy was clearly no longer justifiable, and the time given to the exercise should now be devoted to other 'more enjoyable' musical activities. In spite of the weakness of their case, advocates of child-centred education were aware that fashion supported them; and encouraged by this apparently erudite and historically sound argument unsuccessful teachers of sight-singing were glad to abandon the pursuit.

Tonic Sol-fa, the standby of elementary teachers at the beginning of the century, had never gained wholehearted support from the instrumentally biased teachers who succeeded them. Sol-fa syllables did not help a pianist to find his notes, and the letter-notation designed to help beginners was seen as an old-fashioned expedient which had outlived its usefulness. The first English announcement, early in the 1960s, of Kodály's Method and its successful application in the schools of Hungary aroused a stir of interest – but without revealing to teachers generally that the inspiration of Kodály's achievement lay in their own neglected Tonic Sol-fa. And while a limited number introduced the Kodály Method in their schools, news of Carl Orff 's *Schulwerk* with its instrumental bias – also first circulating at this time – attracted much greater interest and support from the new generation of teachers. It was widely felt that instrumental activity in the classroom satisfactorily replaced sight-singing, making the use of Tonic Sol-fa unnecessary. It was generally abandoned.

Another casualty to current iconoclasm was class singing itself. Former high standards of school singing now earned scornful rejection as being artificially reminiscent of the cathedral chorister – that outmoded elitist.

Already sadly undermined by the introduction of rowdy songs into the repertoire and perhaps even more seriously assailed by the deliberately unformed voices modelled by pop-idols, voice training finally disappeared from most schools. Gruff low-pitched voices producing either an ugly uproar or a husky mutter now regularly went unchecked in junior class-rooms, while older pupils sulkily refused to sing at all.

During the 1970s the wheel turned full circle as former children who had received this impaired musical education themselves became teachers. To the existing problems of the junior school was now added the class teacher who had never learned to sing and who believed that children's voices should not use the upper register. This opinion was echoed in research documents which claimed that (judging by existing standards in schools) all previous theories and experience touching children's singing voices were mistaken, and that the true compass was in the contralto range. At a stroke the entire repertoire of treble songs drawn from the past four centuries was consigned to the dustbin. All told, the future looked far from bright.

THE AFTERMATH

It is not unusual to find the phenomenal growth of new teaching methods which has taken place since the 1950s described as an 'Explosion'. Like other explosions this one has emphatically produced its roll of casualties. But however serious that consequence may have been it is not just what was *destroyed* that gives rise to misgiving in this case: there seems as much cause for concern in the very prodigality of what has been *created*. Although methods and resources have expanded to an unprecedented extent, the allotment for music on the school timetable remains much what it was a century ago; and this means that instead of producing a general broadening of the music curriculum, the range of alternative procedures presented to teachers has left them to decide what to include and what to omit in the time available.

While there is much to be said for enabling individual teachers to bring to their pupils the benefits of their own preferences and enthusiasms, this can only become a satisfactory general policy where a basic core syllabus exists – at least at primary school level. But this, as we have seen, is something entirely lacking as things stand. As a result, indiscriminate growth in the upper reaches of the syllabus has meant fragmentation of effort and a situation where no two secondary schools teach the same range of musical activities. The position of a pupil transferred from one school to another is thus an unenviable one. At the same time the absence of continuity in musical education between Primary and Secondary levels results in failure to realize music's intellectual and educational potential. And the child's own musical experience and sensibility are left to depend less on what is taught at school than on the choice of television channel at home.

The process of disintegration begun in the 1960s was accelerated by an absence of leadership. The withdrawal of HM Inspectorate from its former role as classroom adviser and critic perhaps reflected an awareness of the unfortunate effect of excessive zeal on earlier generations of teachers. Whatever the reason may have been, the resulting vacuum remained unfilled, in spite of the existence of such bodies as the Incorporated Society of Musicians and the more recent United Kingdom Council for Music Education and Training. For though subcommittees were appointed to make recommendations on school music in either case, their findings were constrained by compromise, and lacked weight. No assembly of 'experts' today, it seems, should be expected to agree a forthright statement which might tread on partisan corns. One vexed issue raised at these discussion meetings concerned the development of musical literacy. And while earlier opposition to teaching the use of notation had given way by the seventies to more general realization of the value of this skill in developing aural sensitivity, agreed statements on the subject were yet discreetly worded to recommend only 'the use of an appropriate form of notation' in order to accommodate the experimental music lobby.

The situation which this impasse reveals is a particularly interesting one showing that the fragmentation which has taken place in the pattern of school music is no more than a reflection of the over-specialization which now divides would-be authorities on music education – each of them concentrating his energies upon the establishment and maintenance of an exclusive facet while defending it from encroachment by other factions. Only rarely, it seems, is an 'expert' to be found with a universal attitude toward the whole range of aspects now available – one who is ready, moreover, to agree the detail of a core curriculum around which other optional activity might take place to complement it. Without such a policy the present spiral of thriftlessness and dissipation seems bound to continue.

Meanwhile, there is plenty of evidence to show that between them, the new teaching methods introduced during the 1960s still command support from large numbers of teachers. What is not so readily apparent is how often this support is forthcoming only because such activities keep pupils 'busy', and not because of the educational expectations they arouse. For that matter, when faced with problems of the kind regularly confronting secondary teachers in urban areas today, the teacher whose prime aim in planning a music lesson is to find undemanding ways of filling up the time must earn at least some sympathy. Yet the consequence of this all too common policy has been to treat the music lesson as an occasion for entertainment rather than for learning. When policy is dictated by despair in place of resolve, educational aims necessarily carry little weight. Music has been seriously undervalued as a result.

Yet there are signs that the long flirtation with unorthodoxy in music teaching is waning. Teachers are rediscovering methods and attitudes rejected by their predecessors during the years when excellence was equated with novelty. In-service training has revealed to many junior school teachers that properly directed effort enables them first to overcome their own shortcomings, then to develop children's skills usefully. Subsequent experience with their classes has shown that contrary to hearsay children enjoy learning to use their musical sense, while short regular sessions of aural training soon develop new skills contributing toward that adventure of discovery which plays so important a part in a child's gratification. Quite as much as any other subject in the curriculum, music offers opportunities for enjoyment through achievement. The conviction is now widespread that much of the secondary pupil's lack of enthusiasm for his music lessons is due to the absence of early training in aural-skills. Misguided attempts to make good the starvation years of the primary school with a prodigal menu in the secondary school now merely call to mind Marie Antoinette's harebrained proposal to feed the breadless poor: 'Let them eat cake!'.

Chapter 2

Music education before the National Curriculum

Keith Swanwick

There are several existing characteristics of British music education which make up the context of music in the National Curriculum. Until fairly recently, music educators had a tendency to be professionally inarticulate; preferring a non-explicit attitude to a declared curriculum statement; getting on with organizing and teaching; and leaving school, local education authority (LEA) and national policy formulation to others. Encouraged by the soft-edged attitudes of the 1960s we have tended to favour what is sometimes called the 'process' model, rather than the sharp definition of instructional objectives. However vague this might appear, there is a profound truth here, beautifully and simply expressed by Polanyi in his famous phrase, 'we can know more than we can tell'.[1] Much knowledge may indeed be *tacit*: we do know more than we can tell, or indeed want to be bothered to tell. This luxury of the undeclared; the hidden curriculum, the 'secret garden', is now being invaded by educational accountants who want to know what it is we actually buy and sell and at what price. Music educators are now more articulate, although this burgeoning eloquence is unlikely to displace totally the intuitive sense that characterizes the musician's view of musical encounters. Teachers of music are particularly committed to their 'subject' as an intrinsically rewarding activity. While they may worry about the plodding predictability of a linear curriculum with checklists of chained, sequential competencies, it is only fair that *all* children in school have the chance to be initiated into musical procedures, the realm of musical discourse, in a manner less haphazard than reliance on the idiosyncrasies of individual teachers. This, presumably, is one major purpose behind the National Curriculum.

In many ways music education in Britain compares well with that in other countries, even though it is somewhat erratic. Seen from a comparative perspective attitudes seem generally well-principled, though it is uneven in pactice. It is in the schools that this is strikingly apparent. Music in higher education, particularly in universities and music schools, has models and replicas in other parts of the globe; though even at this level, the growth of courses in polytechnics and colleges of higher education has generated new course structures and has helped to loosen up the processes of music education for adults. But it is mostly in the schools that the pioneering developmental work has taken place. Unfortunately the effects are distributed somewhat unevenly.

The teaching profession has absorbed the effects of the theory and practice of various curriculum initiatives, especially the Schools Council project, *Music in the Secondary School Curriculum*, which began to be influential two decades ago.[2] There was an early advocacy of a serious regard for Afro-American musics, especially jazz and pop music.[3] Many of us have been hard at work trying to establish a credible and serviceable philosophy of music education and have laboured to tease out the psychological and sociological characteristics of musical experience in order to evolve sound working principles for the classroom and the studio.[4] Eventually it was the GCSE national criteria and the detailed format of GCSE examinations that signalled official acceptance of much that had been pioneered before. Throughout this process HM Inspectorate followed along behind, mopping up the ideas and commending 'good practice'.

Consider the range of activities already to be found in school music classrooms. Between 1985 and 1987, the Music Department of the Institute of Education conducted an enquiry into music in schools. Supported by the Gulbenkian Foundation, the aim of this research was to map out the context and practice of music teaching in a wide range of school classrooms and examine the role of music within the wider school community. The research method was by survey and case study. This study gives a picture of attitudes to music in schools and the reality of classroom transactions. It serves as a marker by which to assess the likely impact of proposed change under the novelty of the National Curriculum.[5]

The findings from this investigation suggest that the situation was not then so very different from what is now being proposed. The main divergence lies in the 'national' formulation of curriculum content, rather than leaving all decisions to individual schools and teachers. The actual structure and status of the music curriculum before legislation is not markedly dissimilar from what is now being proposed.

Music was part of the curriculum in every school we investigated, at least until the age of fourteen, with a usual allocation of one period a week which could vary between twenty and eighty minutes. Generally speaking, the younger the pupils the shorter the available time. Among the staff of school communities, music was perceived as being quite highly valued; certainly by heads and other teachers, caretakers, secretaries, librarians and other ancillary staff. Many music teachers also thought that their professional contribution to the general life of the school was significant and were aware of the importance of music in helping to project a positive institutional image. In spite of this recognized and much appreciated 'window dressing', music teachers seemed uncertain, even defensive, about their own standing

within the timetabled curriculum. They identified a professional requirement to justify their subject and felt that classroom work in music was not
properly understood by many colleagues. Music as a 'subject' seemed to
languish in status by being perceived as 'unacademic'; pleasurable rather
than educational. A growing vocational emphasis also appeared to exert a
strong pull against arts subjects and this affected the major resources of
time, space, equipment and staffing. Two-thirds of the sixty teachers
involved in this study thought they were more or less inadequately
resourced.

When we looked carefully into the classrooms we found a recurring
picture. In the primary schools there was an emphasis on aural and
performance skills: imitating rhythms; learning by rote patterns on percussion accompaniments; listening games; identifying metre or the number of
notes in a chord; responding to changes in levels of loudness and learning
new songs. This kind of activity accounted for nearly 51 per cent of the
total teaching time observed in primary schools. Nine per cent of the
overall time was spent in discussion and classroom organization and 18
per cent in other ways, including 14 per cent lost in moving children around
the school. No significant amount of time was recorded as being spent on
imparting information about music or giving historical, social context or
technical facts.

This last trait was also evident in secondary schools, where only 2.5 per
cent of the time was taken up by teachers in transmitting information.
Nearly 18 per cent of the duration of music sessions was employed in
individual, pair, group or whole class composing, half of this 'by ear' (that is
to say, without using any form of written notation). About 9.5 per cent of
available time was given over to music audience-listening and 22 per cent to
rehearsing skills, while 6.7 per cent was taken up in musical performance.[6]

Half of the 7.8 per cent performance time in primary schools saw the
children engaged in singing. In the secondary schools the emphasis was
much more on instrumental work. A major difference in emphasis became
evident across primary and secondary schools, the former making much
more of sequential skill teaching and singing in whole classes while the
latter engaged more in instrumental performance and composing in small
groups.

The belief that music should be a practical subject is, then, already
generally accepted by teachers and the desirability of this is stressed in
the National Curriculum Music Working Group Report.[7] In answers to our
initial questionnaire, teachers from forty-eight of the sixty schools in the
survey reported spending half or more of their time in organizing practical
activities. Subsequent detailed observation in classrooms suggested that
this may well be an underestimation. One thing became clear; relaying
factual information *about* music was an insignificant feature in all thirty-
two schools that we followed up by systematic observation and interviews.

In comparison with other subjects, pupils too had noticed that in music there were 'no paper and pencils', and 'more movement than writing'.

The Working Group strongly advocated singing as an essential part of music education and lists it repeatedly as an activity throughout the Key Stage statements. On the surface this already seems part of practice. More than two-thirds of our respondents claimed that singing was the most frequent classroom activity and thirteen that it occurred fairly often. It was indicated that in no school was singing ignored, although two of the teachers involved specified that singing took place only rarely. Even sight-singing appears to flourish. In only fifteen instances were there teachers who said they never asked pupils to sing at sight from notation, while seventeen teachers said that this took place fairly often. Subsequent observations of 163 lessons in thirty-two of these schools painted a somewhat different picture. Ninety-one of these lessons involved no singing at all. Nor was any sight-singing observed. This is probably a good example of aspirations outstripping actuality. With regard to singing there is a clear difference between the newly proposed and existing curriculum practice. In reality vocal activities have a low position as a classroom activity and the Music Working Group was aware of this.

The Working Group was anxious not to confine musical experience in schools to the western classical tradition. Indeed, in their *Interim Report* they appeared to get their examples of various musical styles slightly out of balance and a small but vociferous group of academics critical of current developments in music education were quick to respond in the press. This balance appears to have been restored in the final version, but there is no sense in which western classical music is to be an exclusive cultural locus. As far as existing practice goes, we found mainly European idioms, along with less easily classified songs and carols, most frequently cited by teachers. However, there was considerable variation between individuals, some never presenting classical music, others never using jazz, rock and pop, or 'ethnic' music, although most people operated a broad curriculum.[8] The use of available published materials was equally diverse, over 130 different titles were mentioned. Nearly everyone devised their own material. No one appeared to follow a published 'method'. Until now the music curriculum has definitely been homespun.

There is a further practical dimension to be considered. In Britain we inherit two traditions of music education, especially in secondary schools. The first of these derives from the private school system and essentially sees the music educator as the 'director of music' who runs the band, choir and orchestra, who manages the chapel choir and organizes individual instrumental teaching. The second tradition stems from the framework of the class lesson where music is treated like any other 'subject' with allocated slots of time for general music education. In most schools the two systems run side by side, with instrumental teaching engaged on a rota basis, withdrawing students from other classes to work with visiting specialist teachers. The regular music teacher wears both hats, that of musical director and class teacher, coping with classes all day and rehearsals, performances and instrumental administration in spare moments and after school. The strain is enormous but difficult to avoid. Teachers feel that the classes are the real reason for their employment and yet the choirs, bands and orchestras are necessary, not only to put the music department on the map of the school in the eyes of staff and parents, but also to give opportunities to those students who have a special interest in and ability with music.

Although music is now unquestionably part of the school curriculum, it is also woven into the fabric of events in the wider community which means that it frequently and necessarily takes place outside of conventional timetabled lessons in schools. I refer specifically to instrumental teaching schemes which operate through local authorities and are articulated by music advisers. Many of our young people find their richest musical experiences not in classrooms but rehearsing and performing in instrumental and vocal groups, often out of school time and sometimes out of school altogether. This activity has been largely staffed by peripatetic teachers working with small groups and individuals. Things are on the move here and we need to be vigilant in case these opportunities waste away by default.

An important element of music in schools is instrumental teaching. Music in schools for many parents, and certainly for the media, often seems to be instrumental lessons. In the secondary school, GCSE music has already influenced the provision of specialist teaching, since musical *performance* is obligatory. By Key Stage 2 in the National Curriculum 'the need for specialist instrumental tuition becomes apparent'.[9]

This desirable state of affairs now comes into tension with contemporary school management. Each school is now responsible through its head teacher (manager) and the governing body for most of the decisions on spending and the budget. Local authorities are becoming educationally marginal and the instrumental services which they created may not be sustained by other agencies. Head teachers will have to consider whether this form of instruction is economically viable, when balanced against other things. Clearly, no school can provide a range of instrumental teachers to cover all the main options and effective schemes can only be operated in places by some new kind of federation, other local schools sharing the supply and funding of instrumental teachers. This is not likely to be a priority with school managers. And what about regional LEA-based orchestras, bands and choirs? Will these still exist? We only have a Ministry of Education, unlike most European countries where there is also a Ministry of Culture to oversee community musical activities and monitor quality.

Policy on this seems hazy and there has been considerable agitation to try to make sure politicians understand what they are doing. One thing is certain, if these facilities disappear or are truncated then the rich British traditions of both professional and amateur music making will gradually be eroded and participation in instrumental and choral music will become even more exclusively the property of a better-off minority who need no persuading about the value of these things and can afford to pay.

In summary the *status quo* is as follows: music in schools is now essentially a practical activity; composing is widely practised and is generally thought to be both desirable and feasible; western staff notation is relegated to a supporting position in music learning, in the awareness that much music is notated in other ways and some not at all; singing, while thought desirable, does not seem to be as universally engaged in as it might be; it is deemed important to engage pupils in music from different cultural backgrounds; teachers distrust 'methods' and tend to devise their own materials; and the two strands of music education – general and instrumental teaching – require greater organizational coherence.

MUSICAL KNOWLEDGE AND THE MUDDLE OF ATTAINMENT TARGETS

Fundamentally, the music teaching profession in both state and private schools has largely accepted that there are but three psychological avenues down which any of us can approach music; these are in the role of composer, performer or audience listener. These are not the inventions of educational theorists but wait to be discovered whenever we carefully reflect on the nature of musical experience. Recognizing these three dimensions has been essential to recent music curriculum development and to the success of the GCSE, and this is acknowledged in the structure of the final Music Report. The theoretical framework was explicated in the mid-1970s, principally in my *A Basis for Music Education* along with the development of the important and related concepts of expressive and structural elements as essential musical features.[10]

The pervasiveness of this work can clearly be seen in the formulation of the attainment targets offered by the Working Group. After some initial confusion in the *Interim Report*, by August 1991 we were offered the now familiar triad of elements which in effect define the fundamental activities of music as a school subject. These are proposed to be Composing, Performing and Appraising. The term appraising is carefully defined and refers specifically to the *audience-listener* role, which I previously carefully called 'audition' to distinguish this particular way of listening from what might be called composing-listening or performing-listening. In the *Report* it is tied in with what is called 'relevant knowledge' of historical and cultural backgrounds. Now, of course, appraisal also takes place when people are composing and performing and might often be best developed through these activities. However, at least a version of the concept of appraisal has been exposed and may prove helpful in justifying the knowledge basis of music to others and in clarifying the minds of music educators. The danger is that contextual, factual knowledge may be seen as central to musical knowing. It is seductively uncomplicated to manage in the classroom and relatively easy to assess. There are other ways of knowing entangled in musical experience and more must be said on this later.

Of course there are logical difficulties about the National Curriculum category set. Clusters of activities really cannot be attainment targets and composing, performing and appraising are essentially *activities*. What has been attained is surely what has been *learned*, the residue left with us, some change of insight, that which is taken away when an activity has, for the time being, ceased. In spite of this, the August 1991 document seems robust and rich enough in possibilities without being too prescriptive or limiting. We need to ask, though, whether educational reform will produce any significant change in the status and resource implications for music education.

TIME AND STATUS UNDER THE NATIONAL CURRICULUM

To get a feeling for the way in which music is regarded by those who are influential in curriculum policy we need to go back just one stage. The earliest statements on the subject basis of the National Curriculum occur in the DES consultative document of 1987[11] and the first *Report* from the Task Group on Assessment and Testing (TGAT).[12] The consultative document lists three core and eight foundation subjects. Music appears at the end of the list of foundation subjects along with art and physical education. Between them all it is recommended they should take up around 10 per cent of curriculum time. These subjects are the last to be brought into the curriculum framework. Both the balance and sequencing reflect the *status quo* of earlier decades and do nothing to make it likely that there will be any radical change from earlier practice in terms of curriculum time and, by implication, allocation of resources.[13]

Assessment is surely the axis of the National Curriculum and here the status of music is once again analogous to that of art and physical education; there are merely to be 'guidelines' rather than specific attainment targets. It is obvious from this that these subjects are not considered to have a knowledge content sufficiently important or developed to merit any serious attempt at assessment. All this was highlighted by Angela Rumbold, then a Minister of State for Education, in a paper given to the National Association for Education in the Arts.[14] Her view of music education is informed and well expressed.

Our aim will be to bring all pupils throughout their primary and secondary school years, into contact with the musician's fundamental activities in a wide range of different kinds of music – performing, singing or playing an instrument, or listening. I would hope that they would gain some experience of musical composition itself.

(Rumbold, 1987: 6)

This last sentence is interesting, especially the word 'itself'. This suggests that there is something refined, difficult or perhaps mysterious about the activity. This ambivalent attitude to composing permeates the whole consultative process. This may be implied in the letter from the Secretary of State, Kenneth Clarke, to the National Curriculum Council on 19 August 1991, where he asks that 'to avoid an excessive degree of complexity and prescriptiveness . . . I should like you also to consider whether there is a case for two attainment targets instead of three'.

Such a theoretical fixation on simplicity is sadly misplaced. Simplicity is not the same as effectiveness. If it were it might seem perfectly reasonable to reduce the essential three colours of red, blue and green that make up a television image to two. Why not get rid of, say, red? Surely, it would make television manufacture simpler? Unfortunately it would also compromise the level of visual reproduction in an unacceptable way.

In the Secretary of State's earlier response to the *Interim Report* he expressed concern for the many pupils 'with a real appreciation of music but a limited aptitude for its practice'.[15] It is clear from this that any shift towards two attainment targets would probably conflate composing and performing, thus shifting the balance away from practical experience. If either activity were thus to be diminished it would probably be composing, which is less understood by outsiders and less prestigious than performing in the eyes of school communities. It is easy to regard composing either as messing about in an aimless 'progressive' way or, conversely, as a process exclusively confined to the exceptionally talented, the Mozarts of this world. Considered either way, composing becomes problematic. To take a parallel case; it seems curious that experimentation in science or invention in technology is considered to be a curriculum essential for everyone, without any suggestion that pupils are just messing about or, on the other hand, that a Ph.D. is required before anyone can undertake practical, scientific or technological investigation.

Even though it may be that the ultimate *aim* of general music education on schools is to promote in an audience an ability to respond to music in a positive way, the process by which this end is achieved has, for most pupils, to be through practical involvement, when pupils engage in what Angela Rumbold called 'the musician's fundamental activities'. To argue that an appreciation of music can be brought about just by listening in audience (even accompanied by relevant information) is analogous to saying that appreciating Shakespeare can be best achieved without any prior active involvement with the English language, which would be nonsensical. Nor should we limit the scope of practical work to performing. As we have seen, composing music is something that most children have engaged in over the last decade and is certainly not a new element in British music classrooms. It is no rarefied activity but a way of engaging with the elements of musical discourse in a constructive and critical manner, making judgements and decisions; in the richest sense of the term, *appraising* music.

We might also notice in the paper by Angela Rumbold, that music education is portrayed as a series of activities without reference to learning outcomes. Pupils are 'to gain experience of '; but to *learn* what? It is the view of music as knowledge or perhaps as *no* knowledge that pervades these attitudes to music in the curriculum and it is this central issue of music as knowledge that requires our attention.

The terms of reference for subject working groups spell out the concept of attainment targets as: 'the knowledge, skills, understanding and aptitudes which pupils of different abilities and maturity should be expected to have acquired at or near certain ages.'[16] The emphasis here is quite rightly upon learning outcomes rather than activities as central elements of assessment. Further weight is given to these in the TGAT Report where the concept of 'profile components' is exposed. 'We recommend that an individual subject should report a small number (of) profile components reflecting the variety of knowledge, skills and understanding to which the subject gives rise.'[17]

Attainment targets are, then, to be seen as the specific elements making up profile components, which in turn are the fundamental strands of knowledge in a subject field. Unfortunately the early 'core' subject Working Groups proceeded to muddy the epistemological water. The English Working Group came up with three profile components: Speaking and Listening; Reading; and Writing. These are obviously categories of activities, not of learning outcomes. Mathematics formulated the following: Using and Applying Mathematics; Number, Algebra; Shape and Space; and Handling Data. These are bunched up into two profile components: Number, Algebra and Measures; and Shape, Space and Data Handling. We have here more or less the usual sections of existing maths curricula redefined for the new context. Science was initially credited with seventeen attainment targets – such a lot of 'knowledge' here. They include activities such as 'Exploration of Science'. These mainly describe scientific topics for the classroom: Forces; Earth and Atmosphere; and so on. Such topics can hardly be the 'knowledge, skills, understanding and aptitudes which pupils of different abilities and maturity should be expected to have acquired' though they may well be projects through which this knowledge is gained.[18]

This general failure to identify the essential deep structures in 'core' subjects may not be surprising. Indeed, it might be inferred that teachers working in these subjects have been so protected by their traditional status and level of resource that there has been little pressure to think through the fundamentals of the epistemological structure, no urgency seriously to ask what are the essential knowledge dimensions, the real profile components of the subjects. The situation is very different in the arts areas. To fend off curriculum marginalization and to find a compelling professional rationale, arts educators are endlessly turning over and disputing the nature and value of their particular activity; trying to articulate a 'philosophy'; and attempting to define the knowledge base.

Much of the difficulty in formulating a sensible curriculum for music stems from the complexity of the different layers of knowledge involved in musical experience and the non-verbal nature of the activity. There is a long philosophical history lurking here which would be too complex and tedious to rehearse in this paper. Suffice it to say that at times it is necessary for us to know *how* to do things; to operate a lathe; to spell a word; to translate a passage; to articulate our thoughts into a structured form; to manipulate a musical instrument; and to use musical notation. Knowing how to do things is essentially the use and development of particular skills. The second commonly understood kind of knowledge is propositional, that is, informational or knowing *that*. For example we may know that two plus seven makes nine, or that Manchester is 200 miles from London, or that *avoir* is the French verb 'to have', or that Beethoven wrote nine symphonies, or where rap originated. A further, though philosophically contested, way of knowing is that of knowledge by acquaintance. We may know Renoir's painting *The Rowers' Lunch*, or know a friend, a pupil or a city. Although such knowledge might to some extent be demonstrated by propositional statements, most acquaintance knowing is likely to be tacit, unarticulated. There is also an awareness of what we value, *attitudinal* knowledge which has been analysed by Bloom and others under the caption of the 'affective domain'.[19] The development of musical value positions relates to such variables as age, gender, social context, personality type and previous life experience, along with the accumulation of musical experience.

However we construe the epistemological map, *knowing* music is much more than processing factual information. In this respect the subject Working Group has been far from clear.

APPRAISING, MUSICAL ANALYSIS AND MUSICAL KNOWING

It is in the context of musical knowing that the National Curriculum term 'appraising' becomes important. Although the term is specifically intended to pick up the skills and information context needed for pupils to respond to music as 'audience listeners', the implications are much wider. Appraising affirms that there is such a thing as musical *knowledge*. There are more or less objective musical criteria for critical judgements: musical appraisal is not a free-for-all. If this were not so it would be very difficult to justify music as a compulsory element of the curriculum and impossible to believe in any fair or meaningful system of assessment. If 'anything goes' then there will be no shared core of knowledge and therefore nothing to assess.

I have argued elsewhere that the development of musical criticism is the special contribution that schools and colleges can make to music education.[20] That is what distinguishes institutionalized music education from music encountered more casually on the street or in the media. Formal music education takes a special interest in critical statements that have *analytical* force – that say something about how a particular piece of music functions. All analysis is musical criticism but not all criticism is analysis. Analysis cannot be simply an expression of preference or a statement about the social or historical context of a piece of music but is essentially discourse about the internal functioning of a specific musical object. It is about the integrity of a particular work. Appraisal as a concept is interchangeable with analysis: it relies on first-hand acquaintance knowledge of particular musical objects. Anything less is either prejudice or inert information.

Musical appraisal is not necessarily promoted in verbal or scholarly ways. It can be elicited and developed at various levels; for example, in practical workshops where children are composing or improvising music. Here a teacher might ask questions to stimulate appraisal: 'What would the effect be if we played a cymbal here instead of a triangle?'; 'What makes that passage sound so brilliant?'; 'Should this phrase be played quite so boldly or be more tentative in character?'; 'Does this passage hold our attention when played so slowly (or so quickly)?'. These kinds of question may be answered in practical ways, by musical experiment or demonstration, though verbal discourse is obviously important in any educational transaction and assists in the formation of critical judgement in music.

If we attend to music carefully and reflectively we shall find that there are four possible dimensions of critical appraisal or analysis. We might even call them profile components: 'the variety of knowledge, skills and understanding to which the subject gives rise'.

1 There can be appraisal of the sound *materials*, that is, of the management of sonorities; of the 'soundscape' of a work, our impressions of timbre, texture, register, or loudness level.
2 There can be appraisal of *expressive character*, the general atmosphere of a piece, its dramatic levels, or the specific gesture of a single phrase.
3 There can be appraisal of *structural relationships*, the way expressive gestures relate to other gestures, how musical works undergo continual metamorphosis and in so doing keep us alert and attentive.

All three dimensions are areas where there can be objective critical judgements and where it is possible to be more or less right or wrong.
4 There can also be appraisal in terms of the *value of work*; not simply a personal prejudice for or against opera or progressive rock as genres, but an awareness for an individual listener of the significance of a particular musical encounter, a realization built on the appraisal of materials, expressive character and structure. It is here that musical experience is at its most subjective and idiosyncratic.

These distinctions need to be clearly understood if meaningful assessment is to become a reality. Things can easily get confused. For example, the music Working Group lists 'structure' along with pitch, duration, chord, or interval.[21] This is simply a category mistake, rather like placing the speech materials of vowels and consonants (speech is not necessarily meaningful) on the same conceptual level as the language elements of nouns or verbs (language is by definition always meaningful). Sound materials are to do with what we might loosely call musical *speech*. Expressive character and structure lie at the heart of musical *language*. They are qualitatively different from the perception and manipulation of sound materials.

It seems impossible to find any analytical or appraisal statement that does not fall into one of these four categories. This assertion can be tested quite easily by analysing any published review of musical performance into discrete statements. If we are really attending to music we are bound to assess the effect and control of sonorities, the management of the sound surface, the quality of the tonal experience itself; we are also conscious of the character of music, whether it is heavy, or light, flowing or angular; we may also look for coherence, ways in which musical gestures evolve, relate, contrast, or suggest or deny a sense of direction. We might also come to judge the place of a musical encounter in our own matrix of values, understanding its significance for us as human beings.

In our research in the Institute of Education, we have observed these modes of critical appraisal in the musical development of children.[22] A focus on sound materials characterizes the early years. Up to about the age of three, young children appear to be primarily responsive to the direct impressiveness of sound phenomena, particularly timbre and dynamic levels. There is much experimentation with and exploration of musical instruments and vocal sound, though the children soon acquire techniques involved in handling sound, organizing regular pulse and using technical devices suggested by the physical structure of instruments.

Expressive characterization becomes most evident in compositions around the ages of four to six years. This becomes particularly apparent through the exploitation of changes of speed and loudness levels. Musical ideas at this time are often programmatic and the process of invention appeared to be quite spontaneous and unstructured. By seven or eight, most of the children we observed had gravitated towards established expressive musical conventions: marches, lullabies and so on. Phrases then tended to fall into standard two, four, or eight bar units with regular metrical and standard tonal organization.

Structural interest first emerges as musical speculation, usually between the ages of nine and eleven. Repetition of commonplace patterns is broken by imaginative deviations. Surprises occur as children deliberately explore structural possibilities, looking to contrast, overturn or vary musical ideas. Around thirteen to fourteen, structural organization becomes more firmly integrated into longer pieces in clearly identifiable idioms, especially though by no means exclusively from the realms of popular music.

At around fifteen or so, particular pieces of music, often certain shapes of phrase or a harmonic progression become symbolically significant for an individual. There is a growing consciousness of music's emotional power and a tendency to reflect on this experience and to communicate something of the strength of these responses to peers. From the documentary evidence of musicians we can see how this significance may later become transformed into a value commitment revealed in novel composing techniques and original historical, musicological, psychological, or philosophical work. Musical compositions may be based on sets of newly generated musical materials; note rows, electronic series and so on.

DEVELOPMENT AND ASSESSMENT

This thumbnail sketch of musical development can offer insights into the knowledge contours of music. If we were to reconstitute the Key Stage statements of the National Curriculum in epigrammatic form within just one (simple!) dimension with reference to the pattern of children's musical development, we would have something like the following.

Key stage 1

Students should be able to recognize and identify different musical materials and use these skilfully to express an atmosphere or dramatic sequence.

Key stage 2

Students should be able to distinguish and discriminate melodic and rhythmic devices found in songs and instrumental pieces and use these expressively.

Key stage 3

Students should be able to draw attention to and exploit repetitions and contrasting musical ideas involving awareness of the expressive potential of harmony.

Key stage 4

Students should be able to discriminate between various idiomatic practices and demonstrate this knowledge in their own musical work and through verbal articulation.

Most of the Key Stage statements in the National Curriculum document are essentially *quantitative* in character rather than *qualitative*. For example, at Key Stage 2, under the activity of performing, children should interpret 'more complex signs' while at Key Stage 3 they should interpret 'a variety of signs'. Generally, the progressive tendency throughout is towards 'more' independence, a 'greater understanding' of music and more 'sophisticated' ideas.

It is essential to recognize that any reliable form of assessment is dependent on the recognition of *qualitative* changes. We need to have criterion statements that pick up qualitative shifts; something more like recognizing changes of gear in a car than trying to assess relative road speeds without adequate instrumentation. Inappropriate ways of assessing musical achievement certainly exist, for example GCSE procedures that involve giving marks for different categories – melody, harmony, texture and so on and then adding them up. This seems a curious way to engage in musical appraisal.

To give just one positive example, here are some draft criteria for assessing musical performance. Each one represents a change of quality. They have already been found useful and reliable.

Criteria for assessing musical performance

Level 1 – sensory

The performance appears to be fairly spontaneous, even erratic. Forward movement is unsteady and variations of tone colour or loudness appear to have no structural or expressive significance.

Level 2 – manipulative

Control is shown by steady speed and consistency in repeating patterns. Managing the insrument appears to be the main priority and there is no evidence of expressive shaping or structural organization.

Level 3 – personal expressiveness

The general impression is of an impulsive and unplanned performance. Expressiveness is exhibited in changes of speed, accentuation and loudness levels. There is a lack of structural coherence.

Level 4 – the vernacular

The performance is tidy and expressive within accepted conventions and in a fairly predictable way. Melodic and rhythmic patterns are repeated with matching articulation and phrases are balanced.

Level 5 – the speculative

A secure and expressive performance includes some imaginative touches. Dynamics and phrase articulation are deliberately contrasted or varied to generate structural interest.

Level 6 – the idiomatic

There is a developed sense of style and an expressive vocabulary convincingly drawn from identifiable idiomatic practice. Technical, expressive and structural control are consistently and reliably demonstrated.

Level 7 – the symbolic

The performance demonstrates confident technical mastery, is stylistic and compelling. There is penetration into expressive and structural detail and a sense of personal commitment.

Level 8 – the systematic

Technical mastery totally serves musical communication. Form and expression are fused into a coherent and personal musical statement. New musical insights are imaginatively and systematically explored.

Further research based on the music-making of Greek children in Cypriot schools confirms that musical development takes place in the predicted sequence and that teachers are able to make confident judgements in assessing musical compositions at a high level of consensus, provided that they are helped by clear criterion statements.[23]

The weight of reporting on pupil progress in the National Curriculum would be considerably reduced if an analysis of the essential elements were the starting point in every subject. Further work is currently in progress evaluating the reliability and validity of this approach, but it begins to appear that such an analysis may have something positive to offer music education, as we try to gauge the effectiveness of school music under the National Curriculum. Indeed it is essential to develop sensitive, effective and economical means of assessment. There are indeed things to *know* in experiencing music and most of these are just not amenable to assessment by paper and pencil tests, any more than is knowing how to drive a motor car or splint a broken leg.

Sensitive music educators may be worried by all this, aware that there seems to be an exclusive focus on product rather than processes. *Process* and *product* are indeed terms that appear in the 1991 music curriculum document under the heading of assessment.[24] Let us not be misled by these terms and waste further time debating their relative importance. Products are simply what we make or say: processes are invisible without products. There is no such thing as an 'end product' in education. To observe the process of an individual requires us to study a wide range of his or her products on more than one occasion. It seems unlikely that we shall or even ought to penetrate very far into trying to assess the processes of people. This would be presumptuous. Even Freud found certainty difficult under the relatively tranquil conditions of one-to-one discussion in his Vienna consulting room. In most classrooms such discernment seems implausible. But we *can* assess products.

It is the products of children, their *work* that we are able to assess in schools, *not* individual children as people. Once accept this important limitation of educational institutions, criterion statements can be seen to be both potentially fair and easy to use, provided that they are carefully devised, really sequential and their meaning clearly understood. We are also brought up with a jolt by this acknowledgement of the limitations of schools. They are just one agent in the education and development of children and can achieve certain things but not others. The most important knowledge may indeed be tacit, unvoiced. We do not, however, need to be sure about this in order to function effectively.

A RATIONALE FOR MUSIC EDUCATION

Beneath the surface details of the classroom and the curriculum lie important issues. That is why even music education is politically sensitive and why professors of philosophy elbow their way into the debate about the music curriculum. A teacher colleague once said that at a parents' evening he was accosted by the father of a pupil at school and asked two questions: 'Is there any value in music?'; 'Why is music in the school curriculum?'. He had to formulate convincing answers in only a few minutes that were available. It is not uncommon for pupils too to want to know why music is in the curriculum. The first answer is the quick and immediate one. It runs something like this. Consider any cohesive community, what we call a culture. We shall find music. Sometimes it will be fused with ceremony, ritual, dance, story telling, even magic. At other times it will be separated out into such entities as symphonies, pop songs or ragas. There is no need to defend the role of music. It is a valued activity in any culture. We may find it difficult to say *why* it is valued but we can certainly demonstrate *that* it is.

The more difficult question is the second. Why is music in the school curriculum? After all, it might be argued that there is plenty of music taking place in the wider community and that school is an inappropriate place for musical activities. Here the justification hinges on the quality of what is actually done in the school. There can be no case for music done badly. On the other hand, there is every justification for supporting music education when it is well done. Schools extend the scope of knowledge that is casually acquired elsewhere and there is a fund of human knowledge (perhaps better and more accurately designated as *knowing*) embodied in musical discourse that cannot be left to chance. If schools are to be regarded as basing their curricula on important and significant activities in any culture, then music is an obvious candidate, unless we happen to believe that the role of schools should be limited to certain basic activities such as reading, writing and arithmetic. If this is the case, then the school day could be radically shortened and the school leaving age lowered.

It is one thing to give answers at this level, it is another to understand their significance for professional practice. In order to be clear we need to strip away some dead wood of tangled 'philosophies' that have cluttered music education over the last decade or so. It will be necessary to be fairly cryptic in outlining these positions.

There are two apparently conflicting views that have confounded music education, dividing professional aspirations. The first of these is the perspective that sees education primarily as the transmission of cultural heritage. Accordingly, people undergoing education, and especially children in school, are to be given information and skills that will enable them to participate in the accepted cultural conventions. This in turn helps to perpetuate and confirm the structure and content of the culture. The implications for music education are obvious. We would look for a growing familiarity with the master works, for an historical perspective on music, for factual knowledge about music and possibly skill with musical instruments, for a degree of musical literacy, for concert-going and record-buying habits. In the case of the student learning to play an instrument under specialist guidance, we hope we would be initiating him or her more rigorously into a long tradition of craftsmanship through a developed system of instruction assessed by carefully graded examinations.

All of these activities can have immense value, but only if they are undertaken for better reasons than passing on the cultural heritage as though it were a kind of property or territory, and if they are seen in a stronger educational perspective. As it stands things often go wrong. Many students become alienated from the master-works and appear to collide with the cultural values that the teacher represents. If they acquiesce they may become knowledgeable about composers and their works without there being any commitment to real experience of them. For the instrumental player, sensitivity is frequently obliged to go underground in deference to the acquisition of skills at a rate that exceeds the growth of musical understanding. Far too many students give up instrumental lessons than would be the case if there were something intrinsically satisfying in the activity. Furthermore, the quest for any common cultural heritage in multicultural settings seems doomed to failure and the most powerful musical experiences seem most frequently to occur outside of the constraints of formal education.

The second view, sometimes called 'progressive', is in sharp contradiction to the traditional picture, so rudely caricatured above. The central article of faith here is that we begin with the child as an unfolding personality and not a mere recipient of a culture. Accordingly, the emphasis is on learning rather than teaching, on the development of the imagination, on discovery and above all, on creativity. Thus, instead of accepting and perpetuating the status quo, we look for development of the ability to influence and change the culture. In music education we would place an emphasis on composition or improvisation, on experimentation with new sound materials, on small-group or individual activities rather than large choirs or bands. We would look for involvement with contemporary music, defined alternatively as either the music of contemporary composers or pop music. General music in schools is seen as very different from specialist instrumental tuition and the whole apparatus of examinations and tests becomes suspect because it not only imposes an unwelcome uniformity, but also attempts to measure the unmeasurable – the personal development of different individuals. Is this why music is valued then: because it helps pupils to develop as people in their own way?

Once again, the underlying assumptions of this theory may give rise to distortion of otherwise valuable activities and objectives. Teachers may even abdicate from teaching altogether in the interests of children 'discovering' for themselves, or from a misguided sensitivity to the creative processes of students. The music of the avant-garde is not espoused by many and a good proportion of the students may feel that the school has no right to institutionalize popular music. The instrumental player goes his or her own way and shrugs off the low-level activity of the classroom, preferring to stay with the classical tradition, the rewards of examination passes and public acclaim. Worse still, most students may not seem at all interested in the development of their own personalities through music.

Following the philosopher Karl Popper, I would offer a less distorting perspective that signals the interactive nature of tradition and renewal and at the same time gives us a sense of direction.[25] This is derived from noticing a relationship between the two extreme views already examined. It is essentially human to be at once an inheritor, part of a culture, and an innovator, creatively striving within or against tradition. We assimilate the world to our own perspective but also accommodate to new realities. Each of us is moulded by the society in which we find ourselves but we also shape that culture through our individual actions. We are able to interact with the world precisely because we utilize such symbolic forms as language, maths, art and music. This symbol-making facility enables us to become aware of and articulate our personal history, the elements of our culture, the thought, the perceived feelings and actions of other people, the movement of planets, the natural world around us; all the forms and strands of human knowledge. It also allows us to speculate, to predict, to make attempts to shape the future. Symbol-making and symbol-taking are the supreme human gifts. The psychological space between one person and another, between an individual and the environment is mapped out through symbolic forms.

Music is one way in which people symbolically articulate their responses to experience and share their observations and insights with others. It has something though not everything in common with the other arts, in that it is particularly well-adapted to illuminate those elements of human feeling which are fleeting and complex and the universal aspirations which most people share, whatever their culture.

Why we value music is ultimately not to do with belonging to a particular tradition or with self-development, but depends on a recognition that music is one of the great symbolic modes available to us. Initiation into this activity is what education is about. We might find ourselves drawn incidentally into a tradition or sub-culture, or may realize that we are developing as individuals: but these outcomes are by-products of doing music for its own sake, just as happiness is a by-product of something else, not a legitimate objective in itself.

No one has yet been able to explain in a totally satisfactory way how the arts function as symbolic forms, though many have tried. I shall not even attempt to open up that enigma here but simply note that musicians have taken extraordinary trouble to make sustained, complex and carefully articulated works and that people have responded to them as though they were significant, meaningful, symbolizing something. Through them something is communicated, something is transmitted, something is known. When any work of art stirs us it is more than simply sensory stimulation or some kind of emotional indulgence. We are gaining knowledge and expanding our experience. The same is true when we form music as composers or perform it: the act of shaping music is a purposeful attempt to articulate something meaningful. It need not be complex or profound, earth-shattering or of cosmic proportions but it will be articulate, expressive and structured and just as 'objective' as the spoken or written word, an equation or a map.

THE FUTURE

Children know how to learn. Schools can impede this impulse. We have to avoid the danger of predicating a curriculum upon a narrow view of musical knowledge and musical learning. In our studies of the musical development of children we have described a swing between assimilation and accommodation, between the personal world of the individual and the public domain of knowledge and experience 'out there'. The surface pleasure of sounds – the sensory – personal expressiveness and the experimentally speculative are all necessary energies and motivation flowing from the student. Acquiring aural and manipulative skills, entering the shared discourse of a musical vernacular and participating in idiomatic procedures are elements that schools and teachers can bring to the educational encounter. If we carefully observe what children actually do with music, we shall notice this constant crossing from one side or the other. The realities of human aspiration and development are not to be compromised or waylaid by apparently conflicting doctrines.

There is much to do now to equip primary school teachers to take on the role of music critic, to become sensitive appraisers and to organize the music curriculum of primary schools in a planned, developmental sequence. This is where there are major resource implications and a need for imaginative teacher education. The main problem for secondary schools is that pupils arrive with radically different levels of ability and experience, often with diminishing enthusiasm for general music courses and are grouped in classes of thirty or so. Options within music are essential to match the range of idiomatic engagement. The music curriculum may need to be thought of in a modular rather than a completely sequential way. The advantage of this is flexibility. Each project can be started at a level which is relevant to a group of pupils and which uses available expertise and resources. There can be culminating points, which may be a series of small-group performances, a whole class composition assembled from small-group contributions or a performance on record and tape of related items composed by children and 'professional' composers. A range of instrumental teachers and community musicians can and should be involved in this process. We must avoid any suggestion of perpetuating a separate musical sub-culture in schools, detached from music in the wider world.

However music in the curriculum is to be organized in the new framework, it will ultimately be defined, refined and managed by teachers supported by others in the field. Whitehall, Westminster and the National Curriculum Council (NCC) have to acknowledge this. Through the Working Group a fairly serviceable structure has been articulated. Doubtless this could have been improved, for instance by moving towards outcomes statements as prime components when stating attainment targets, while specifying classroom activities as a second dimension. This is not to be. In January 1992 the National Curriculum Council, treating music in the same way as art, reduced the attainment targets to two, once again muddling up activities and outcomes – an elementary mistake that makes logical curriculum development difficult if not impossible. The Secretary of State's theoretical fixation with 'simplicity', revealed in his asking the NCC to consider whether there was a case for two attainment targets instead of three, has led to a conceptual mess. The NCC, by reducing music attainment targets to two, is committing an elementary error that makes coherent curriculum documentation nearly impossible. Performing and composing cannot be seen as targets standing separately in the same dimension as knowledge and understanding. Musical knowledge and understanding are learning outcomes that are fostered and *demonstrated* in these activities, and less clearly in audience-listening.

We were offered this framework.

Attainment target 1 – performing and composing

The development of the ability to perform and compose music.

Attainment target 2 – knowledge and understanding

The development of knowledge and understanding of musical history and theory, including the ability to listen to and appraise music.

The import of the NCC model, that knowledge and understanding have to be *about* music is simply nonsensical. Knowledge and understanding can also be *of* music, directly experienced. Such rudimentary reasoning will push the school music curriculum back to the same 'chalk and talk' that fifteen years ago was making music so unattractive to pupils and will foster a belief in the value of acquiring inert information. If the NCC really wanted to go for simplicity, it could have settled for just *one* attainment target – *musical knowledge and musical understanding*, properly defined. The main curriculum activity strands can then be performing, composing and audience-listening.

This unprofessional piece of work, which seems to owe more to the dictates of politicians and civil servants than to an adequate understanding of the subject, has provoked a storm of protest, including responses from musicians such as the conductor Simon Rattle and the Chair of the Music Working Group. The integrity of the NCC is now seriously compromised.

Four leading professional associations, representing musicians and music education experts throughout the United Kingdom, have called on Kenneth Clarke, the then Secretary for State, to reject the National Curriculum Council's advice that the music teaching in schools should have only two Attainment Targets, rather than the three recommended in

1991 by the National Curriculum Working Group for Music. The Incorporated Society of Musicians, the UK Council for Music Education and Training and the Music Advisers' National Association, responded with concern to the NCC's Report, published on the 13 January 1992.

The following press release makes their position clear:

The ISM, UKCMET, MANA and SMA are dismayed by the NCC's advice to the Secretary of State for Education and Science that the National Curriculum for Music should have only two Attainment Targets – 'Performing and Composing' and 'Knowledge and Understanding' rather than the three – Performing, Composing and Appraising – recommended last year by the authoritative National Curriculum Working Group for Music.

First, there has been a total disregard of the consultative process set up in relation to the Working Group reports, whose advice to the Secretary of State took into account the realities and successes of acknowledged advances in music education. The attempts by the NCC to interpret their own statistics which indicated that 80 per cent supported the Working Groups's recommendations – are demonstrably unconvincing.

Second, there is neither musical nor educational logic in favour of adopting only two attainment targets. The three targets recommended by the Working Group represent a means of achieving a broad and balanced musical education, as originally specified by the Secretary of State. The two targets preferred by the NCC lump together the important activities of performing music and composing; while seeking, for the sake of symmetry, to draw a spurious relationship between factual knowledge and the understanding of a subject. Parents will be more accurately and fully informed about pupils' musical knowledge and understanding if teachers assess these through the activities of performing, composing and appraising.

Third, while we take no exception to the end of Key Stage Statements, the Programmes of Study contain items which are totally inappropriate as a legal requirement. The worst of these misjudgements exist in Attainment Target 2, with its heavy emphasis on elements of musical history and theory. For example, at age eleven 'recognize the distinctive characteristics of music from the following periods: medieval, renaissance, baroque, classical, romantic, recent and contemporary' and 'identify the characteristics of music from different styles and genres, including opera, ballet, folk and jazz and different cultures and traditions'.

Such prescriptiveness is contrary to the Secretary of State's terms of reference to the Music Working Group, which we endorsed, requiring the Group 'to advise on a statutory framework which is sufficiently broad and flexible to allow schools wide discretion in relation to matters to be studied'.

The citation of examples are also over-prescriptive and impractical to a point where we can have no confidence in the capacity of the National Curriculum Council as presently constituted, to formulate curriculum proposals and produce workable non-statutory guidance for classroom teachers of music.

Our associations are, of course, more than willing to co-operate in the development of the music curriculum and more into line with the Secretary of State's original intention of clarity and practicality.

In a letter from the author to the Secretary of State it was pointed out that the NCC was promulgating educational nonsense. The following formulation was suggested (see Postscript below):

Attainment target 1 – performing and composing

The development of the ability to perform and compose music with understanding.

Attainment target 2 – listening and appraising

The development of the ability to listen to and appraise music, including knowledge of musical history.

This formulation was assimilated word for word into the Draft Order, though whether the professionals will now accept a two target model is questionable, especially since the Secretary of State has announced that these changes are more a matter of 'packaging' than of 'substance'.

What will happen now is, at the time of writing, very uncertain. It really is essential for politicians, civil servants, right-wing philosophers and other amateurs to withdraw. There are times when professional judgement has to be respected. Ultimately, curriculum development is teacher development and it is here that real curriculum change will be shaped and articulated, just as it always has been.

POSTSCRIPT

The author sent a fax to the Secretary of State on 21 January 1992. The substance of this was carried by *The Times Educational Supplement* on the 24 January 1992. It was an attempt to place the music curriculum within a decent theory of musical knowledge and to push back the advancing tide of inert information implicit in the NCC's attainment target: 'Knowledge and understanding – the development of knowledge and understanding of musical history and theory, including the ability to listen and to appraise music'.

The fax ran as follows:

Dear Secretary of State,

You will by now be aware of the widespread and profound disquiet over the NCC recommendations on the music curriculum. I write in the hope that action can be taken to avert professional alienation at the end of a process of committed consultation which appears to have been over-turned by the NCC.

Without getting into unnecessary detail or subscribing to the appalling ideological warfare which has characterized some of the writing in the press, I shall identify the main difficulties and a possible way forward which would recover the confidence of musicians and music educators, on whom the future development of the music curriculum depends.

1 Attainment targets

The major impediment to professional acceptance of the report is the implication in the attainment targets that knowledge and understanding is essentially tied up with knowing *about* music and does not enter into performing and composing. This may not have been intended but it is inescapable in the way that the attainment targets are defined. Further-more, the balance has been tipped heavily towards factual knowledge about music rather than knowledge of music by the actual wording of the second attaiment target. This will have the effect of increasing the amount of factual information within a subject already restricted to a small corner of time in the school curriculum. Listening to music and appraising it is the key to understanding music history. It should not be slipped in at the end of the target statement after the word 'including'. The use of the word 'theory' is also misleading. I take it that this mainly means knowing about music notation, which is of course no substitute for being able to actually read and write music notation when composing and performing.

Clarification of the wording in the NCC's proposed attainment targets and the accompanying definitions would remove all of these objections and would, I believe, be supported across a wide spectrum of views.

AT1 Performing and composing

The development of the ability to perform and compose music with understanding.

AT2 Listening and appraising

The development of the ability to listen to and appraise music, including knowledge of musical history.

This formulation is logically, educationally, musically and practically acceptable and I would make every effort to persuade colleagues in the music and music education professions that it is so. If these ATs were to be given an approximate curriculum weighting of 60 (AT1) to 40 (AT2) the balance would be about right for most schools.

The programmes of study

There is specific concern about the second attainment target, especially at Key Stage 2. As it stands this is cluttered. There are four different items relating to different periods, styles and historical background. This is informational overkill for 8 to 11-year-old children and would be impossible to sustain in the primary school music curriculum.

The examples

These are non-statutory and I hope they can be re-worked. Some are likely to be meaningless to many children and in any case, taken together they are culturally over-prescriptive.

Sincerely,

On Monday 27 January 1992, Kenneth Clarke, the then Secretary of State, announced that he accepted this formulation of the attainment targets and agreed a weighting towards composing and performing of 2:1. Further work is expected during the consultation process on reducing the information load, especially during Key Stage 2. In the end, the advice of a 'professional' appears to have been of value in a confused situation of do-it-yourself curriculum writers intruding into an area without experience or expertise.

NOTES

1 Polanyi, M. (1967) *The Tacit Dimension*, London: Routledge.
2 See Paynter, J. (1982) *Music in the Secondary School*, Cambridge: Cambridge University Press.
3 An early considered discussion of this issue is in Swanwick, K. (1968) *Popular Music and the Teacher*, Oxford: Pergamon.
4 Swanwick, K. (1977) 'Belief and action in music education', in M. Burnett, (ed.) *Music Education Review*, London: Chappell.

 5 Swanwick, K. (ed.) (1987) *Music in Schools: A Study of Context and Curriculum Practice*, London: Institute of Education.
 6 The observation method was to record only those activities lasting for five minutes or more.
 7 Department of Education and Science (DES) (1991) *Music for Ages 5–16*, London: HMSO.
 8 The term 'ethnic music' is used to indicate music from non-European musical traditions. The term is unfortunate and misleading, since all music is 'ethnic' in origin. However, at the time of the research it was in common use and was understood by teachers and others.
 9 DES (1991) *op. cit.*, p. 57.
10 Swanwick, K. (1979) *A Basis for Music Education*, Windsor: NFER-Nelson.
11 DES (1987a) *The National Curriculum 5–16*, London: HMSO.
12 DES (1987b) *The National Curriculum Task Group on Assessment and Testing – A Report*, London: HMSO.
13 As to the other arts, Drama is seen as part of English and Dance a part of Physical Education.
14 Angela Rumbold, October 1987, in 'The arts and education' in Swanwick, K. (ed.), *Papers from the National Association of Education in the Arts 1983–1990*, NFAE.
15 A letter from the Secretary of State for Education to Sir John Manduell, 14 February 1991.
16 DES (1987a) *op. cit.*, Annex A.
17 DES (1987b) *op. cit.*, Section 35.
18 The Science attainment target 14, *Sound and Music*, seems very odd. It seems that music is to be defined in terms of pitched sounds. A tambourine and a side drum would presumably be ruled out as musical instruments and a police siren could be counted in.
19 Bloom, B. *et al.* (1964) *Taxonomy of Educational Objectives, Book 2, Affective Domain*, New York: David McKay & Co.
20 Swanwick, K. (1988) *Music, Mind and Education*, London: Routledge.
21 DES (1991) *op. cit.*, p. 7.
22 Swanwick, K. and Tillman, J. (1986) 'The sequence of musical development', *British Journal of Music Education*, 3 (3), Cambridge: Cambridge University Press.
23 Swanwick, K. (1991) 'Further research on the musical development sequence', *Journal of the Psychology of Music* 19: 22–3.
24 DES (1991) *op. cit.*, p. 45.
25 Popper, K. (1972) *Objective Knowledge*, Oxford: Clarendon Press.

Part II

Teaching and learning in music

Chapter 3

The developmental psychology of music

Scope and aims

David Hargreaves

There can be no doubt that there has been an explosion of interest in music psychology over the last decade: three journals have been launched and several textbooks published, most recently by Sloboda (1985), Howell *et al.* (1985), Dowling and Harwood (1986) and Storr (1992), for example. This boom, perhaps inevitably, has led to greater specialization within the field. We are now much more likely to refer specifically to the cognitive psychology of music, or to the social psychology of music (Paul R. Farnsworth (1969) was well ahead of his time in this latter instance!), and I see the developmental psychology of music as a natural addition. These subdisciplines are not primarily new collections of facts, but rather new theoretical perspectives, or 'angles', on existing material.

In one important respect, the application of the developmental perspective is long overdue. In primary school mathematics and science, for example, developmental psychology provides a clear theoretical foundation upon which pedagogical practices are based: several curriculum schemes are explicitly based on Piagetian principles, for example Harlen (1975). Although many aspects of this approach are currently being called into question by psychologists and educators, there can be no doubt that Piaget's broad view of the nature and development of logical thinking has had a profound influence upon science education. In the arts subjects in general and music in particular, on the other hand, any comparable foundation is almost completely absent. There is no common body of developmental theory which guides pedagogical practice. As Keith Swanwick says:

> To read through articles in the music education journals and to scan the books that advocate classroom practices is to enter a world that has apparently never assimilated the thinking of people who have influenced and still influence the climate of educational thought and practice.
> (Swanwick, 1977: 65)

My own attempt to survey the developmental foundations that *can* be identified for music education has two main guiding principles. First, I think it is essential that the course of research should be theory-driven: that we should constantly be trying to develop and refine our explanatory framework for musical development, and that this should guide our strategy and planning. There is little point in collecting research data, or in devising teaching methods, without any underlying rationale. There are several (sometimes mutually contradictory) frameworks to choose from, of course, but one of our primary tasks should be to identify and clarify their common themes and their contrasts. Tackling large-scale, thorny issues such as the nature of developmental change as either a continuous or a discontinuous process, or the effects of early experience on later development, demands the resources and insights of all the theories at our disposal.

Second, it is clear from current research that the cognitive, social and affective aspects of development cannot be considered in isolation from one another, as has been the case in the past. The upsurge of research in social cognition, for example, reveals that psychologists are at last beginning to get to grips with the full complexities of human development, and this is particularly important in such a mysterious, abstract and multifaceted domain as music. This change in emphasis stems from several deep-seated changes that have taken place in developmental psychology over the last thirty years or so. There are three main lines of thinking which have transformed the discipline from a relatively quiet backwater of psychology into one of its most vigorous, active branches.

There can be no doubt, first, that children take an *active* part in determining the course of their own development. Young babies frequently take the lead in initiating sequences of reciprocal action with their caregivers, that is, in 'turn-taking', in their gestures, vocalizations and facial expressions (see, for example, Stern, 1977). Researchers in this area have suggested that such phenomena may well be mediated by 'intersubjectivity', that is, the mutual construction of meaning between infant and caregiver; this reflects the second predominant influence upon contemporary developmental psychology, that of the *cognitive* approach. Infants are now seen to 'train their parents' just as much as vice versa, and this new view of development as a joint enterprise is radically different from that which was taken in the earlier 'child-rearing' research in which socialization was essentially thought of as a one-way process.

The third main trend in the discipline is towards a full and comprehensive analysis of human development as a whole. The *ecological* approach involves the consideration of all of the interacting influences upon the developing child, including siblings, peers, caregivers, relatives and so on. Until fairly recently, most research attention had been devoted to the mother–child relationship in a kind of 'social vacuum', that is, with very little consideration being given to the interpersonal network in which this relationship was set. It is also only recently that the *life-span* approach has begun to have a significant impact within the discipline. Developmental psychologists have concentrated very heavily upon the changes that take place between infancy and adolescence, and have only just begun to pay attention to those occurring after the age of sixteen or so.

The developmental psychology of music should presumably bring these insights to bear upon the specific topics of musical development, that is, upon the changes that take over the life span in the perception and production of pitch, melody, rhythm, tonality, harmony, style and form. These topics form the heart of the subject, and we would expect the more rapid and striking developments to occur in childhood. More broadly, however, it could be argued that almost any area of music psychology is 'developmental' in the sense that people's perceptions and capabilities are ever-changing, as are the situations in which they find (or place) themselves. For this reason, there will be many overlaps with other branches of psychology. It goes almost without saying, for example, that there will be a considerable amount of cross-fertilization with the perspectives upon music of cognitive and social psychology, as well as with that of behavioural psychology. More specifically, my own account of the developmental psychology of music draws upon findings from experimental aesthetics and psychobiology, from auditory perception and psychophysics and from psychometrics, the latter raising the issues of environmental and social influences upon musical ability, creativity and personality. Let me try next to outline what I see as the three main theoretical perspectives in the developmental psychology of music, and to identify some key areas of growing research within each.

COGNITIVE PSYCHOLOGY

'Cognitive psychology' is a term which is now used so widely, and in so many different senses, that it embraces most of today's human experimental psychology. Eysenck, for example, writes that 'virtually all those interested in perception, learning, memory, language, concept formation, problem solving, or thinking call themselves cognitive psychologists, despite the great diversity of experimental and theoretical approaches to be found in these various areas' (Eysenck, 1984: 1). The general emphasis of cognitive psychology is upon the internal rules, strategies and operations that people employ in intelligent behaviour, as well as upon the external outcomes of these processes. Part of the original impetus for this approach came from the analogy with computers: psychologists might be thought of as studying the flow of information through the human processing system, as well as trying to specify what happens in the various intermediate stages between input and output. Although there is still a good deal of interest in the computer analogy, especially in the field of artificial intelligence, many cognitive psychologists have begun to question its validity.

The cognitive approach has become a dominant one within music psychology, as the contents of recent textbooks clearly illustrate. In Deutsch's (1982) influential volume, for example, there is a pronounced emphasis on psychophysical studies of tones, intervals and scales; on research on melodic perception and memory; and on representational models of musical structure. Now most cognitive psychologists working within this tradition, who might well follow Deutsch's lead in referring to 'musical processing', have not *primarily* been interested in developmental questions. These questions have mainly been addressed by researchers working within the *cognitive-developmental* tradition, which is most closely associated with the theory and research of Jean Piaget. Piagetian and neo-Piagetian theories are essentially part of the enterprise of cognitive psychology, and they share many concepts and assumptions with the information-processing approach, but they nevertheless derive from a quite different European structuralist tradition. I should like to take a separate look at the cognitive-developmental approach in the next section, and to devote the remainder of the present section to three areas of growing research which derive from the mainstream of cognitive psychology.

The first of these is concerned with the development of melodic perception, or melodic processing, in children. Chang and Trehub (1977a), for example, repeatedly played short, single-note melodies to five-month-old babies, and identified those whose heartrates showed a clear pattern of 'startle' (deceleration) followed by habituation to the melodies. These babies, about one-half of the original sample, were next played versions of the melodies which were transformed either by pitch transposition, or by a change in melodic contour, and their reactions once again assessed by the heartrate measure. Chang and Trehub found that these infants could detect changes in melodic contour, and subsequent research (Chang and Trehub, 1977b; Trehub *et al.*, 1984) showed that infants of this age could also detect changes in the rhythmic patterns and frequency ranges of melodies, which is much earlier than previous research might predict. These investigators suggest that young infants employ a 'global strategy' for processing melodies which is based on their overall shape, or contour.

The work of Dowling and his associates on the acquisition of tonality in later childhood (Bartlett and Dowling, 1980; Dowling, 1982) supports and extends this line of research. Using a similar research strategy, they played familiar melodies along with various transformations of them to children of different ages, and found some consistent developmental changes in processing strategy. Broadly speaking, we might conclude that the 'global' strategies of early childhood, with their concentration upon gross melodic features such as contour and pitch level, are gradually replaced by more 'analytic' strategies which involve the grasp of tonality. Dowling (1982) suggests that the hierarchy of melodic features – pitch, contour, tonality and interval size – appears as a sequence of developmental acquisitions in children, and it is interesting to note that this same sequence seems to appear in adults' perception of unfamiliar melodies.

The study of children's singing has a long history, and the descriptive studies of Moog (1976) and Moorhead and Pond (1978) are deservedly well-known, but this topic has recently been given a new impetus by the cognitive approach. Dowling's (1982, 1984) research on singing is complementary to his general account of developmental change in melodic processing strategies, mentioned above; he has produced some empirical evidence for a similar age-related move from a predominance of gross features such as melodic contour in early songs towards the incorporation of more precise features such as tonality and intervals. Another significant body of recent research on children's singing has been carried out by members of the Harvard University Project Zero group (for example, Davidson et al., 1981). Both research programmes take their methodological lead from the psycholinguistic research of Roger Brown: their common approach has been to make a detailed, comprehensive and naturalistic record of the song output of a small number of children over a period of some few years.

The Project Zero researchers suggest, like Dowling, that the child's initial grasp of a song is 'topological': that its global 'outline' properties are more salient than its precise details. By the age of around three, they suggest, children produce song 'outlines' or 'frames' into which regularities of rhythm and contour are gradually incorporated. These song 'frames' gradually merge with the standard songs of the culture, such as nursery rhymes: spontaneous songs incorporate an increasing proportion of phrases and patterns from standard songs, and vice versa, as children get older. In this way, Davidson et al. suggest that what they call 'first draft' songs emerge by the age of five years or so. The 'song frames' of the three-year-old have been 'filled in' to a significant degree, and the child possesses a wide repertoire of standard songs, but these are still far from completely accurate in terms of tonality and interval size.

A central explanatory concept in the accounts of both Dowling and the Project Zero researchers is that of the cognitive *scheme*, or *schema*. Though their explanations differ in some respects, both see musical schemes as abstract, internal representations of knowledge about musical structure. The child's 'song frame' is a general form of scheme, for example, and Davidson (1983) has proposed a more detailed theory of the organization of early song which is based on the concept of the *contour scheme*. Schemes have been part of cognitive psychology for some time, of course: Neisser described them as 'cognitive structures that prepare the perceiver to accept certain kinds of information rather than others' (Neisser, 1976: 20), for example, and they are at the heart of Piagetian theory.

One ingenious way of investigating children's musical schemes is by approaching them via other non-musical media: by studying children's *representations* of music. There is a small but very promising area of research on children's drawings of simple musical patterns, such as rhythmic sequences. Goodnow (1971) and Bamberger (1982), for example, have played sequences of taps and claps to children at different age levels, and asked them to write down or draw what they heard. There seem to be quite distinct developmental trends in the drawing strategies adopted, and Bamberger's account of these is quite elaborate. One key distinction which emerges from her description is that between *figural* and *metric* modes of representation. Young children's *figural* strategies focus on the function of events *within* drawn figures: they represent the individual's *global* interpretation of the sequence, such that each musical event is coded by reference to its immediate context. The *metric* strategies of older children are correspondingly *analytic*: they pay more precise attention to the exact duration of each event, and to the underlying reference beat.

I think that this line of research is important for two reasons. First, the cross-modal approach to musical representation might well lead to insights which could not emerge from research conducted from within a single medium. Second, Bamberger's distinction between figural and metric strategies of representation throws light on a much wider issue in music education. Metric drawings approximate to conventional musical notation, and would thus be regarded by many as displaying a higher level of musical thinking than figural ones: we might say that they reveal evidence of *formal* musical understanding. At the same time, figural strategies can convey the *intuitive* musical sense of a stimulus or piece, in particular its phrasing, in a way that metric strategies cannot. Bamberger (1982) observes that as children's formal ability to read and write music accurately gradually increases, there may well be a corresponding decline in their intuitive feeling for a piece: that if teachers are not careful, intuitive musical understanding can easily be stifled. I shall return to this important issue in the final section.

COGNITIVE-DEVELOPMENTAL PSYCHOLOGY

Cognitive-developmental psychology is the branch of cognitive psychology which is most readily applicable to music education, and this has largely occurred in musical applications of Piaget's theory. It is not appropriate for me to elaborate upon the essentials of the theory here, and I would refer the interested reader to one of the many excellent general texts which are available (for example, Boden, 1979), as well as to Serafine's (1980) penetrating review of Piagetian research on music. Suffice it to say that Piaget's theory is *cognitive* in its proposition that children make sense of their environment by means of internal *schemes*, the 'building blocks' of cognition which constantly evolve and change as the child assimilates new objects and events; and that it is *developmental* in its concern with age-related changes, which take place in a well-known sequence of *stages*. The largest area of research is that on 'music conservation', which involves the direct application of a central Piagetian concept to children's musical thinking, and there is also a growing body of research on the development of aesthetic appreciation which adopts a Piagetian-type stage approach.

The idea of 'music conservation' was pioneered by Marilyn Pflederer Zimmerman of the University of Illinois, who devised a series of musical tasks which are intended to be analogous to Piaget's non-musical conservation tasks (Pflederer, 1964). Children are typically played a short melody, followed by a version of it in which one property (such as 'durational values' or 'pitch level') is transformed whilst all other properties remain the same. They are asked to say whether the two versions are 'the same', or 'different', or both; conservation is inferred to be present if they recognize that the melodies are both the same *and* different in certain respects. The basis of the analogy is that pre-operational children (who cannot conserve) should inappropriately *centre* either upon the common properties of the two versions or upon the transformed property, and that concrete operational children should be able to *decentre*.

Pflederer Zimmerman has formally developed the analogy with Piaget's theory of concrete operations in proposing five 'conservation-type laws' for the development of musical intelligence (Pflederer, 1967), and a considerable body of evidence has accumulated in support of the predictions that these laws make about age-related improvements on the musical tasks (see Serafine, 1980). Even though this includes some of my own evidence (Hargreaves *et al.*, 1986), I share with others (for example, Gardner, 1973; Serafine, 1980) some serious doubts about the validity of the Piagetian analogy. These revolve around the fact that musical transformations, being time-based, are not comparable with transformations performed upon one member of a pair of concrete objects which are simultaneously present.

Establishing causal explanations is always notoriously difficult when age is the independent variable, as it is in this case. The fact that older children do better than younger ones on tasks which are described as measures of 'music conservation' gives no guarantee that a Piagetian-type explanation is correct: many other concurrent developments, such as in attentional skills, verbal fluency, memory, or auditory sensitivity could equally well produce the same result. Pflederer Zimmerman's tasks are virtually identical in form to those employed by Dowling and others in the 'melodic processing' literature, and I would like to suggest that some cross-fertilization between these two parallel streams of research might go quite a long way towards the resolution of this problem.

Piaget's stage theory forms the basis of Kohlberg's cognitive-developmental account of moral thinking, and both models have been applied to the development of aesthetic appreciation in children. Gardner *et al.* (1975), for example, tape-recorded open-ended interviews about pictures, poems and music with children aged between four and sixteen years. Analysis of the transcriptions showed that children's responses could be grouped into three broad categories, reflecting *immature, transitional* and *mature* artistic reasoning respectively: this was interpreted as supporting the predictions of cognitive-developmental theory. Parsons (1976) has also proposed a Kohlberg-based stage theory of the development of aesthetic appreciation which largely concentrates upon visual art.

By far the largest body of empirical data in this area is that which has been gathered by the Harvard Project Zero group, to which I referred earlier. Howard Gardner and his associates have focused on the development of sensitivity to artistic styles, and their main research strategy has been to ask children of different ages to make stylistic discriminations and judgements about original and transformed works from various artistic media (including literature, visual art and music; see Winner (1982) for a full account). Although Gardner's theoretical approach is clearly cognitive-developmental, he disagrees with Piaget in two important respects. First, he claims that Piaget's view of logical-rational scientific thought as the apex, or 'end state' of mature cognition is inappropriate: that a great deal more consideration should be given to the irrational, intuitive forms of thought that are demanded by the arts. Second, he believes that Piaget pays insufficient attention to the *content* of cognitive development: that we ought to study the specific problems of verbal development, mathematical development, musical development, graphic development, etc., on their own merits rather than attempting a global explanation which attempts to cut across all media.

With these issues in mind, Gardner (1973) has formulated an alternative theory of artistic development which centres on the child's acquisition of *symbols*. He defines and describes the properties of *symbol systems*, suggesting that the preschooler's acquisition and use of words, drawings, make-believe and other symbols is the main developmental foundation for later artistic development. This leads to the provocative implication that most children have acquired all the essential characteristics of the audience member, artist and performer by the age of seven or so, such that 'the groupings, groups and operations described by Piaget do not seem essential for mastery or understanding of human language, music, or plastic arts' (Piaget, 1973: 45). Gardner proposes an alternative model of artistic development with just two broad stages, that is, a 'presymbolic period' of sensorimotor development in early infancy, and a 'period of symbol use' from ages two to seven.

The research of the Project Zero group has provided a good deal of empirical evidence for developmental increases in sensitivity to artistic styles, and most of these have been identified *within* the symbol systems provided by each artistic medium. One recent study (Winner *et al.*, 1986) has attempted an ambitious exploration of the development of sensitivity to three aesthetic properties *across* three art forms (drawing, music and literature), and has reached the conclusion that aesthetic sensitivity develops *within* symbol systems, such that there is no need to postulate general underlying cognitive processes such as those of Piaget. This is not the place to debate the relative merits of the two rival theories: I would simply like to suggest that their approaches are perhaps not as divergent as Gardner implies. The symbolic function is after all at the heart of Piaget's account of the pre-operational period, and Gardner's approach is essentially a cognitive-developmental one. The difference may turn out to be one of detail and emphasis rather than of substance.

BEHAVIOURAL PSYCHOLOGY

One distinctive theoretical approach in developmental psychology derives from the *behaviourism* of J. B. Watson (Watson, 1924). One of Watson's tenets was that psychologists should be concerned with publicly-observable aspects of behaviour, and not with internal mental states: this represents the antithesis of modern cognitive psychology. Watson's original theory gave rise to numerous subsequent variations, which might collectively be termed *reinforcement*, or *learning* theories (see Bower and Hilgard, 1981). Some of these theories maintain that all of human development can be explained by the laws of operant and classical conditioning: that behaviour can ultimately be reduced to sets of learnt associations between stimuli and responses. Variations such as *social learning theory* (Bandura, 1977), on the other hand, acknowledge that the full complexity of human development can only adequately be dealt with by incorporating certain mentalistic or cognitive constructs, such that the resulting theory falls somewhere in between the two views.

Although numerous shades of theoretical opinion exist, and although conceptual and terminological confusion abounds, it is nevertheless quite possible for music educators to make practical applications of the various *principles of learning* without a commitment to any particular point of view. Some music educators have applied their knowledge of positive and negative reinforcement, modelling and behaviour shaping, stimulus discrimination and generalization, extinction and so on to meet immediate practical needs, and I have chosen the broad term 'behavioural psychology' to convey this eclecticism of approach.

Behavioural methods have been applied in music therapy and in programmed music instruction as well as in the classroom, and a good deal of the progress in this field derives from the work of R. D. Greer, C. K. Madsen and their collaborators (see for example, Madsen *et al.*, 1975). Greer (1978) points out that a good deal of the behavioural research on music learning in the classroom has been concerned either with *motivation* or with *affect*. Studies of the former have investigated the use of music itself as a reinforcer, for example, to improve children's performance on non-musical scholastic tasks, or to facilitate social skills. Another body of research, perhaps more directly relevant to music educators, has looked at the effects on music learning of various extrinsic reinforcers such as teacher approval/disapproval, modelling, progress charts and tokens (see Greer, 1978). Research on affect has used the concept of the *reinforcement value* of music in investigations of the development of musical taste.

One indisputable advantage of the behavioural approach to music learning is that it is extremely practical: it works directly upon behaviour in the classroom. Greer's (1980) *Design for Music Learning* presents a thorough and explicit statement of the practicalities involved. Using behavioural principles, the music learning task is analysed and hierarchically categorized. Strategies of teaching are devised, based on learning principles, to chart the learner's precise course through the task hierarchy; the teachers themselves practise these strategies in the classroom, and the learner's progress is consistently monitored. This monitoring serves as feedback motivation for the mastery of subsequent tasks by the learner, and so the cycle continues; feedback and assessment are an integral and continuous part of the learning process.

The behavioural approach clearly provides one answer to the call for a rapprochement between theory and practice, though it is a peculiarly North American answer of which many non-American educators would disapprove. The precise specification and assessment of learning forms the essence of the *competency-based* approach to music education (see for example, Madsen and Yarbrough, 1980), and this is highly compatible with behavioural psychology. Behavioural techniques are undoubtedly effective in the teaching of lower-level performance skills which can easily be specified, but higher-order skills such as those involved in composition and improvisation almost certainly cannot be dealt with in the same way.

MUSIC EDUCATION AND THE DEVELOPMENTAL PSYCHOLOGY OF MUSIC

In this article, I have tried to throw some light on Sloboda's (1986) original questions by pointing out some of the key points of contact between music education and the developmental psychology of music. Behavioural psychology in a sense exists by virtue of its application to the classroom, and thus side-steps the problem – but it has some severe limitations, as I have tried to indicate. Most of the rest of our knowledge of musical development, it must be admitted, is of indirect rather than of direct help. Music teachers are more likely to need to evaluate and compare the different *pedagogical* techniques and theories that they might draw on, such as those of Orff, Kodaly, and Suzuki, for example, in their everyday work. Nevertheless, I think that there are some issues of immediate concern to music educators to which developmental psychologists can make a direct contribution.

The first of these concerns the distinction between the 'formal' and 'intuitive' aspects of musical understanding. The recommendation in the HMI document *Music 5–16* (DES, 1985: 1) that 'the mastery of techniques should be subservient to experiencing music itself ' goes all the way back to Rousseau, Jacques-Dalcroze and others, of course, and yet it still provokes disagreement and even hostility. The fact that the British Schools Council Project Music in the Secondary School Curriculum (Paynter, 1982) remains controversial underlines this point: Many teachers still emphasize the academic, formal aspects of music rather than its intuitive, creative aspects, and may thus be putting the cart before the horse. My hope is that scientific evidence about children's use of formal and intuitive cognitive strategies in musical development, such as in the work of Bamberger, should have an important part to play in the practical pros and cons of this argument.

The second issue is closely related to this, and concerns the curriculum. Here again, Her Majesty's Inspectors are (perhaps surprisingly!) forward-looking in proposing that composition and improvisation should be integral, assessed parts of the music syllabus: playing by ear and creative music-making are considered to be just as important as the ability to read and write formal notation, and to perform from a score. This leads to a second point, which is that the former may be much *more* important in certain areas, such as pop, jazz or folk music. The Inspectors suggest that '*what* music is taught is only slightly more important than the *way* it is taught' (1985: 2), and it goes almost without saying that different skills are demanded by different musics. Formal notational skills are required in many forms of tonal music; programming, recording and studio production skills are essential in many forms of electronic and experimental music; jazz, pop and many non-Western forms of music rely on aural skills and improvisation; traditional and ethnic musics may well demand an understanding of their historical and cultural contexts: and so on. I would make the simple point that psychologists should be able to provide us with an understanding of the interrelationships between these different skills, and also perhaps of the general developmental principles underlying them. (I would also add, in passing, that the musical materials used by many experimenters in music psychology are as conventional as in the most traditional of classrooms!)

The third issue concerns the role of evaluation and assessment. One of the largest single areas of music psychology deals with ability testing and personality assessment, as we have seen, and contemporary psychology offers a comprehensive, sophisticated armoury of techniques of psychometric assessment and statistical analysis. It does not seem unreasonable that music educators should expect some help from psychologists in this respect. This might enable them to assess pupil progress, so that particular teaching programmes can be devised accordingly: to evaluate the effectiveness of teachers, or at least to enable teachers to appraise their own effectiveness: and to evaluate the objectives of the course of instruction itself. I am not sure that British music educators could or should aspire to the ideals of North American-style competency-based music education, but a rigorous analysis of existing practice along these lines would do no harm in the present disorganized context.

REFERENCES

Bamberger, J. (1982) 'Revisiting children's drawings of simple rhythms: a function for reflection-in-action, in S. Strauss and R. Stavy (eds) *U-Shaped Behavioral Growth*, New York: Academic Press.

Bandura, A. (1977) *Social Learning Theory*, Englewood Cliffs, NJ: Prentice-Hall.

Bartlett, J. C. and Dowling, W. J. (1980) 'The recognition of transposed melodies: a key-distance effect in developmental perspective', *Journal of Experimental Psychology: Human Perception and Performance* 6: 501–15.

Boden, M. A. (1979) *Piaget*, London: Fontana.

Bower, G. H. and Hilgard, E. R. (1981) *Theories of Learning* (5th edn), *Englewood Cliffs, NJ: Prentice-Hall.*

Chang, H. and Trehub, S. E. (1977a) 'Auditory processing of relational information by young infants', *Journal of Experimental Child Psychology* 24: 324–31.

Chang, H. and Trehub, S. E. (1977b) 'Infants' perception of temporal grouping in auditory patterns', *Child Development* 48: 1666–70.

Davidson, L. (1983) 'Tonal structures of children's early songs', paper presented at the International Conference on Psychology and the Arts, Cardiff, *Bulletin of the British Psychological Society* 36: A119–A120.

Davidson, L., McKernon, P. and Gardner, H. (1981) 'The acquisition of song: a developmental approach', in *Documentary Report of the Ann Arbor Symposium on the Applications of Psychology to the Teaching and Learning of Music*, Reston, VA: MENC.

DES (1985) *Music from 5–16*, Curriculum Matters 4, London: HMSO.

Deutsch, D. (ed.) (1982) *The Psychology of Music*, New York: Academic Press.

Dowling, W. J. (1982) 'Melodic information processing and its development', in D. Deutsch (ed.) *The Psychology of Music*, New York: Academic Press.

Dowling, W. J. (1984) 'Development of musical schemata in children's spontaneous singing', in W. R. Crozier and A. J. Chapman (eds) *Cognitive Processes in the Perception of Art*, Amsterdam: Elsevier.

Dowling, W. J. and Harwood, D. L. (1986) *Music Cognition*, New York: Academic Press.

Eysenck, M. W. (1984) *A Handbook of Cognitive Psychology*. London: Lawrence Erlbaum.

Farnsworth, P. R. (1969) *The Social Psychology of Music* (2nd edn), Ames, Ia: Iowa State University Press.

Gardner, H. (1973) *The Arts and Human Development*, New York: Wiley.

Gardner, H., Winner, E. and Kircher, M. (1975) 'Children's conceptions of the arts', *Journal of Aesthetic Education* 9: 60–77.

Goodnow, J. (1971) 'Auditory–visual matching: modality problem or translation problem?' *Child Development* 42: 1187–201.

Greer, R. D. (1978) 'An operant approach to motivation and affect: ten years of research in music learning', paper presented at the National Symposium for the Application of Learning Theory to Music Education, Ann Arbor, MI; Reston, VA: MENC, 1981.

Greer, R. D. (1980) *Design for Music Learning*, New York: Teachers' College Press.

Hargreaves, D. J. (1986) *The Developmental Psychology of Music*, Cambridge: Cambridge University Press.

Hargreaves, D. J., Castell, K. C. and Crowther, R. D. (1986) 'The effects of stimulus familiarity on conservation-type responses to tone sequences: a cross-cultural study', *Journal of Research in Music Education* 34: 88–100.

Harlen, W. (1975) *Science 5–13: A Formative Evaluation*, Schools Council Research Studies, London: Macmillan.

Howell, P., Cross, I. and West, R. (eds) (1985) *Musical Structure and Cognition*, London: Academic Press.

Madsen, C. K., Greer, R. D. and Madsen, C. H. (eds) (1975) *Research in Music Behavior: Modifying Music Behavior in the Classroom*, New York: Teachers' College Press

Madsen, C. K. and Yarbrough, C. (1980) *Competency-Based Music Education*, Englewood Cliffs, NJ: Prentice-Hall.

Moog, H. (1976) *The Musical Experience of the Pre-School Child*, trans. C. Clarke, London: Schott.

Moorhead, G. E. and Pond, D. (1978) *Music of Young Children*, Santa Barbara, CA: Pillsbury Foundation, 1941–51.

Neisser, U. (1976) *Cognition and Reality: Principles and Implications of Cognitive Psychology*, San Francisco: W. H. Freeman.

Parsons, M. (1976) 'A suggestion concerning the development of aesthetic experience in children', *Journal of Aesthetics and Art Criticism* 34: 305–14.

Paynter, J. (1982) *Music in the Secondary School Curriculum*, Cambridge: Cambridge University Press.

Pflederer, M. (1964) 'The responses of children to musical tasks embodying Piaget's principle of conservation', *Journal of Research in Music Education* 12: 251–68.

Pflederer, M. (1967) 'Conservation laws applied to the development of musical intelligence', *Journal of Research in Music Education* 15: 215–23.

Serafine, M. L. (1980) 'Piagetian research in music', *Council for Research in Music Education Bulletin* 62: 1–21.

Sloboda, J. A. (1985) *The Musical Mind: The Cognitive Psychology of Music*, Oxford: Oxford University Press.

Sloboda, J. A. (1986) 'Achieving our aims in music education research', *Psychology of Music* 14 (2): 144–5.

Stern, D. (1977) *The First Relationship: Infant and Mother*, London: Fontana/Open Books.

Storr, A. (1992) *Music and the Mind*, London: HarperCollins.

Swanwick, K. (1977) 'Belief and action in music education', in M. Burnett (ed.) *Music Education Review*, vol. 1, London: Chappell.

Trehub, S. E., Bull, D. and Thorpe, L. A. (1984) 'Infants' perception of melodies: the role of melodic contour', *Child Development* 55: 821–30.

Watson, J. B. (1924) *Behaviorism*, New York: Norton.

Winner, E. (1982) *Invented Worlds: The Psychology of the Arts*, Cambridge, MA: Harvard University Press.

Winner, E., Rosenblatt, W., Windmueller, G., Davidson, L. and Gardner, H. (1986) 'Children's perception of "aesthetic" properties of the arts: domain-specific or pan-artistic?', *British Journal of Developmental Psychology* 4: 149–60.

Chapter 4

Music education and the natural learning model

Margaret Barrett

In recent years the work of a number of researchers in the field of language acquisition, has greatly influenced our understanding of how children learn oral language. Smith (1978), Holdaway (1979) and, more recently, Cambourne (1988) appear to have reached agreement about certain factors connected with the ways in which children learn oral language. These factors have had a major impact on the way in which we think about children's language acquisition in its spoken form and, consequently, the way in which we think about children's acquisition of the written form of language. This has resulted in a number of initiatives within education with particular reference to the understanding of the development of literacy skills in children. Consequently, the study of how children acquire language has provided the basis for the development of a model of learning in a number of curriculum areas.

In the view of these researchers, learning is regarded as a natural behaviour. 'Learning is not an occasional event, to be stimulated, provoked or reinforced. Learning is what the brain does naturally' (Smith, 1980: 88). Natural, or developmental learning, as Holdaway (1979) describes it, has a number of characteristics which are apparent, regardless of the skills to be acquired.

Perhaps the most powerful example of natural learning is that of the young child learning to talk. Children acquire this skill with no apparent formal instruction and, provided there are no physical or mental impediments, are competent and successful in the acquisition and execution of this skill. As Cambourne (1988) states: 'Learning how to talk . . . is a stunning intellectual achievement, almost universally successful, extremely rapid, usually effortless, painless and durable'.

A number of factors emerge as commonalities in the development of the skill of talking. The child is in a supportive environment, surrounded by models of the skills to be acquired, in action. These models occur in a natural and meaningful context, and are part of the fabric of the child's life. Attempts by the child to copy the skills are encouraged, indeed celebrated, however far from the 'correct' response the initial attempt may have been. Such encouragement is interactional and non-judgemental, as the child's attempts at language are responded to, and at times, extended. The child is universally expected to acquire the skills with a resultant diminution of feelings of fear or negativity on the part of the learner. The child is encouraged to operate independently, and to take responsibility for his learning and is able to practise the skill at his own pace. Holdaway describes this type of learning as:

> highly individual and non-competitive; it is short on teaching and long on learning; it is self-regulated rather than adult-regulated; it goes hand in hand with the fulfilment of real life purposes; it emulates the behaviour of people who model the skill in natural use.
>
> (Holdaway, 1979: 14)

From these observations and understandings of how a child acquires spoken language, Holdaway (1979) developed a model for natural language learning of which the following summarizes the major characteristics:

- The learning begins with immersion in an environment in which the skill is being used in purposeful ways.
- The environment is an emulative rather than an instructional one, providing lively examples of the skill in action.
- Reinforcement contingencies, both intrinsic and extrinsic, approach the ideal of immediate rewards for almost every approximation regardless of the distance of the initial response from the ideal response.
- Bad approximations . . . are not reinforced.
- Practice of the task is determined largely by the learner.
- The environment is secure and supportive . . . free from any threat associated with the learning task.
- Development tends to proceed continuously in an orderly sequence marked by considerable difference from individual to individual.

> (*ibid.*: 23)

Cambourne (1988) has further refined this model of natural language learning and has identified a number of conditions which are fundamental to the development of learning as a natural behaviour. While relating the natural learning model specifically to the acquisition of literacy, it is Cambourne's belief that these conditions are not exclusively those of language learning, but provide a framework for learning in general. Cambourne believes:

> that there is a single unitary very effective process of learning which is exemplified by learning to talk and, that over the long period of human evolution, the brain has evolved so that it prefers to learn this way and that most learning, especially language-related learning, proceeds most effectively under these conditions.
>
> (Cambourne, 1988: 42)

These conditions: immersion; demonstration; engagement; expectation; responsibility; approximation; and use and response have formed the basis of a number of literacy programmes in Tasmanian schools. The development of teaching strategies and learning experiences which emulate the natural way in which children acquire oral language has had a major impact not only on the ways in which literacy skills are taught, but has also affected changes in the ways in which learning and teaching are regarded in other curriculum areas, for example, in the Arts Education areas of the Visual Arts (Education Department of Tasmania, 1988); Expressive Movement (Education Department of Tasmania, 1980a); Experiential Drama (Education Department of Tasmania, 1980b); Music (Department of Education and the Arts, 1990); and Mathematics (Edmunds and Stoessinger, 1987). Although the conditions which are characteristic of the natural development of children's language acquisition may not be exactly replicated within the classroom, teachers may draw on the principles which are exemplified by them.

When the conditions described above are considered within the context of music education, the basis for the development of a powerful curriculum model is provided. This curriculum model, reflective of Cambourne's (1988) belief in a single process of learning, is applicable at all levels of education, and is not restricted to a specific range defined by age or ability. In the following discussion, each of the conditions identified by Cambourne are discussed and related specifically to music education.

IMMERSION

Immersion in an environment which is rich in musical experiences is perhaps one of the most important prerequisites for developing the understandings and skills necessary for learning to use and control the materials of music. Initially, this immersion may take the form of exposing children to appropriate sound-making materials. A range of interesting tuned and untuned percussion instruments of good quality provides children with immense possibilities for developing an original and individual vocabulary of sound, a fundamental aspect of the development of understanding in music.

A popular activity in the music classroom has been that of making musical instruments. Often the instruments which result from these activities bear only an outward resemblance to a musical instrument. For example, suggestions such as the manufacture of a tambourine by gluing two paper plates together and attaching bottle tops to the outer edges, while producing an object which resembles a tambourine, do not in any way address the sound-producing properties of the instruments in question. The imposition of materials foreign to 'serious' or 'adult' music-making, such as shakers made from bottles filled with pebbles, and similar home-made instruments may appear irrelevant and pointless to the learner when attempting to develop original compositions. Therefore, it is essential that children have the opportunity to deal with appropriate materials at all times. Although valid music compositions may result from the employment of materials which are not initially considered to be musical instruments, it is suggested that these compositions are usually the work of composers who have an extensive knowledge of the concepts of music, and are therefore able to address these concepts through the innovative use of unusual sound-making materials.

Quality examples of the work of adult and professional musicians which illustrate a wide range of musical styles and forms should be provided in order to encourage children to develop an understanding of the diversity of musical experiences and opportunities which may be made available to them.

When considering the concept of immersion, it must be emphasized that the notions of opportunities for engagement in musical experience, and availability of musical materials, are paramount. Children may be engaged in musical experience through listening to a performance, developing an original composition, participating in an ensemble, following a notation, devising a notation, singing a song, or sharing a composition with peers. Immersion needs to be sustained and sequential in order to be effective. Isolated incidents which occur at irregular intervals throughout the child's learning experiences may be regarded as transitory and ineffectual in developing understanding. Furthermore, children need opportunities to talk about music, to learn about music from other cultures and times and to become familiar with the materials and processes of music-making.

DEMONSTRATION

Demonstrations may be regarded as the models of behaviours from which we learn. These demonstrations do not necessarily have to take the form of a series of actions, such as a live performance, or the construction of a composition, but may be embedded in the artefacts which arise from these actions. The score of a composition, whether notated conventionally or with graphic notation, is a demonstration in itself of a musical process. Similarly, a recording of a performance, an artefact which preserves the most fundamental of musical behaviours, that of playing, is a powerful demonstration. Engagement with the artefact is synonymous with engagement in a specific set of actions. 'The world continually provides demonstrations, through people and through their products, by acts and by artefacts . . .' (Smith, 1980: 89), and it is when we engage with one of those demonstrations which surround us, that we may begin to internalize some aspect of that specific demonstration.

When the above is taken into consideration, theoretically everything that occurs in the classroom is a demonstration. However, learners will only engage with those demonstrations that are perceived to be relevant to their needs and interests. Learners may select, interpret, organize and reorient their thinking through engagement with demonstrations. For example, the observation of the variety of ways in which a peer produces sound from an instrument, or the demonstration of some alternative ways of notating duration, may influence the learner's subsequent work. The imitative use of stylistic musical conventions within a student's composition provides an example of the importance of demonstrations in developing musical understandings. As Bunting states: 'a composer may seek out new ideas by speculating on accepted musical conventions' (in Swanwick and Tillman, 1986: 324).

When engaged in music experiences, the individual takes up a number of roles. These roles are described by Swanwick (1979) as those of the composer, the auditor and the performer and are based on the areas of music experience of composition, audition and performance (CAP). Swanwick expands on these three areas of music experience by including those of literature studies, that is the 'literature of and about music' (1979: 45) and skill acquisition, specifically those relating to aural, instrumental and notational issues (CLASP). In order to develop the skills and understandings associated with music education, children need to be immersed in an environment rich in musical experiences, where all the skills are being used in meaningful and purposeful ways, and where they are encouraged to take on all the roles of musical experience, that is, those of composer, auditor and performer. Ideally, this environment should include lively demonstrations of the areas of musical experience by professionals, amateurs, peers and people who play a significant role in the lives of children, such as parents and teachers. For example, a teacher who listens to a composition with the children in her care, rather than using such times as an opportunity to complete another task (for example, completing the roll!) is effectively demonstrating one of the many purposes of music.

Children should be able not only to observe professionals at work, such as performers or composers, but to be able to talk with them, discuss their lives and their work, and meet with examples of their work on a reasonably regular basis. In this manner, children may learn that there is a variety of ways of approaching the medium, and seemingly limitless possibilities for the use of the materials of music. Techniques used by professional composers, such as the keeping of notebooks in which to notate ideas or motives, or the recording of original work, may be adopted by children, encouraging them to listen to their environment and their musical experiences more acutely and more accurately.

Performances from visiting artists, local identities and fellow students; listening experiences which expose children to a variety of musical forms and styles; opportunities to participate in a range of musical experiences;

and, perhaps most importantly, the opportunity to experiment with the materials of music in order to discover their possibilities and limitations, provide children with a number of examples of how music may become meaningful to them, and a powerful part of their daily lives.

ENGAGEMENT

Immersion and demonstration may be considered to be necessary conditions within the learning environment. However, in themselves, they may not be sufficient to ensure that any learning takes place. Some children may be patient observers of numerous demonstrations, and be immersed in an environment rich in musical experience, and yet appear to be unable to engage meaningfully with any of these experiences, incapable of making them 'their own'.

Prior to engagement occurring, a number of factors need to be taken into consideration. Children need to perceive themselves as potential 'doers' of whatever is being demonstrated; as potential musicians, composers and auditors. This is one of the most important factors; that children have confidence in their ability to make a statement in music which will be accepted, regardless of the sophistication, or simplicity of the response. Children need to perceive that the acquisition of the skills being demonstrated is personally meaningful, and that they may '. . . somehow further the purposes of their lives' (Cambourne, 1988: 52). Finally, children should feel that any 'risks' associated with the task are endurable, and that it is safe to attempt the task.

EXPECTATIONS

Expectations are messages provided by the teacher, that communicate the confidence that the teacher displays in the child's abilities to be ultimately successful, and as such are fundamental aspects of the process of engagement. It is important that the teacher conveys to children that the development of an understanding of music, its materials and processes and the ability to use these purposefully, are potentially some of the most important things in their lives.

Children need to perceive that the skills and understandings that they are trying to master are valuable, relevant, functional and useful. They need to develop an understanding of music as a fundamental aspect of human culture that empowers the individual to articulate original statements, and to communicate meanings through another medium. The transmission to the learner of the message that music is more than vicarious entertainment; that it is a way of thinking and a way of knowing is essential.

Expectations are intimately connected to the development of self-esteem in the child, and the establishment of a relationship founded in trust and mutual respect between the teacher and the child. The teacher needs to know each individual in the class, and plan appropriately, in order to ascertain expectations which are pertinent to the individual's needs. Motivational factors are highly relevant in this context, and learning experiences which provide the opportunity for individual problem-solving may be regarded as the most intrinsically satisfying. Children involved in open-ended problem solving, are required to engage in a number of intellectual processes such as inferring, envisioning possibilities and exploring possible courses of action whilst developing the skills and techniques which will enable them to arrive at a satisfying response.

RESPONSIBILITY

The fostering of independent learners who are capable of identifying problems, determining courses of action and subsequently implementing appropriate strategies in order to seek a resolution to the problem may be regarded as one of the responsibilities of the teacher. Evaluation of the effectiveness of a solution is also an important aspect of the process, and it is the teacher's task to ensure that the learner is provided with a safe and supportive environment which is conducive to the promotion of such decision-making.

In order to promote independent learning, individuals need to be given opportunities to operate independently. Children need to be placed in situations where it is necessary to make decisions independently of the teacher. The implication for the teacher is that the child must be trusted to make some decisions independently, to engage with demonstrations and to select from those demonstrations those aspects which are perceived to be most pertinent at that time, consequently deciding what is most necessary to explore further.

Of course, within the context of music this does not mean that the teacher abandons the child after making sure that a sufficient number of instruments are available! Initially it may mean that materials are provided for guided exploratory experiences to enable the child to become familiar with and develop the ability to control the characteristics of the medium. When the child has developed a sufficient vocabulary of possibilities, a number of simple open-ended challenges designed by the teacher which may be met at the individual's level of understanding and experience may be provided. Gradually, challenges of increasing complexity may be introduced until the child is capable of initiating his or her own musical statements.

Assistance from an expert, often the teacher, or a peer whose musical capacities are more highly developed, should be available at all times. The experience of explaining, or teaching an item to another is often instrumental in clarifying the issues within the mind of the learner, and peer tutoring should be encouraged as a commonplace occurrence within the learning environment. When tutoring a peer, emphasis needs to be placed upon the processes of problem-solving, not upon the provision of a solution. Consideration of the above factors should lead to a learning environment in which the learner has a number of options from which to choose, and where decision-making becomes an integral part of the learning process.

APPROXIMATION

In its most basic form, the condition of 'approximation' may be considered as the franchise to 'have a go'. Within any learning environment, it is evident that the opportunity to 'have a go', to attempt an approximation, is crucial to the learning process. It is only through the element of approximation that the learner has an opportunity to evaluate his work and its proximity to the desired outcome, and, as a result, refine the response in an effort to meet the desired response more accurately. In a more regimented view, approximation may be defined as 'mistakes'. However, when learning is regarded as a problem-solving experience in which the individual is involved in the process of testing out a number of possible solutions to a problem, it becomes evident that approximations, or 'mistakes' are a vital part of the process. The 'tyranny' of emphasis on, and expectation of the correct answer may be counter-productive in promoting true understanding, and mistakes should be accepted as a natural part of learning.

The development of understandings and competencies in music is not achieved through unleashing learners upon the basic materials of music and justifying the lack of guidance in terms of specific challenges, with the general catchcries of 'allowing the individual's creativity to develop', or of 'providing another avenue for personal expression'. Working with music as a creative medium is an intellectually challenging and stimulating task, and needs to be recognized as such. Students need to be provided with challenges which extend their understandings, involve the individual in making choices and promote the individual's confidence in making personal judgements. The acquisition of these and more specifically musically oriented skills is time-consuming and requires frequent opportunities for exploration, repetition, continuity of experience and practice. 'Freedom to approximate is an essential ingredient of all successful learning' (Cambourne, 1988: 70).

Inevitably, at some stage of the learning process, the learner's approximations of the skill will become public. This may be an occurrence as simple as looking at a peer's notation of a composition, or the planned performance of a finished work. Whatever the context for this public sharing, the individual needs to feel safe in the knowledge that his or her approximation will be accepted upon its merits. As a consequence of this, the teacher may decide that the work is not indicative of the quality of which the individual is capable, and may accept the response whilst reminding the individual that he or she is capable of some further refinement. For example, when discussing a notation, the teacher may remind the student of some of the conventions which are known to be part of that individual's repertoire, and make suggestions for the incorporation of these into the work.

USE

One of the most essential aspects of the learning process is the opportunity for the learner to put into practice the skills and understandings that have been developed. As a consequence of this, the learner needs sufficient time in which to implement these newly acquired practices and knowledge. Continuity of experience is essential when providing a comprehensive music programme for the learner, and such continuity should promote the sustained and continued use of the practices of music. Within music education, 'use' may encompass the development of an original composition, the practising of a piece of music for sharing, the performance itself, or listening to music for a variety of purposes. While engaged in any of these uses, the learners should be encouraged to evaluate their experience in terms of their developing understandings and skills.

RESPONSE

Learners need to receive 'feedback' about their efforts from exchanges with 'experts' or more knowledgeable 'others'. The teacher, peers, or other musicians and composers may provide this necessary component. When an 'expert' comments on a learner's approximation, a response occurs. Responses provided by the teachers or the expert should be relevant, appropriately timed, readily available and, above all, non-threatening.

A response may take a variety of forms: (i) acceptance of the learner's musical statement, regardless of the distance from the 'correct' response at the initial stage; (ii) a simple celebration of the learner's attempt and appreciation of the efforts that have been made; (iii) an evaluation in terms of the extent to which the stated goals have been achieved, and the degree to which the learner has demonstrated some mastery and control of the medium; and (iv) a demonstration of other possibilities, and a more refined approximation if appropriate.

It is essential to bear in mind that evaluation should be a continuous component of the learning experience, and as such should occur at various times throughout the development of a piece of work, be it a composition, a notation, or preparation for a performance. Ongoing evaluation initiated by the learner is a major factor in clarifying the purposes and defining the problems of a learning experience, and of refining a piece of work. Learners should be encouraged to rely increasingly on their own judgements, and develop the ability to analyse their own work critically.

CONCLUSION

Music learning experiences in the primary classroom may take a range of forms. For example, whole class practical sessions may be planned in which children work through a series of individual, pair or small group compositional challenges. Throughout these sessions, the teacher is available to assist when help is requested. During the development of challenges, the teacher may move between the children, listening to work in progress, discussing problems and modelling skills that individuals are perceived to need. At the end of each session, a brief period of time may be set aside in order to hear the works that have been developed and subsequently to reflect on the processes in which the children have been engaged, and the musical issues which have arisen from the challenges.

Alternatively, within a general primary classroom, teachers are able to make provision for children to continue working on a task, to practise skills and to use these in developing their own compsitional challenges by allotting time during the day, or later in the week, for the completion or development of a task. Displays of children's work, the provision of learning centres which may be left for children to work with in their own time and the display of artefacts which are exemplary of specific practices are powerful ways of reinforcing some of the issues identified above and may be incorporated easily into the classroom environment. Listening centres in which adult exemplars of issues with which children are working may be provided, thereby establishing a context for listening experiences whilst introducing children to some of the adult literature of music.

In developing a learning environment for music which supports the conditions of natural learning identified by Cambourne, a number of elements may be identified. Teaching practices acknowledge the value of emulative rather than purely instructional behaviour, as the teacher is providing a model of appropriate behaviours. The learning environment is characterized by a sense of security, and support and assistance is readily available to the learner. Appropriate, positive feedback is provided for the learner for all approximation, reinforcement being a continuous aspect of the programme. The learner is encouraged to assume responsibility for his own learning, with frequent opportunities provided for the continuous practice of skills. An individual's strengths and needs are recognized, and promotion of these is effected through the development of appropriate individual challenges.

The development of a 'natural' learning environment for music provides an effective context for music education within the classroom. In addition, the philosophy and consequent practice of music education may be seen to be consistent with that of other curricular areas. Such consistency can only strengthen the place of music in the curriculum.

REFERENCES

Cambourne, B. (1988) *The Whole Story: Natural Learning and the Acquisition of Literacy in the Classroom*, Auckland: Ashton Scholastic.

Department of Education and the Arts, Tasmania (1990) *Music in the Classroom*, Hobart: Department of Education and the Arts.

Edmunds, J. and Stoessinger, R. (1987) 'Investigating a process approach to mathematics', (unpublished manuscript), Education Department of Tasmania.

Education Department of Tasmania (1980a) *A Framework for Speech and Drama: Expressive Movement*, Hobart: Eduation Department of Tasmania.

Education Department of Tasmania (1980b) *A Framework for Speech and Drama: Drama*, Hobart: Education Department of Tasmania.

Education Department of Tasmania (1988) *The Visual Arts in Primary Schools*, Hobart: Education Department of Tasmania.

Holdaway, D. (1979) *The Foundations of Literacy*, Gosford: Ashton Scholastic.

Smith, F. (1978) *Joining the Literacy Club: Further Essays into Education*. London: Heinemann.

Smith, F. (1980) 'What shall we teach when we teach reading?' in *Proceedings of the 1984 Annual Conference of the Australian Reading Association*. Canberra: Australian Reading Association.

Swanwick, K. (1979) *A Basis for Music Education*. Slough: NFER – Nelson.

Swanwick, K. and Tillman, J. (1986) 'The sequence of music development: a study of children's composition', *British Journal of Music Education* 3 (3):305–39.

Chapter 5

In search of a child's musical imagination

Robert Walker

OVERTURE

In searching for a child's musical imagination, some questions spring to mind as being important preliminaries. If we identify musical imagination in adults, can we draw some conclusions that would be applicable to children? Furthermore, can we expect the same type of behaviour as manifests musical imagination in adults to occur in children? Do we expect children to do the same things as adults? What kind of behaviour contains evidence of musical imagination as far as both children and adults are concerned?

Some would be tempted to agree that a child of pre-school age who could play an unaccompanied violin sonata by J. S. Bach displayed more musical imagination than one who could merely bang tin cans and play-bricks together, accompanied by shouts and screams, or even a reasonably well-sung song. Yet if we can recognize children's musical imagination only in behaviour we call musical in the adult sense, then there are certain implications. First, and perhaps most important, is the odd position this gives music in a child's range of behaviours. We might accept 'childish' drawings on their merit as important sources of information about children's mentality and visual representation in the way Rudolf Arnheim has done, but 'childish' musical actions would be rejected as such. And it would mean that as far as musical behaviour is concerned, we expect children to be like little adults; that is, we can take them seriously only when they play or compose adult music like a Bach violin sonata. Applied to visual art, it would mean looking for children who could paint a *Blue Boy* or *The Adoration of the Magi*, and so on. Such a view would mean that very few children are capable of either displaying or even possessing musical imagination. One feels intuitively that something must be wrong with this view of music and children.

THEME 1

Gardner (1983) regards what he calls musical intelligence as one of man's finite number of intelligences, along with spatial, logical-mathematical, and others. Interestingly, he explains the term by reference to the behaviour of unassailably musical adults. In claiming that no other intelligence 'emerges earlier than musical talent' (1983: 99), he cites examples of precocious behaviour in children as the manifestation of musical intelligence, at least in western culture or, more precisely, recent western culture.

But, as if aware of the problem inherent in the precocity argument, he goes on to explain that the music of other cultures contains different acoustic emphases than that of the western traditions. This is quite a crucial point, which needs exploring further.

Some African tribal music contains enormously complex or tediously repetitive (to the western ear) rhythms played on sticks and drums and voices chanting pitches that western music does not utilize. Some North American Indian music uses different vocal timbres and minute frequency changes near the threshold of auditory functioning in humans, which have never been employed in recent western traditions, except in the work of some of today's avant-garde musicians. Many singers in other cultures across the world can produce more than one note simultaneously, a practice never used in the west, and in some South Pacific islands there is a flute that is played with the nose. Some cultures revere the sound of the rattle above all else as possessing special powers, particularly when it is shaken by the most powerful persons in their society. Thus the rattling together of bits of metal, slivers of bone or shell, or dried seeds is thought by many to contain deep spiritual significance. Similarly, in some societies dried skins from the backs of humans, seasoned with the urine of descendents, are thought to make drums of frightening power and which have the ability to communicate with spirits of the dead (Sachs, 1942).

Considering music in such a world context, it can be argued that for some cultures, at least, a child banging tin cans and play-bricks may well be regarded as displaying musical imagination in a more comprehensible manner than a child playing a violin. But there is another point: the type of technique required to make some of the musical sounds of cultures outside the western tradition of high art is of different order than that needed to play a Bach violin sonata. So the role of specialized training and access to it assume some importance. Little technical training appears necessary to make some of the sounds heard in some non-western cultures, compared with the rigour and scope of that needed to play the violin, and certainly little training appears necessary for success in the pop-rock scene – a form of musical communication that seems to transcend cultural barriers in a way no other musical behaviour may be capable of doing. Therefore, apart from any lingering nineteenth-century notions of western cultural superiority, there seems little to suggest that mere skill acquisition through rigorous training can contribute much to the development of musical imagination. Irrespective of the possibility that pre-school children who can play Bach sonatas are 'freaks', *ipso facto*, it must follow that precocity cannot be the only behavioural attribute in which musical imagination is manifest. If that were so, musical imagination would be found only in such freaks. It is, of course, quite conceivable that some freaks, like any other subgrouping, may display musical imagination, but it is surely unacceptable that only musical freaks can.

In fact, it is possible to illustrate this point through reference to child prodigies and musicians in history. One of the most celebrated of all time was Wolfgang Amadeus Mozart. At least this is how history has brought him down to us. Those in the eighteenth century might have seen things differently! There were literally hundreds of child prodigies at the time, of whom Mozart was but one, even though he was highly regarded. In England, for example, there was William Crotch of Norwich, who in 1778, at the age of three, was giving recitals in London and Cambridge. The 1954 edition of Grove's *Dictionary of Music* states that 'Crotch's precocity is almost unparalleled in music; even Mozart and Mendelssohn hardly equalled him in this respect'. He was also precocious in drawing and painting and was the subject of an enquiry by the Royal Society at the age of five.

If anyone can be said to display musical imagination, it must be Mozart, whose compositions and legendary fame at improvising and making fun of others' musical mannerisms earned him, respectively, posthumous and contemporaneous reputations. He even made fun of the young Beethoven, much to the latter's annoyance, imitating his excessively loud playing and furious sounds. The same cannot be said of William Crotch, who has been all but forgotten as a prodigy and is not known at all as a composer, except in the organ lofts of some English cathedrals. If we contrast this with a most unprecocious French composer, Hector Berlioz, whose music is discussed under headings like 'Berlioz and the Romantic imagination', we are surely able to draw some conclusions!

Berlioz could almost be said to have been the antithesis of a precociously talented youngster. He could not play any instrument really well, and he showed a certain lack of aptitude at his musical studies. One of the professors (Cherubini) at the Paris Conservatoire actually had him thrown out. Berlioz attempted to study music somewhat illegally, while a student of medicine, and his angry father cut off his allowance on hearing of his musical activities. Yet few now would disagree that the mature Berlioz displayed outstanding musical imagination in his compositions.

From this we can say with some assurance that precocious behaviour in music is by no means a *sine qua non* for manifestations of musical imagination. We might even say that it should be possible to identify musical imagination in nonprecocious children. Berlioz was certainly not the only imaginative musician to lack a precocious beginning.

THEME 2

It is no easy task to identify musical imagination in adults, even within an artistic tradition like western high art. For example, would we consider a composer whose music was described by his contemporaries as 'obscene' or 'obscure, idle balderdash' as imaginative? These were just some of the opinions expressed about Berlioz's symphonies (Strunk, 1950). If we read the terms 'madness' and 'musical contortions' about someone's music, would we be likely to say the composer displayed musical imagination? A prominent nineteenth-century German music critic wrote such things about Tchaikovsky's music for orchestra, and Liszt's piano music was described as 'the invitation to stamping and hissing' (Sitwell, 1967).

DEVELOPMENT AND VARIATIONS

Today, in contrast, no one would have any compunction at agreeing that all three composers displayed what can be called musical imagination, and not just in comparison with any mediocrity that surrounded them. We say things like Berlioz's music plumbs the depths of individual sensibility by pitting itself against the collective insensitivity in unique ways, and that Liszt and Tchaikovsky provide musical transportations into realms of consciousness not achieved or even attempted previously. We might also add that their imitators in this century have earned millions by providing diluted resemblances of such musical imagination for the movies and television.

Judging by these contemporary opinions of the three composers, we can say that they represented disturbing departures from acceptable norms of musical expectation to some people in the nineteenth century, even though to their supporters they exemplified the epitome of musical and romantic imagination. It is significant that the names of those many musicians who tended to conform to societal expectations do not appear in retrospect as exemplars of musical imagination in the commentaries of those who write about such things. We do not see chapter headings such as 'Cherubini and the Romantic imagination'. One supposes this has nothing to do with the fact that it was this gentleman who was responsible for getting Berlioz thrown out of the Paris Conservatoire library, not only as a nuisance but as an 'untalented wastrel'.

There certainly seems to be something worth following up in the observation that those who conform to expected norms in music do not earn reputations for being imaginative in the way that those who create their own independent expressions do. Many could learn to write music like Cherubini, and still do in some music academies, but few, if any, could learn to write like Berlioz, Tchaikovsky, or Liszt. It is this presence in music of a disparity between the mediocre and the unique and brilliant that has fired people's imaginations for two or three centuries in western European musical culture. Mozart delighted or infuriated his contemporaries with his brilliant powers of mimicry as he exposed unimaginativeness, mannerism and transparency in others, while producing music incapable of such imitation himself. The very fact that his music was so unassailable in this way is testimony to its perfect synthesis with his entire being, his whole consciousness and his single-mindedness. He could not have written music for someone else's tastes if he tried. In fact, he did try without success.

At the age of fourteen, he visited Bologna and met the eminent teacher Padre Martini. It was suggested that he sit the examination for the Diploma in Music, Bologna's highest academic honour. The task involved writing three parts above a given antiphon melody 'in istile osservats' – strict counterpoint. Mozart failed miserably (Einstein, 1945). He was unable to write in any style save his own, and Martini had to show him the correct answers. The archives of the Accademia Filarmonica and the Liceo Musicale at Bologna retain the manuscripts of this event (Einstein, 1945: 147).

These examples do not mean that anarchy and a total lack of any continuity and uniformity characterize musical imagination, but they do suggest that we are not able to draw any conclusions about identifying musical imagination simply by looking for norms. We could almost make a case for looking for deviations from norms as a first prerequisite to discovering musical imagination. We certainly cannot derive any clear relationship between actions that may contain evidence of musical imagination and laws of musical art distilled from musical practices at a given time or place. We can no more recognize a Mozart until he is dead than we can an Elvis Presley or a John Lennon until the sales figures tell us. It is against this background of an apparent uniqueness and a nonconformity with established norms that I want to suggest alternative ways of viewing musical imagination as it might appear in children.

EPISODE AND FUGUE

Generally speaking, not many people associate music with children making their own compositions, in the way they associate visual art with children drawing and painting, or myth and literature with children telling their own stories. To claim that music is different, or is regarded differently, may seem like a lame excuse for being unable to explain why all children are not regarded as capable of composing a piece of music in the way they are of drawing a picture. Nevertheless, it is a fact that adults in western culture generally either regard musical activity as something that has to be taught or consider that to make up his or her own music, a child would have to be a genius.

Look around any school and there will be evidence of children's activities in drawing, painting and writing stories, but virtually none of their musical inventions. So the first thing to establish is that, apart from trying to identify how imagination manifests itself in children's music making, there is the problem of actually finding and observing the musical equivalent to children drawing and telling their own stories. Children are not encouraged to make up their own music; instead, they are made to play someone else's, who always happens to be an adult.

This is not to suggest that there is universal regard for children's inventions in visual art and storytelling, but none for music. To many, all such activities appear to be a category of 'things children do' until they grow up, rather like listening to pop-rock, wearing jeans, getting dirty frequently, or throwing stones at birds or into ponds. Despite the work of many researchers into children's behaviour, there is still a lack of general understanding of what is seen by some people as disorganized, un-adult creative play that should perhaps be tolerated, at least until children learn something of greater value. This is a far cry from regarding children's behaviour in producing 'scribbly' drawings or cacophonous sounds as a category that might be different from mere worthless children's play. Yet it is probably not an exaggeration to claim that far more attention has been paid by researchers to children's drawings and storytelling than to their exploration and expression using sound, despite the work of Harvard's Project Zero team between 1977 and 1987. There is no large corpus of research into children's musical behaviour among psychologists, in spite of the growing numbers who are now entering the field of music psychology. Those who do attempt to fill this gap have the difficulty of dealing with an historically biased population among both musical practitioners and observers. This bias is largely because of the nature of musical art: it is a performance activity in which a composer cannot be heard without performers, many of whom have spent years perfecting historical techniques. Musical taste and preference consequently tend to oscillate between classical rigidities founded upon notions of quality derived from Plato and Aristotle, and a bewildered acceptance of anything, in the face of the overwhelming influence of pop-rock music. The feeling of safety in attributing musical imagination to the precocious four-year-old who can play Bach is a product of ancient Greek views of music buried deep in western belief systems.

In the *Republic*, Plato warns that we must:

> identify those rhythms appropriate to illiberality and insolence or madness or other evils so that we can use the opposite . . . good speech, then good accord and good grace and good rhythm wait upon a good disposition . . . music has power to affect his spirit, his soul, disposition, and abilities in all things.
>
> (Strunk, 1950: 7–11)

And Aristotle, in *The Politics*, explains that 'rhythms and melodies contain representations of anger, mildness, courage, temperance and all their opposites and other moral qualities' (Strunk, 1950: 18).

Upon such foundations there developed a belief in a relationship between character, personality, or moral worth and types of musical sound. In such a belief system, music actually represented these various qualities. Thus it was possible for American jazz to be outlawed in the 1920s and 1930s. Similarly, there was the outrage that greeted the rise of rock and roll in the 1950s, when one governor in the United States issued a warrant for the arrest of Elvis Presley on the grounds of corrupting the morals of minors. The eminent cellist Pablo Casals summed up the feeling of many when he described rock and roll as 'poison put to sound'.

The obverse of such attitudes is exemplified in the sanctification of 'great' composers, such as Beethoven, who was almost deified by some because of his noble music and a belief in an inextricable link between his personal behaviour and his music. We still do not like our musicians to be as revolutionary or antisocial as our visual artists, in whom we tolerate such behaviour. The musician is expected to be dressed in a dinner suit; the visual artist can wear jeans and sloppy sweaters.

This has remained in our education systems as a legacy from history. And so it is perhaps not so much a desire to see every child play a violin sonata by Bach that motivates such views, as a lingering belief in the connection between the music one plays and type of person he or she is. We still tend to believe in a relationship between a noble or saintly exterior, as someone plays a 'great' piece of music, and his or her inner being. It is the same legacy that makes us prize logical thought, in the fashion of the ancient Greeks, above all other types of mental activity. This in turn causes us to pay more attention to a child's music making that most nearly resembles an adult's rationalizations about music than to his or her expressive use of sound not conforming to such notions.

Many obviously unique talents have suffered throughout recent history from such attitudes. They prompted some of William Blake's contemporaries to regard his paintings and poetry as the daubings and rantings of a madman; similarly, some people were convinced Beethoven had lost his wits, when they heard his later quartets and piano sonatas. It is not just the battle between the rational and intuitive that is referred to here, but rather a modern legacy of this ancient debate. Children's activities in music today are regarded by some people in much the same way that music of the Romanticists was regarded by the empiricists and rationalists of the nineteenth century. In fact, many attempts at explaining artistic activity of any kind in a logical framework have produced a number of theories and formulae.

Joshua Reynolds, for example, was convinced that blue was a cold colour and could never be used as the centre of a successful painting. Thomas

Gainsborough's response was to paint the now celebrated *Blue Boy* (Saw, 1972). Birkhoff (1933), inspired by ancient Greek notions of balance, proportion, and harmony, produced the formula $M = O/C$, where M is the aesthetic measure, O the degree of order, and C the degree of complexity. There are obvious difficulties in assigning a number to concepts like order or complexity in a painting or a piece of music, yet later researchers have modified the equation to $M = O \times C$ (Eysenck, 1968; Smets, 1973). Such ideas can be traced back to Euclid, from whom the notion of the 'Golden Section' was developed. This is expressed as a ratio of approximately 62:38 between opposing elements.

It is difficult to see how such applications of mathematical methodology can yield anything of significance as far as artists are concerned. Certainly, there has been no such measure applied to real art, and it is doubtful that any will be attempted. Art cannot be measured in such a way, and such methods seem of little value in identifying imagination at work.

Of more use, it is suggested, are questions about the content of actual art works. For example, does musical imagination lie in the fury of a last movement of a Beethoven piano sonata, or the almost static harmonies and rhythmic motionlessness of Erik Satie's *Gymnopedies* or *Sarabandes*, or the elegant sonata structures of Mendelssohn, or the wit and clarity of Mozart, or the musical happenings of John Cage? Can it lie in the mixture of blues, country, and hillbilly that is Elvis Presley's style or the throaty patriotic sounds of Bruce Springsteen? Or does it in fact lie in the very diversity of musical practices all these represent? Illogicality, arbitrariness, contradiction, and the unexpected seem far more helpful clues to seeking out imagination in the music of western culture than logical explanations or mathematical formulae. But this is the problem of aesthetics: it is more a matter of looking at what artists do than of applying some external measure.

SONATA

In describing music from a more multi-cultural standpoint, Wachsmann (1971) explains it as a 'special kind of time, and the creation of musical time is a universal pre-occupation of man'. The notion of the creation of musical time, one's own personal musical time, seems far more applicable to what actually happens in music than does anything mathematical. It also seems far more appropriate in trying to understand what children may do with sound when they create their own 'musical time' than does looking for evidence of incipient greatness or adult behaviour.

Children can do with sound what they do with two-dimensional space in drawing and painting or with words in creating their stories. But to a child, the texture of a sound is more important than an adult concept like pitch or melody, and the duration of a sound is more significant than the concept of rhythm. Sergeant (1983) demonstrates that the basic unit of pitch in western music, the octave (a frequency ratio of 2:1), is a concept, not a percept. He explains that young children tend to identify similarities between tones by listening for similarities of sound rather than for a more logical octave generalization. In other research (Walker, 1978, 1981, 1985) there is evidence that visual matchings for sound textures, duration and loudness yield more consistency in young children than do those of pitch differentiation.

This would seem to point in the direction of children having greater involvement with elements of musical textures, durations and loudness than with concepts like pitch, derived from high art, in the early stages of their activities in music. It also suggests that musical imagination in children should be sought in observing their use of the basic parameters of musical sound (loudness, timbre, duration and pitch) in creating their own 'musical time'. In such observations, one should bear in mind the relationships between the great artists of the past and the norms of expectancy from which they diverged, each in their own unique manner as they created their own musical time.

Looked at in this way, some of the extant studies of children's musical explorations provide some relevant insights. John Paynter (1971) describes an experiment in which he observed a number of five-and six-year-olds in an open-ended task. The children were given freedom to explore a variety of tuned and untuned percussion instruments over a period of several weeks. Paynter reports that after an initial exploration in apparently random and somewhat chaotic manner, the children began to settle down to purposeful activities. These are described in the children's own words. A little girl explained that she was looking out of the window and watching the rain falling off the roof of the bicycle sheds into a puddle, so that she could play the rain on her chime bar. A pair of children described how they were 'playing' a conversation between themselves on their instruments. Other children were composing stories or describing events in music.

In another set of observations, Bamberger (1982) describes how a fourth-grade class invented their own drawings for the rhythm of a class composition. The class took about ten minutes to produce the drawings, which were categorized into two types by Bamberger: figural and metric. A second experiment included more children and a greater age range. Although the two types of drawing were to some degree confirmed, there were some interesting deviations, particularly among younger children aged around four years. Bamberger describes them as 'the children's invention for externalizing their "knowledge in action" – that is what they know how to do but had not before tried to put down in some external, static way' (1982: 193–4).

Bamberger hypothesizes in some detail about the motivations for the various drawings, using Piaget's models of children's behaviour. These include imitation of the movements needed to produce the rhythm acoustically. The interest for this writer lies in the clear indication that the children could perceive movements in musical time that contained varied loudness due to rhythmic accents, as well as repetition, and could externalize the mental images that resulted. The rhythm used was a simple four-beat pattern with an accent on the first beat. Many children tended to write a larger shape for each first beat, with correspondingly smaller ones for the remaining three. Thus there was evidence of a proclivity to use figural representations of loudness rather than metric representations of rhythm. Bamberger comments that musicians will tend to see rhythms in purely metric terms, having forgotten their own earlier figural interpretations because of their musical training. In Bamberger's view, these conflicts between figural and metric domains 'remain tacit barriers, especially to effective teaching' (1982: 225).

Other studies (Walker, 1978, 1981) indicate that children will readily provide drawings that faithfully represent, in visual metaphors, auditory movement in the basic parameters of sound: frequency, wave shape, amplitude and duration. A consistency of visual representation was reported in all age groups from five-year-olds to adult, though age was clearly a factor in maintaining the consistency of representation of frequency by vertical placement, wave-shape by visual pattern or texture, amplitude by size and duration by horizontal length. The same consistency was observed in congenitally blind subjects (Walker, 1985) and across different cultures (Walker, 1986).

This seems to imply that children respond to the sensuous parameters of sound rather than to adult musical concepts, and that musical sounds are perceived by children as auditory expressions. In fact, there is some indication in these studies that children are attracted to the sensuous properties of sound and by their potential for personal expressive use. It is to this latter aspect that I finally want to turn, for this, it is maintained, constitutes a basic ingredient of musicality.

It is a fairly reliable assertion that if children are asked to invent some music – which may be just 'a piece' or might describe their friends or their parents – they will use the sounds available rather than search for some Mozartian melody or Bach-like counterpoint. In one such session observed by the writer, a six-year-old described her friend by a loud, long continuous tapping on a variety of instruments. When asked why, she replied that her friend was always talking, and never stopped even in her sleep. Another girl described her mother as alternately like a glockenspiel played softly on a variety of notes and a loud banging on a drum. This related to her perception of her mother as often calm and loving, but sometimes angry.

In using stories as a basis for making music with children, the same proclivity to use what was available, but with as much variety in sound as possible, was noticed. For example, the story of Beowulf fighting the monster Grendel elicited an interesting range of sounds. Young children depicted the walk of the monster Grendel by a combination of cymbal, drum and woodblocks to indicate its weirdness, unnaturalness and terror. An older group, including some well-educated and accomplished musicians, produced a five-beat *ostinato* pattern with accents shifting at random to any of the five beats in a measure, and a combination of cello, double bass, piano, drum, trumpet and clarinet playing a fugue-like structure above this.

These and many other examples serve to illustrate a dichotomy in musical eduction. It lies between what Bamberger calls the figural and the metric in rhythm – what is referred to earlier in this chapter as the adult conception of music based upon Greek notions of refinement and the perception of the auditory parameters of sound that comprises musical expression – and what Langer calls expressive form as opposed to the abstraction of a concept for discursive thought (1969: 139).

CODA

In case this might seem like an argument in favour of educational strategies in music that are based on progressions from concrete to abstract experiences, it is important to emphasize the nature of musical communication. It is not like verbal language. The letters *c-a-t* have a specific symbolic and syntactic function of communication in language. In contrast, a musical element such as the chord of C major has no symbolic function and no syntactic constraints of the kind the noun *cat* has. Moreover, the word *cat* can be translated exactly into other languages whose speakers will instantly recognize the small, four-legged domestic pet it symbolizes. There is no equivalent to a C major chord in any other music save the tradition of the west. Moreover, it just isn't possible to translate musical elements from one culture to another by means of identifying their symbolic function and meaning. In western music, slow, sad music is played at funerals and gay, happy music at weddings. In Dervish music, fast, happy-sounding music is played at funerals as well as at weddings. There is no matching of musical variety with occasion. They never had a Plato to categorize musical sounds and attribute specific representational qualities to them.

The point is that the kind of abstract and concrete experiences referred to by writers on educational development, while clearly relating to language or mathematical activity, have no relevance to music. When a child hears a tune in C major that modulates to the dominant and back, the meaning he or she derives has nothing to do with C major or the dominant. It has to do with the sound being what Langer calls 'expressive form'. How different it is with language or mathematics! The child does not abstract meaning from the expressive form of the sound of words in a story, for example, but from the fixed meaning of words. He or she may note the tone of voice and manner of delivery, but it is the ideas symbolized in the words that contain the meaning. Entirely the opposite is true of music. There are no ideas as such expressed in the symbolism of tones, chords, or rhythms. They express only themselves, in the opinion of many musicians and writers about music. But it must be added that there was, historically, some support for a capacity of music to express a certain level of generality of meaning. This was found particularly in the nineteenth-century tradition of Romantic music following the writings of Schopenhauer. The arguments are long and tedious on both sides. Suffice it to say that few composers actually believe that what they write in music has any significance outside of the sounds and structures of music (see Strunk, 1950; Langer, 1969), in the way that words do.

So for this reason, despite the nineteenth-century belief in music having some representational powers, it seems reasonable to say that current educational practices, based as they seem to be on notions of language acquisition, not only are inappropriate to an activity like music, but are possibly inimical to the true nature of musical expression and perception as it occurs in cultural tradition. The very lack of children's musical compositions in schools is testimony to the misconceptions about music referred to here, and to the timorous attitudes toward children's activities with sound, particularly those that do not result in recognizable rhythms or melodies.

REFERENCES

Bamberger, J. (1982) 'Revisiting children's drawings of simple rhythms: a function for reflection-in-action', in S. Strauss (ed.) *U-shaped Behavioural growth*, New York: Academic Press.

Birkhoff, G. (1933) Cited in D. E. Berlyne 1974 *Studies in the New Experimental Aesthetics*, New York: Wiley.

Einstein, A. (1945) *Mozart*, London: Oxford University Press.

Eysenck, H. J. (1968) Cited in D. E. Berlyne 1974 *Studies in the New Experimental Aesthetics*, New York: Wiley.

Gardner, H. (1983) *Frames of Mind*, New York: Basic Books.

Langer, S. K. (1969) *Philosophy in a New Key*, Cambridge, MA: Harvard University Press.

Paynter, J. (1971) 'Creative music in the classroom', unpublished Ph.D. dissertation, University of York, England.

Sachs, Curt. (1942) *The History of Musical Instruments*, London: Dent.

Saw, R. L. (1972) *Aesthetics: An Introduction*, London: Macmillan.

Sergeant, D. (1983) 'The octave – percept or concept?' *Psychology of Music* 2(1): 3–18.

Sitwell, S. (1967) *Liszt*, New York: Dover.

Smets, D. (1973) Cited in D. E. Berlyne 1974 *Studies in the New Experimental Aesthetics*, New York: Wiley.

Strunk, O. (1950) *Source Readings in Music History*, New York: W. W. Norton.

Wachsmann, K, P. (1971), 'Universal perspectives in music', *Ethnomusicology*, 15(3) September, Middletown, CT: Wesleyan University Press.

Walker, R. (1978) 'Perception and music notation', *Psychology of Music* 6.

Walker, R. (1981) 'The presence of internalized images for musical sounds and their relevance to music education', *Council for Research in Music Education USA Bulletin* 66/67.

Walker, R. (1985) 'Mental imagery and musical concept formation', *Council for Research in Music Education*, special issue of papers read to the Tenth International Research Seminar on Music Education.

Walker, R. (1986) 'Some differences between pitch perception and basic auditory functioning in children of different cultural and musical backgrounds', paper invited to the Eleventh International Research Seminar on Music Education, Frankfurt, West Germany, July 1986. Council for Research in Music Education.

Chapter 6

Creativity as creative thinking

Peter Webster

There are few topics in music teaching and learning that are as fundamentally important as creativity. Thousands of words have been written about this subject. It has influenced the forming of philosophy, the writing of goals and objectives and the design of countless lesson plans. One bibliography of literature that deals with creativity in music education contains over a hundred annotated citations organized into theoretical, practical and empirical categories.[1]

Much of this literature focuses on practice. Important monographs on creative teaching have been written, including books on traditional composition techniques as well as unusual approaches. Many of the major texts on teaching practice deal directly with creative strategies.

In terms of student outcomes, approaches such as those of Carl Orff and Emile Jacques-Dalcroze stress certain kinds of creative activity. The Contemporary Music Project and Manhattanville Music Curriculum Project, two well-known efforts of the 1960s, contained detailed descriptions of creative strategies as a central focus of curriculum design. The Ann Arbor Symposium III and the Suncoast Music Education Forum are examples of professional meetings that have dealt exclusively with this topic.[2]

CONTINUED CONFUSION

Although much of this work has been helpful in understanding the complexities of creativity and in helping to formulate practice, confusion continues about just what the word means. For instance, a ten-year-old child's Sunday piano recital might be termed a milestone of creativity by some, while others might view the same child's Orff improvisation during Monday's music class in the same terms. Some view the very presence of music in the schools as an example of educational commitment to creativity, while others gauge creativity solely by the products of these programmes or by the awards they win. Some regard creativity as a term best reserved for geniuses, while others look to the spontaneous songs of the three year old or the daydreams of the adolescent.

Many questions about creativity continue to prevail. Is creativity product, or process, or both? Should it be considered primarily as something that takes place in composition? Can it be readily measured? Does it have anything to do with music aptitude? Isn't it the same as intelligence? Isn't it really only a 'general music' activity? Can it be taught? There remains little doubt about the importance of creativity in the music education profession, but little collective sense of what it is.

NEW THINKING

Music educators and psychologists interested in artistic development have recently supplied answers to these and many other questions. Many of their studies are based, in part, on a more focused view of creativity – one that centres on the *mental processes* associated with creative production. One of the main problems we face is the word 'creativity' itself. It has been used in so many different contexts that it has lost much of its meaning and power, especially in terms of music and children. In the educational context, it might be more prudent to use the term 'creative thinking'. There are a number of reasons for this.

By focusing on creative thinking, we place the emphasis on the process itself and on its role in music teaching and learning. We are challenged to seek answers to how the mind works with musical material to produce creative results.[3] This approach demystifies creativeness, places it in context with other kinds of abilities and external influences and – perhaps most important – makes our job as educators much clearer.

There are four characteristics of the recent literature on creative thinking that are worthy of consideration: it shows (i) an emphasis on the role of musical imagination or musical imagery; (ii) theoretical modelling of the creative process; (iii) new approaches to the measurement of creative aptitude; and (iv) systematic observation of creative behaviour, often in natural settings. A fifth characteristic is now emerging: the use of computers and sound technology as tools for recording and stimulating creative thought. Each of these characteristics has important implications for practice and each helps in its own way to clarify what we really mean by the term 'creativity'.

MUSICAL IMAGINATION

The mind's ability to 'think in sound' has been an important issue for musical achievement for some time. For example, the private trumpet teacher might encourage a student to 'hear' a musical line internally before playing it to improve the quality of performance. A general music specialist can often encourage a sixth grade class to 'remember' a musical passage during a listening lesson in order to compare the passage to an occurrence later. Conducting teachers encourage students to 'imagine' the sound of a score before rehearsal.

This ability to internally imagine sound meaningfully is not only important for music achievement and *convergent* tasks (tasks designed to yield a single right answer), but is also critical for creative thinking ability and specifically for *divergent* tasks (tasks for which several answers are possible). What is of interest is the encouragement of imaginative, divergent thinking in the classroom, rehearsal hall and the private studio. Typical questions and statements that encourage this kind of thinking are: 'imagine how the composer might have changed the ending to sound more tentative. How could this be done?'; 'think of what it would sound like without the strings – with just the tuba and piccolo playing together'; 'can you think of another accompaniment pattern for that melody? Play it for me', 'clarinets, imagine what that fugue subject would sound like if it had been written a century later'.

It is this kind of imaginative problem solving with musical sound that plays such an important role in the creative process and that has captured the attention of many music professionals interested in the formal study of creativity. Ironically, it is precisely this kind of thinking that is so often not stressed by music teachers – often ignored in favour of factual or skill-orientated content. Factual information is, of course, critical for imaginative thinking, but we must provide students with opportunities for applying this conceptual understanding in creative tasks. It is equally ironic that mathematics or history teachers might be more effective in getting students to think imaginatively about their subjects than is the music teacher.

MODEL OF THE CREATIVE PROCESS

How does this imaginative thinking relate to the big picture? Figure 6.1 displays one view of the creative thinking process. Such attempts at conceptual modelling are useful for teachers and researchers. They suggest relationships that imply possible teaching strategy and give direction to research. They can also generate a platform for debate in the profession – always a healthy sign. This model is designed to be representative of creative thinking by both children and adults, although certain aspects of the model might be qualitatively different at various stages of development.[4]

Product intention

Composition performance/improvisation and analysis (written and listening) can be considered at the outset of creative thinking as goals or

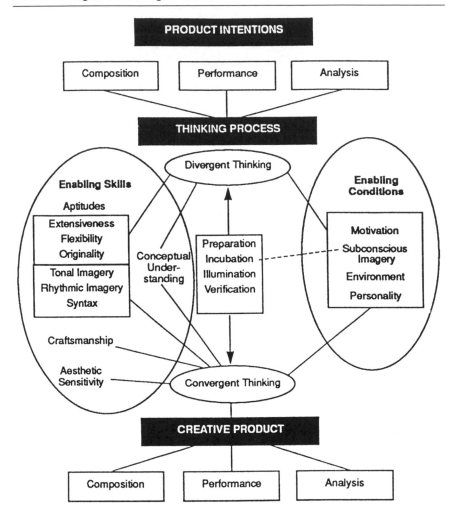

Figure 6.1 Model of creative thinking in music

'intentions' of the creator. At the same time, they represent the final product of creation. The product intentions of school-aged children are usually limited under our current educational system to performance/ improvisation and listening, a fact that hopefully will change as schools encourage more written composition and analysis. Each product intention results in subtle differences during the creative process, but the inner workings of the process are probably quite similar. An important point for music education is that creative thinking is part of the total curriculum effort and should not be viewed as just a classroom activity.

Enabling skills

With the intention established, the creator must rely on a set of skills that allow for the thinking process to occur. These skills form the basis of a musical intelligence and interact with the thinking process in a rich variety of ways.

First among these skills is the necessary collection of *musical aptitudes*. These are individual skills that are subject to influence by the environment during the early years of development and possibly into early adult life. They include such convergent thinking skills as the ability to recognize rhythmic and tonal patterns and musical syntax (sensitivity to musical whole). Certain divergent, imaginative skills are also critical, such as musical extensiveness (the amount of time invested in creative imaging); flexibility (the range of musical expression in terms of dynamics, tempo, and pitch); and originality (unusualness of expression). These musical aptitudes are largely innate, although they are subject to developmental improvement with training.

Another enabling skill is conceptual understanding: the *knowledge of facts* that comprise the substance of musical understanding. Furthermore, the possession of two more types of ability fall into this category: *craftsmanship* (the ability to apply factual knowledge in the service of a complex musical task) and *aesthetic sensitivity* (the ability to shape sound structures to capture the deepest levels of personal feeling – an ability that is demonstrated over the full length of a musical work).

Conceptual understanding, craftsmanship and aesthetic sensitivity obviously grow with age and experience, but transfer of these abilities into the mosaic of creative thinking does not often occur naturally. This transfer might well be an important goal of formal music education.

Enabling conditions

In addition to the personal skills that drive the creative thinking process, there are a number of variables involved that are *not* musical. These influences vary greatly from person to person and mingle with musical skills in delicate and complicated ways.

One of these, *motivation*, comprises those drives (both external and internal) that help keep the creator on task. Another, *subconscious imagery*, is the presence of mental activity that occurs quite apart from the conscious mind and that may help to inform the creative process during times when the creator is occupied consciously with other concerns.

Another, *personality*, describes factors such as risk-taking, spontaneity, openness, perspicacity, sense of humour and preferences for complexity, that seem to exist in many creative persons and that may hold some significance for enabling the creative process. *Environment* is the host of characteristics that define the creator's working conditions and contribute to the creative process, including financial support, family conditions, musical instruments, acoustics, media, societal expectations, peer pressure and many others.

Thinking process in the central core

The centre of the model in Figure 1 indicates movement, in stages, between divergent and convergent thinking. These stages involve time to play with ideas (preparation); time to have away from the tasks (incubation); and time to work in structured ways through the ideas (verification) after solutions have presented themselves (illumination). A very important implication for music teaching is that we must allow enough time for creative thinking to occur.

There are a number of important connections between this process and the enabling skills and conditions. Of the musical aptitudes, some (those of tonal and rhythmic imagery and musical syntax) are most clearly connected to convergent thinking. Tonal and rhythmic imagery concern the ability to perceive sound in relation to change and involve the representation of sound in memory. Musical syntax is the ability to shape musical expressions in a logical manner according to patterns of musical repetition, contrast, and sequencing. In this sense, a grasp of syntax is closely related to aesthetic sensitivity and is an early indication of this skill before extensive formal training. The aptitudes of extensiveness, flexibility, and originality are clearly connected to divergent thinking. Conceptual understanding directly impacts both divergent and convergent thinking. (Divergent thinking requires the mind to survey its data banks for possible musical content, so the more that is in those banks, the better. It is impossible to expect individuals to think creatively if nothing is there with which to think creatively!) Craftsmanship and aesthetic sensitivity are also connected to convergent thinking because they require careful manipulation of musical material in sequential ways. Divergency is directly related to aesthetic sensitivity as well.

Another major implication shown in this model for music teaching is the idea that environments that encourage divergent thinking in music are just as important as environments that encourage convergency of thought. Are we doing enough in our rehearsals, private studios and classrooms to ensure the very heart of this model?

MEASURES OF CREATIVE APTITUDE

Only recently have attempts to actually measure creative aptitude in music begun. Much of this work has focused on young children, ages six to ten, and has sought to identify divergent and convergent thinking skills in music using musical tasks in game-like contexts. For example, a measure I developed uses an amplified *voce*, a round sponge ball with a piano, and a set of temple blocks to engage children in musical imagery.[5] The tasks begin very simply and progress to higher levels of difficulty in terms of divergent thinking. There are no right or wrong answers to the tasks.

The first section of this evaluation procedure is designed to help the children become familiar with the instruments used and how they are arranged. The children explore the parameters of 'high/low', 'fast/slow', and 'loud/soft' in this section and throughout the measure. The way they manipulate these parameters is, in turn, used as one of the bases for scoring. They are given tasks that involve images of rain in a water bucket, magical elevators, and the sounds of trucks.

The middle section asks the children to engage in more challenging activities with the instruments and to focus on the creation of music using each of the instruments singly. Children enter, into a kind of musical question/answer dialogue with the mallet and temple blocks, and they create songs with the round ball on the piano and with the voice and the microphone. They use images that include the concept of 'frog' music (accomplished by hopping and rolling the ball on the piano) and that of a robot singing in the shower (realized with the child's voice through the microphone).

In the last section of the procedure, the children are encouraged to use multiple instruments in tasks whose settings are less structured. They tell a space story in sounds, using drawings as a visual aid. The final task asks the children to create a composition that uses all the instruments and that has a beginning, a middle, and an end.

This measure, and others like it, yields scores for such factors as musical originality, extensiveness, and flexibility, as well as musical syntax. Measurement strategies are based on the careful analysis of video or audio tapes of children actually engaged in the activities. Objective criteria as well as rating scales are used: musical extensiveness, for example, is measured by the time involved in the creative tasks, while evaluators rate originality by observing the manner in which pitch, tempo, and dynamics are manipulated.

Results based on administration of the test to over 300 children have been encouraging. Reliability and validity data seem to suggest that the children's responses follow consistent patterns and that the content of the tasks is appropriate. The tasks are not measuring the same skills as traditional musical aptitude tests (which measure tonal and rhythmic imagery) nor are they related with any statistical degree of significance to general intelligence. The scores on the tests do not seem to be grouped according to differences in gender, race, or socio-economic background.

Perhaps the most important point surrounding this work, however, is that what was once thought to be unapproachable and mysterious is now being studied. The actual tasks in these measures also serve as models for

What is happening in this picture?
(child responds)
Can you show me with your hand
the way a frog moves?
(child responds)
Using this sponge ball on the piano,
can you make up some frog music
that begins soft and, little by little,
gets louder and louder?
(child responds)
Now can you make some smooth,
rolling sounds with the ball?
(child responds)

Great! Now it's time to make some more frog music! I would like you to make up a piece of music that has jumpy sounds and smooth sounds, soft and loud sounds, and fast and slow sounds. Feel free to use all the keys on the piano and to make your piece as long as you want. Now think about your frog music for a while and when you think you're ready, I would like to hear about it.
(child responds)

The administrator should move to the rear and to the side of the child during performance so that the child will not be tempted to seek approval from the administrator for the various parts of the composition.

After this task is finished, proceed immediately to the concluding set of tasks by placing the first space picture on the piano music stand.

Figure 6.2 Administrator's instructions, illustration from *Measure of Creative Thinking in Music*

music teaching strategy as educators seek to engage children in imaginative thinking about music. (See figure 6.2)

OBSERVATION

Some of the most interesting writing in recent times has come from studies that have systematically observed the products and processes of children's creative expression in music and have attempted to analyse what happens as children create. The aim is to provide a sense of how the mind represents sound at various stages in development and how the music educator might benefit from this knowledge. Strategies involve engaging children in either compositional, improvisatory, or quasi-improvisatory tasks; recording the results; and then studying the characteristics of the music the children produce. Unlike efforts that are designed to create a standardized measure as described above, these studies essentially describe content as it is happening.[6]

We already see some interesting trends. Until children are five or six, their rhythmic and melodic material is somewhat idiosyncratic, with no predictable pattern. It is not clear if this is because of motor co-ordination problems in the production of sounds or if it is a true representation of the children's inner hearing. After this age, both rhythmic and melodic structures seem to be more predictable. Between the ages of six and ten, changing or mixed metres occur, giving way to quite consistent patterns after age ten. Duple metre seems to be preferred by most older children.

After age five or six, consistent melodic and tonal characteristics also become more pronounced. The music of six- to ten-year-old children exhibits a gradual development of feeling for cadence structures and a growing awareness of tonal centre within melodies. It seems clear that as children imitate the songs in their environment, their own music is influenced accordingly. After the age of ten, children become much more conscious of 'correctness' of musical structure and tend to create music that is more organized in terms of rules, but not necessarily more original.

There appears to be a general rise in the use of both rhythmic and melodic motives from age five to eleven. Interest in the actual musical development of a melodic motive rises as children reach age eleven, but rhythmic development seems to remain relatively unchanged at all levels.

Much of this information is preliminary and more careful study is needed. What is most important for music education is the fact that there do appear to be patterns of thinking and behaviour that can be studied. By asking children to solve musical problems with the goal of creating a musical product, we have an opportunity to learn more about the creative process while at the same time engaging children in tasks that are fundamental to music as art.

TECHNOLOGY: ITS FUTURE ROLE

Musical imagination, conceptual modelling, measurement and observation are four keys to a better understanding of creative thinking in music. Each of these keys stands to gain immeasurably from technology. Much has been said about computers, electronic keyboards, software and MIDI as teaching tools for convergent goals in music education. It is *not*, however, with this kind of education that such technology holds its greatest promise. It is rather with the encouragement and careful study of divergent, imaginative musical thinking.

Imagine a child seated at a music keyboard with a computer screen providing the score. This child composes a brief fragment of music by playing on the music keyboard. This fragment is displayed on the screen (in traditional notation or in other forms) and is played through speakers. The child continues to expand the fragment, working with many different timbres, additional voices, dynamics and phrase patterns. At one point the child becomes frustrated and quits, saving the work in a file. The child returns later to the saved composition and continues work until a final version is ready to be shared with the teacher and the class. The child then prints a copy of the score and takes it home for the refrigerator door, and transfers the recording to cassette tape for the child's parents to hear. Throughout the entire process, the computer has saved every moment of the child's work and can 'replay' the 'electronic sketches' in exacting detail. Although this is of little interest to the child, it is of great interest to the teacher, who can use these electronic sketches to evaluate the student's progress.

Just a few years ago, such a scenario would have seemed financially and technologically out of the question. Not so today. With software and hardware to support multimedia applications, music work stations of this sort now exist in music labs in several schools. Similar projects will be easily designed by the teacher for performers and listeners as well. This technology will soon help us to expand our understanding of musical imagination, to challenge our concepts of the creative process, and to measure and observe creative thinking in ways never thought possible. The real question is, will we be able to take advantage of this power?

PROVIDING THE ANSWERS

Creative thinking, then, is a dynamic mental process that alternates between divergent (imaginative) and convergent (factual) thinking, moving in stages over time. It is enabled by internal musical skills and outside conditions and results in a final musical product which is new for the creator. Focusing on creative thinking is an important beginning to our understanding of creativity and may yield important answers to the questions raised at the beginning of this article.

A child's potential for creative thinking is not so complex that it cannot be measured and should be considered as part of an expanded view of traditional musical aptitude. It is not the same as general intelligence or musical achievement skill. Composition is not the only end product of the creative thinking process. Performances of precomposed music, improvisation, and careful listening and analysis all involve the creative thinking process. The rehearsal hall, private studio, and the classroom are all sites for such thinking. Creative thinking can be taught by providing children with chances to explore musical images and by applying them in problem solving tasks. Technology may play an important role in our teaching strategy.

In the final analysis, we are limited only by our own creative thinking as teachers. Exciting the imagination of our children about music is what it is all about. Facts and skills will not do it alone.

NOTES

1 Peter R. Webster (1988) 'Creative thinking in music: approaches to research', in *Music Education in the United States: Contemporary Issues*, ed. Terry Gates (Tuscaloosa: University of Alabama Press, 1988), 66–81.
2 *Documentary Report of the Ann Arbor Symposium on the Applications of Psychology to the Teaching and Learning of Music: Session III* (Washington, DC: Music Educators National Conference, 1983); *Proceedings from the Suncoast Music Education Forum on Creativity* (Tampa, Florida: Department of Music, University of South Florida, in press).
3 This approach is in line with current work in music cognition and is part of a larger effort in the social and behavioural sciences, neurosciences and computer science. For a general overview, see Howard Gardner, *The Mind's New Science* (New York: Basic Books, 1987).
4 For a fuller description of this model, see Peter R. Webster, 'Conceptual bases for creative thinking in music', in *Music and Child Development*, ed. J. Craig Peery, Irene Peery, and Thomas Draper (New York: Springer-Verlag, 1987), 158–74.
5 Peter R. Webster, 'Refinement of a measure of creative thinking in music', in *Applications of Research in Music Behaviour*, ed. Clifford Madsen and Carol Prickett (Tuscaloosa: University of Alabama Press, 1987), 257–71.
6 For an excellent review of this literature, see John Kratus, 'A time analysis of the compositional processes used by children ages 7–11'. *Journal of Research in Music Education* 37 (1) (Spring 1989), 5–20.

Chapter 7

Creativity and special needs
A suggested framework for technology applications

David Collins

I first met Adele Drake in 1986 when I invited her to speak at a two-day conference on music technology and special needs in Sheffield. Although that is only a few years ago, the rate of change in technology applications has been immense. We were then demonstrating basic packages using BBC computers, monophonic keyboards (others were far too expensive) and very few MIDI applications. Adele had a vision of the ways in which technology would enhance the opportunities of access into expressive music for people with handicap, a vision which went ahead of the then current technology. Whereas the Drake Research Foundation is generally concerned with physically handicapped people, I have been, in the main, involved with children who experience moderate learning difficulties, although this label in itself covers a huge variety of need; children with less severe physical impairment such as epilepsy, or visual impairment; children who have a background of abuse and stressful home conditions; others for whom a large mainstream school is too overpowering and leads to phobia. These factors in themselves lead to a complexity of needs, none of which can be categorized, and which present to the special needs teacher problems as unique as the individuals themselves. We all, however, carry with us our own sets of special needs, a fact which I hope remains at the background of anything we plan or do.

From my experience of working with young people in music education incorporating technology wherever possible and necessary I hope that this chapter may pull together several strands of thought, and furthermore that it will help practitioners, researchers, software and hardware designers and authors of corresponding documentation and classroom methodology to achieve a greater commonality of thought and application.

The emphasis here will be on the process of music composition: I am aware that I am not experienced in the realm of music therapy, but I believe that such therapy, where creatively applied, can achieve marvellous results. The emphasis is upon individuals being responsible for their own music composition – a kind of intrinsic therapy, where they may experience for themselves the cathartic, expressive power of music, rather than it being applied extrinsically. If they are to be enabled to do this, then we have to look at some of the conditions for creativity.

CONDITIONS FOR CREATIVITY

If we begin from the premise that each one of us possesses potential for expression in sound, perhaps we can echo the statement of Torrance that creativity is a 'natural human process motivated by strong human needs', and that in the process of enabling people to be creative, ever present 'is the question of just how much and what we are teaching and how much of the progress we observe is due to facilitating conditions that free natural processes to operate' (Torrance, 1972).

It is these facilitating conditions for creativity which I would hope to look at; conditions applicable to anyone, irrespective of handicap; then to examine some of the ways in which those with special needs may have been denied the choice to align themselves with any or all of these conditions, and subsequently to consider the enabling role of technology in the context of these factors. Underlying this, I believe any development of technology must serve well established educational criteria, and not the other way round.

As I have said, my emphasis is upon music composition in its broadest sense, from the smallest and most modest musical statements to more worked out compositions. Malcolm Ross (1980) has suggested some principles upon which one may base the conditions for creativity:

Initiating

This is the beginning of the creative impulse in music composition, and frequently seems to arise from tactile exploration and playing around with ideas. Although it might be pleasant to think that every member of the human race has a mind like Mozart, who seemed to have preformulated compositions in his head, so that composition to him was merely the transference of this to paper, it is unfortunately not the case. Most of us need some kind of physical engagement with a sound-making device to trigger off or galvanize ideas. This is an extension of play: play is essential in the act of creation, and Torrance points out that 'creative children are often learning and thinking when they appear to be playing around, often in manipulative or exploratory activities. Musical imagination is not entirely what Vygotsky describes as 'play without action' – action is part and parcel of this initial imaginative stage. Stravinsky has spoken eloquently of this need for action:

> The very act of putting my work on paper . . . is for me inseparable from the pleasure of creation. So far as I am concerned, I cannot separate the spiritual effort from the psychological and physical effort.
>
> (Stravinsky, 1974: 67)

In a recent piece of research on writing, called 'Hand, eye, brain: some basics in the writing process', Emig (1983) recounts a statement by Ernest Hemingway, made after an automobile accident when he feared that he had lost the use of his right arm. 'Hemingway commented simply that he thought he would probably have to give up writing. For how many others of us is the action of the hand, the literal act of writing, the motoric component, equally crucial?'

Emig goes on to suggest four reasons why the motoric component may be so crucial in the creative process, the primary being that: 'the literal act of writing is activating, mobilizing. It physically thrusts the writer from a state of inaction into engagement with the process and with the task. We have actually, physically, begun to do something'.

The early stage of engagement with the medium of sound may take the form of doodling, which in itself may incorporate unintended events. Ross places a great deal of importance on this doodling activity:

> the doodling initiates a form of relaxed, perceptual scanning that eventually detects the possibility of affective centring – it could be that some happy accident of movement catches the imagination, a cluster of notes, a rhythmical pulse, a phrase or movement of speed.
>
> (Ross, 1980: 112)

Chance happening within the playful activity (at whatever age/developmental level), seems to be essential; playing around on the keyboard one may discover an unintended yet desired set of notes; a melody may acquire greater personal meaning merely through the slip of a finger.

Stravinsky again:

> Invention presupposes imagination but should not be confused with it. For the act of invention implies the necessity of a lucky find and of achieving full realization of this find . . . creative imagination [is] the faculty that helps us pass from the level of conception to the level of realization. In the course of my labours I suddenly stumble upon something unexpected. This unexpected element strikes me. I make a note of it. At the proper time I put it to profitable use. This gift of chance is . . . bound up with the creative process.
>
> (Stravinsky, 1974: 69)

This initiating or precipitation of musical creativity probably represents one of the greatest stumbling blocks for music educators and their pupils.

Acquainting

Not only is there a necessity to play around with ideas, but also to be conversant, sensitive, with the medium. Just as in calligraphy one needs to know how much ink to load the pen or brush with, or in pottery, how wet to make the clay, so in the medium of sound one needs to be conversant with such things as the effect of combining two or more notes, or the effect of a particular note juxtaposed against various differing harmonies, or the way in which various instruments create their own timbres. This process of becoming conversant with the medium can only arise out of active involvement, which to a greater or lesser extent continues to involve physical activity. To experience the effects of various notes against others, or simply the emotional power of a note-cluster on a keyboard played alternatively with force, or pianissimo and sustained, a personal (and tactile) engagement with the medium of sound, seems very important.

Controlling

Such activities, however, may be a creative cul-de-sac without a degree of mastery of basic skills and techniques to manipulate the medium. One may know exactly how much ink a brush or pen will hold without blotting, but be unable to use that skill to draw a Chinese character. Similarly, simply knowing what is the best consistency for modelling in clay will not enable us to produce a pot.

Manipulating the medium of ink, clay or sound requires mastery of certain techniques, but the mastery of a technique presupposes limitations on one's freedom. This does not mean, conversely, that the creative act is rule-directed, but that, paradoxically, it creates conditions for creativity:

> In music, the prescription of sets of sound materials has always been an obvious feature of compositional processes. It seems essential for composers to limit available resources, to make music manageable, to get themselves started. Thus we have the tonal system, twelve note techniques, pentatonic scales, Indian ragas and even more limited sets of sound, as we find when Debussy makes a piano prelude out of the interval of a third, or when Bartók writes pieces in his *Mikrokosmos* based on fifth chords, or triplets in 9/8 time, or when jazz musicians improvise on the foundation of a well known standard tune or a limited chord sequence.
>
> (Swanwick, 1982: 22)

Stravinsky spoke further, in his *Poetics of Music*, of his same need for self-imposed limitations as part of the creative enabling process: 'the more art is controlled, limited, worked over, the more it is free . . . my freedom will be more meaningful the more narrowly I limit my field of vision and the more I surround myself with obstacles, (Stravinsky, 1974: 85). An equally perceptive, but slightly comical, advertisement for music software based on algorithmic principles (*Ludwig* by Hybrid Arts) runs as follows: 'the blank page . . . it's a composer's nightmare. It doesn't matter whether you're a novice with one or two synths, or a seasoned pro with a mountain of MIDI gear . . . sooner or later you'll face the blank page'. Thus amongst our conditions for creativity, controlling or manipulating the medium (sound) carries with it the need for imposed limitations.

Structuring

The final process in any art-making activity is structuring; a gathering into a comprehensible whole. As Fischer states: 'not only must art derive from an intense experience of reality, it must also be constructed, it must gain form through objectivity. The free play of art is the result of mastery' (Fischer, 1963).

Witkin points out that:

> A work of art is a significant pattern of events, a pattern of changes, variations and contrasts in light, sound, gesture or whatever. In and through the changes that constitute the work we sense a continuity, a relatedness. . . . The meaning or significance of the work is bound up with this relatedness as realized in the events that constitute the work. However, this relatedness is not the product of mechanically adding or combining constituent elements. Rather, each element is perceived as it is because of the relatedness of the whole.

> (Witkin, 1974)

Structuring an art work (whether it is a simple four-bar melody, or a young child's early attempt at creative writing, or a large scale musical piece) requires the art maker to manipulate the various elements (or building blocks) until the relatedness is achieved. This in itself requires the action of obtaining an overview of the work. With a visual artwork the marker is able to take in, to comprehend, the complete object at one particular moment. In a piece of creative writing the author may need to rescan, revise the elements. Much anecdotal evidence of the use of word-processors in creative, imaginative writing highlights the usefulness of being able to move and play around with chunks of ideas, in the same way that the user of a computer graphics system can manipulate groups and objects. Because the form of music exists with reference to the parameter of time, it is less easy to achieve an overview of the structure. Stravinsky, I believe, used to paper his wall with ongoing compositions in order to be able to stand back and gain some objective understanding of the overall composition. Thus structuring requires not only the manipulation of the constituent elements, the chunks or building blocks, but also a *Gestalt* or intelligent overview of the complete work in time.

If these four elements – initiating, acquainting, controlling and structure – constitute a basis of art activity (and of course, they do not necessarily occur sequentially; recursion from one to another may happen since creativity is not a neat, linear sequence of events), then our aim as

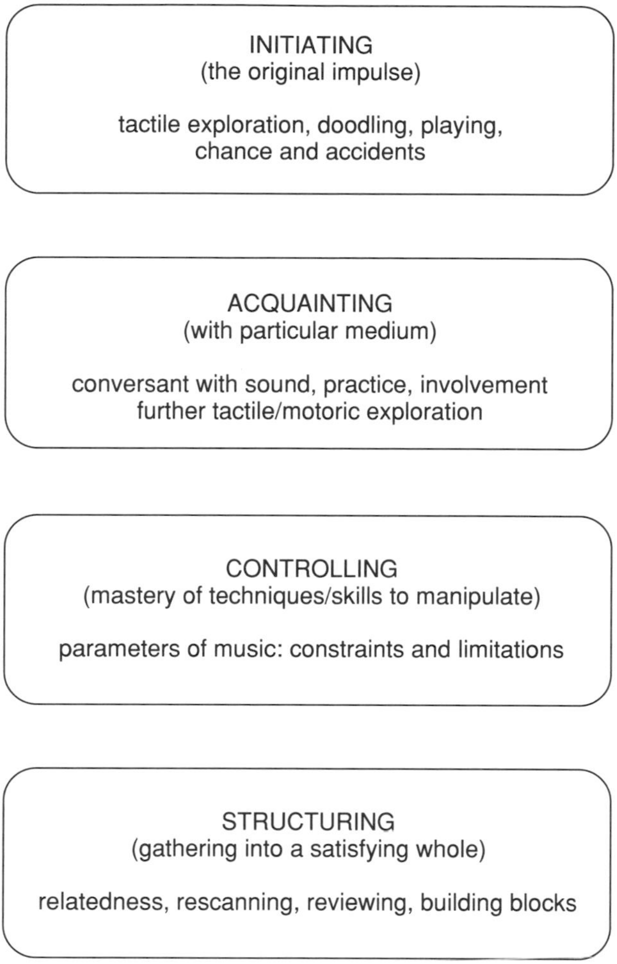

INITIATING
(the original impulse)

tactile exploration, doodling, playing,
chance and accidents

ACQUAINTING
(with particular medium)

conversant with sound, practice, involvement
further tactile/motoric exploration

CONTROLLING
(mastery of techniques/skills to manipulate)

parameters of music: constraints and limitations

STRUCTURING
(gathering into a satisfying whole)

relatedness, rescanning, reviewing, building blocks

Figure 7.1

educators is to enable our pupils to have opportunities to engage with
these elements (see figure 7.1).

THE SPECIAL NEEDS FACTOR

Because a person has special needs it does not necessarily follow that we
have to abandon this basis for creative thinking and action. We have to ask
the question: in what ways do this person's particular needs inhibit any or all
of the four processes; what do we observe, as trained educators, to be the

major stumbling blocks to allowing this person to realize their full creative potential?

Thus there has to be an identification of need, before further progress can be made. This is not as straightforward as it may appear at first, due in the main to a multiplicity of disability; that is, a person's physical handicap may have interfered with the processes of learning due to continued hospitalization; or in another, disaffection, or a passivity towards learning may have arisen out of home and personal circumstances, which in itself may subsequently have led to imagination blockages, or an inability to attend to a task. We cannot simply apply technology (or even conventional music therapy) without being aware of each individual's disablement, whether visible or invisible, physical or emotional.

In the context of the four elements of initiating, acquainting, controlling and structuring, we may then see that two fundamental issues arise for research and development in technological applications.

HARDWARE/INTERFACE DESIGN ISSUES

First, it becomes apparent that both the initiating process and the acquainting process seem to be predominantly governed by motoric/tactile interaction with the medium of sound. Playing with ideas, doodling, experimenting: in the act of music composition these are physically dominated activities, not abstract conceptual stages (I would find it very difficult to conceive of doodling in one's head!) Looking at the role of technology, therefore, both these processes transfer into hardware/interface research and design issues. In what ways can developments in these areas be used to give those who are denied the opportunities for this physical engagement with sound? (as mentioned earlier this may be due to severe physical handicap or an inability to develop fine motor control. Hence the importance of identifying the need). How can we best design the hardware to allow the user to have the opportunity to play around with melodies, chords, timbres, and do so with the built in possibility of discovery through chance accidents?

SOFTWARE DESIGN ISSUES

However, to stay at the level of hardware design would only be to address half the issue of creativity and special needs; the domains of controlling the medium and structuring, whilst still requiring reference to hardware/ interface issues, necessarily require us to look at software design issues. By way of example, a device called 'Gesture' has recently been developed which, through a MIDI interface to a sound module/synthesizer, allows the user to generate sound by interrupting a conical beam of ultrasound. This interface between the user and a digital instrument has exciting possibilities, and may allow the person with disability both to initiate and to become acquainted with sound. None the less, it does not necessarily lead to the conceptual processes of controlling and structuring. There would be a need for storage of material and further manipulation of the constituent sound elements.

Referring again to research in creative writing, Emig argues that, in education, the current model which permeates much thinking is that children must be taught to write atomistically from parts to whole, in a linear sequence. She argues, however, that findings from developmental research indicate that children often write as frequently from whole to parts as from parts to wholes, and that the processes of writing are not linear but recursive. This is reflected in much software which functions at an atomistic not holistic level. Current research in music cognition indicates that we process musical information in comprehensible units. Our perception of what Lerdahl (1988) terms a 'musical surface' requires that surface to be parsed into a sequence of discrete events. These events are embedded within larger organizational features. Individual notes or sounds taken out of context are meaningless, and only gain significance in context with other notes or sounds (see Chew *et al.*, 1982 among others). There is a strong case for working towards object-orientated music composition software which will allow the user to deal with building blocks of sound parameters, not necessarily in a linear sequence and will positively enable the user to move from the initiating stage to the structuring stage in a natural progression.

THE OVERALL TEACHING/LEARNING ENVIRONMENT

I hope that it has been possible to identify the necessity for research and development, and application, in both hardware and software domains. For successful implementation in the musical education of those with special needs they are complementary in interreactive factors. Because of the multiplicity of special needs, it is highly unlikely that one particular package would meet all needs satisfactorily. This in itself is not a bad thing, however, because it forces us to take heed of the human element – the specialist trained music teacher for whom a particular set of technological tools is only part of an overall creative teaching strategy. I do not believe that we can expect to return to the teaching machine model, where the learner was left alone with a computer, and the teacher, as Sharples (1985) points out, acted as a kind of shepherd tending a flock of teaching machines. The aim of some AI researchers, desperately attempting to produce a computer which will emulate creative processes, only reflects one aspect: the nature of intelligence and how a machine can replicate this. But as Self (1985) indicates: 'there are many areas . . . teacher training, the curriculum, school case studies . . . where AI has little to offer'.

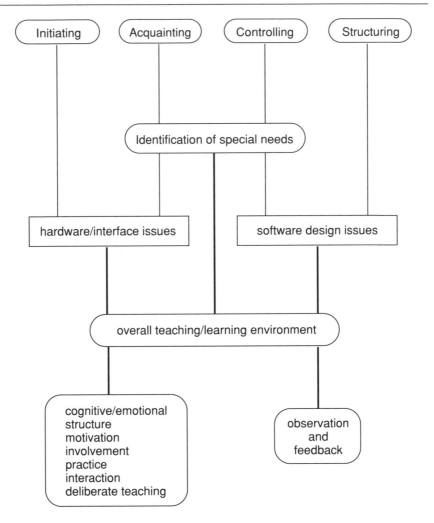

Figure 7.2

The role of the teacher cannot be abandoned in the teaching, or at least stimulus, of creativity. In a major study Torrance (1972) came to the conclusion that, despite claims that 'nobody can teach anybody anything', there was the paramount necessity to develop skills which would create facilitating conditions to allow what he termed 'free creative processes'. His study led to the conclusion that these facilitating conditions would be those which 'involve both cognitive and emotional functioning, provide adequate structure and motivation, and give opportunities for involvement, practice and interaction with teachers and other children'. Motivating and facilitating conditions certainly seemed to make major differences, but he claimed that differences in creative functioning 'seem to be greater when deliberate teaching is involved'. Not only is the role of the teacher to cultivate appropriate conditions for creativity, through these approaches and in tandem with technology, but also to provide highly important feedback to those involved in hardware and software design; a continuous shop-floor update on the effectiveness of the tools they are using.

We have an obligation to give those with disability a voice; a liberation from the world of silence which Adele Drake speaks of in her poem:

Breaking barriers of sound with language of a different kind.
Silence filled with melody and harmony, carrying the voice within.

I believe that if we can make some move to adopting some of the issues I have mentioned, then we may at least be some way forward in fulfilling this obligation.

REFERENCES

Chew, S. L. *et al.* (1982) 'The abstraction of musical ideas', *Memory and Cognition* 10 (5): 413–23.

Collins, D. (1990) 'Music education and technology: towards a broader perspective', *Roland/IMPAC Conference Proceedings.*

Emig, J. (1983) *The Web of Meaning: Essays on Writing, Teaching, Learning and Thinking,* Boynton-Cook.

Fischer, E. (1963) *The Necessity of Art,* Harmondsworth: Penguin.

Lerdahl, F. (1988) 'Cognitive constraints on compositional systems', in J. A. Sloboda (ed.), *Generative Processes in Music – the Psychology of Performance, Improvisation and Composition,* Oxford: Science Publications.

Ross, M. (1980) *The Arts and Personal Growth,* London: Pergamon Press.

Self, J. (1985) Micros in education – the AI dimension', in D. J. Smith (ed.), *Information Technology and Education: Signposts and Research Directions.* London: ESRC.

Sharples, M. (1985) 'Tools for learning', *Greater Manchester Primary Contact, Special Issue* no. 3.

Stravinsky, I. (1974) *The Poetics of Music,* Cambridge, MA: Harvard University Press.

Swanwick, K. (1982) 'The arts in education: dreaming or wide awake?', *University of London, Institute of Education, Special Professorial Lecture.*

Torrance, E. P. (1972) 'Can we teach children to think creatively?', *Journal of Creative Behaviour,* 8 (2): 114–42.

Witkin, R. W. (1974) *The Intelligence of Feeling,* London: Heinemann.

Chapter 8

Musical development in the primary years

Janet Mills

RESEARCH IN MUSICAL DEVELOPMENT

During this century, and particularly over the last thirty or so years, psychological research into children's musical qualities has mushroomed. Early research, such as that carried out by Carl Seashore at the turn of this century, was in the tradition of psychometric testing, and took place under carefully controlled conditions. It explored research questions concerned with musical perception. What is the highest note that can be perceived? What is the smallest pitch interval that can be recognized? Do the answers to these two questions depend on age? Measurement often required the use of sophisticated apparatus, and sometimes took place in laboratories.

Research into perception continues to this day and has a relevance to music education which is sometimes overlooked. But, alongside this, a tradition of exploring children's activity as musicians is developing. Here, the research questions are more directly related to composing, performing, listening and classrooms. How do children develop as composers? In what circumstances do children learn to sing in tune? And so on.

These two research traditions are not necessarily in opposition. The results of investigations in one tradition sometimes inform the questions asked in the other. Indeed, some researchers have worked in both areas at various points of their career. But because the questions asked are so different, and because the relevance of the research to music education is of a different nature, I consider the two areas separately.

CHILDREN AS PERCEIVERS

Research in aural perception can be concerned with any of the parameters of sound, such as pitch, loudness or timbre. I shall focus on just one aspect of perception: pitch discrimination. This is the ability to assess that there is a difference in the pitch of two tones. Investigations of pitch discrimination often explore how close in pitch tones must be before they are judged to be the same. They may also explore whether the direction of the pitch movement can be assessed accurately. Thus an individual having his or her pitch discrimination assessed might be asked to listen to two tones and say whether the second one is the same, higher, or lower. One's ability in pitch discrimination depends on the frequency range used. Very high and very low intervals are harder to discriminate. The investigations referred to below use a frequency range in which children find discrimination particularly easy: their vocal range.

Children's pitch discrimination has been investigated by many researchers. The pattern that has emerged is as follows:

Children can discriminate very small intervals

In 1893, J. A. Gilbert (Shuter-Dyson and Gabriel, 1981) found that chlidren aged seven could, on average, assess the direction of some intervals as small as two-thirds of a semitone. In the early 1960s, Arnold Bentley (1966) found they could assess one-third of a semitone. In the early 1980s, I found (Mills, 1988a) that the average 7-year-old could assess an interval as small as one-sixth of a semitone, that is, a 1 per cent difference in frequency. Thus several researchers have agreed that normal 7-year-olds can discriminate very small intervals. Quite how small, does not matter for the purposes of this argument. The discrepancies between the three sets of findings are probably attributable to the differing quality of the recording and replay equipment available at the time (Mills, 1984); there is no reason to suppose that the children of the 1990s necessarily have pitch discrimination any finer than those of the 1890s.

Researchers of pitch discrimination have often reported the results of work with children aged at least six years. This is usually simply because younger children might have difficulty coping with the test situation, which often requires children to write their responses. There is no evidence that younger children do not perceive fine differences in pitch. Indeed, Bridger (1961) observed that some babies aged under five days notice pitch differences of about four semitones, and they may be able to perceive much smaller intervals. It is difficult to understand how children could acquire language, and particularly accent, without some pitch discrimination.

Children's discrimination improves with age

Bentley and Gilbert both wrote of marked improvement over the junior years and into the secondary years. I found that the average 11-year-old is able to assess the direction of an interval of about a 0.85 per cent difference in frequency. Thus the average 11-year-old ear competes with much scientific equipment for sensitivity.

In any age group, there is a considerable range of ability

This has been observed by many researchers. I found some children as young as 9 who could judge the direction of an interval as small as one-tenth of a semitone; that is, about a 0.6 per cent difference in frequency.

What is the use of these findings? Researchers (for example, Seashore, 1938; Bentley, 1966; Mills, 1988a) used the range of ability, coupled with the observation that successful performers tend to have superior discrimination, as a basis for devising musical ability tests that include tests of pitch discrimination. The generally fine discrimination of children was, if anything, a nuisance. It meant that tests had to include very small intervals if they were to differentiate between children. And very small intervals are difficult to record accurately.

But some other implications of the three points I have drawn from the pitch discrimination research have more immediate relevance to class teachers.

Teaching the concept of pitch (up/down)

Pitch is one of the basic concepts of music. Understanding of pitch is one of the objectives set for 7-year-olds in *Music from 5 to 16* (DES, 1985a). Yet many 7-year-olds do not understand it. We might suppose that a child who has yet to achieve this objective is unable to perceive the pitch differences we are presenting. Our reaction might be to present progressively larger pitch differences to children, in the hope of finding an interval wide enough for them to notice. But as the research shows that the average 7-year-old can discriminate differences much smaller than those usually used in music, the child's problem may be labelling, not perception (see Crowther and Durkin, 1982). 'Up' and 'down' are terms associated with spatial movement. Their application to a musical context may need explanation and illustration. Teachers often approach this through the association of musical movement with spatial movement. Children may be asked to sing up a scale as they walk up some steps. They may use a hand to draw the contour of the pitch of a melody that they are listening to or singing.

Many children learn the concept of pitch easily using these sorts of techniques. Where problems persist into the junior phase, a teacher may wish to test a child's pitch discrimination using a published test (for example, Mills, 1988a). In any case, it would be unwise to assume that a child who does not sing well in tune necessarily has any problem with discrimination (see page 65).

One question remains. If children have problems with the labelling of pitch movement, how do they manage to do pitch discrimination tests? The answer is, I think, linked with the recorded instructions that children are given as part of the test. These seem to be sufficient to enable children to apply the concept throughout the test, even if the children do not remember it, or become able to apply it on other more musical occasions. Certainly, some children who do not seem to understand the concept in a musical context display it during the test. Of course, there may be other children who would benefit from even more comprehensive instructions.

Coping with musically able children

The considerable variation in pitch discrimination in any age group means that some children have finer pitch discrimination than some teachers. This means that tuning tasks that are difficult for teachers are not necessarily difficult for children. A teacher is not necessarily the best arbiter of what is, or is not, in tune. This has some immediate implications. When children assert that two seemingly identical notes are different, we need to take them seriously. A child who complains that a guitar that her teacher has just tuned is out of tune may be justified. If such children are suppressed by statements such as 'it will do' or 'there's nothing the matter with it', they may not bother to listen so closely in future. Rather, their ability can be employed to the teacher's advantage: the children can assist the teacher with tuning.

There are all sorts of musical activities in which teachers can find that some children are more able then they are. This happens to everyone, not just those who have not had much formal musical experience. The most highly qualified music graduates still find children who play some instrument or other better than they do. We have to suppress a natural reaction to be threatened by this, and instead work out how to use some children's ability to promote the development of less fortunate children, and also ourselves.

Diagnosing children's musical problems

The masking of fine pitch discrimination by difficulty with verbal labelling shows the need to think carefully about the causes of children's musical problems. Does inability to echo a clapped rhythm indicate poor rhythmic memory, or some difficulty with motor co-ordination? Does failure to walk in time with a piece of music necessarily mean that a child cannot hear its regular pulse? Musical perception takes place inside the brain; we cannot tap directly into it. If we want to know whether someone is perceiving accurately or not, we have to ask them to sing, speak, write or move, for instance, and then measure how well they do that. Any problem may result from difficulty with the singing, speaking, writing or moving itself, rather than the perception.

Setting expectations for children

The significant variation in children's discrimination is a reminder of the need to guard against setting expectations of children so low that they become unable to show us what they can do. Recognition of the dangers of underestimating children is crucial to the effectiveness of curriculum planning.

The implications I have drawn from this research are personal. I have made use of the researchers' findings according to my particular circumstances as a music teacher. Teachers in different situations may see other implications as more significant. The point is that research questions that seem not to address concerns central to music education can still yield answers that are both relevant and useful. In particular, investigation of a characteristic that is at best only a component of musical activity can have implications relevant to music education.

That said, there are many research questions that can be answered more effectively through investigation of real music making by children. We now turn to a selection of these.

CHILDREN AS MUSICIANS

In this section, I focus on three studies. Each is based on children's ordinary musical activity in classrooms; in two the children are composing, and in the third they are performing. In each case, I draw out some implications of relevance to teaching and curriculum planning. The emphasis here is mine, not the researchers'. The first study, an investigation of children's sequential development as composers, culminates in the proposition of a model of composing development which may also have wider applicability. The second, an investigation of children's development as song composers, serves also as a reminder of the danger of adherence to a simple model; development is inevitably multi-faceted, and not always apparently sequential. The third, an investigation of infants' developing vocal accuracy, points to the fact that a music curriculum intended for one group of children may be inappropriate for others.

CHILDREN'S SEQUENTIAL DEVELOPMENT AS COMPOSERS

How do children develop as composers? If children were all to follow the same pattern in their development as composers, then life as a music teacher would be straightforward. Given that a child had produced a composition at some particular position in this pattern, we would know where she or he was destined to move next; our job would be simply to lead the child there. As we all know, no aspect of child development – or even human development – is like that. Every model of learning is the result of some generalization, and few individuals follow any so-called normal patterns of development literally for more than the briefest period. There are many curriculum activities in which we accept this. Although we discern general patterns of development in children's writing or painting, we learn to respond to the expressive and technical aspects of work that seem to be out of sequence. We adapt reading and mathematics schemes to suit children's individual needs by adding a book here, or missing out a section there. The idea of a sequential model of children's musical development may be attractive, but we cannot expect it to answer all our questions about response to children's music making.

In their article The sequence of musical development: a study of children's composition (Swanwick and Tillman, 1986), Keith Swanwick and June Tillman describe a spiral model of development represented by

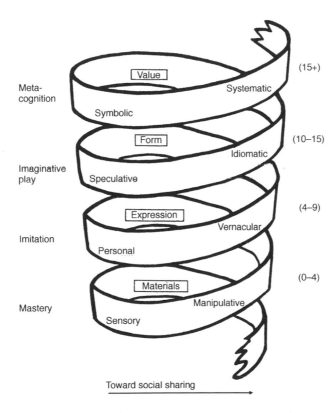

Figure 8.1 The Swanwick/Tillman model of musical development.
Source K. Swanwick and J. Tillman (1986) 'The sequence of musical develop-ment: a study of children's composition', *British Journal of Music Education*, 3 (3): 331.

the helix shown in Figure 8.1. The theoretical basis of the spiral arises from consideration of the psychological concepts of mastery, imitation, imaginative play and metacognition, and draws on the work of writers including Jean Piaget (1951), Helmut Moog (1976), Robert Bunting (1977) and Malcolm Ross (1984). The empirical evidence for the spiral arises from observation of several hundred compositions by forty-eight children taught, at various stages, by June Tillman.

The figures at the right-hand side of the helix correspond to the approximate ages at which Swanwick and Tillman believe children pass through the turns. Although only the first three turns are likely to be seen in primary school, I shall, for the sake of completeness, summarize all four. Using the explanation and examples provided by Tillman (1988: 85–6), let us follow a fictional child, Julie, as she progresses, over ten years or so, from the sensory mode, and a concern with materials, through to the systematic mode, and a concern with value.

Turn 1: materials

Sensory mode

As Julie explores the tone colour of instruments in a seemingly random manner, she seems to be asking the question: 'what sound does it make?'. She is fascinated by the rattle of a tambourine, and the rasping sound of the scraper.

Manipulative mode

Now, Julie seems to want to organize the sound she makes. Sometimes she beats out a steady pulse. Some of the patterns that she chooses – such as a glide up and down a xylophone – seem influenced by instrument shape.

Turn 2: expression

Julie's concern with materials continues. But two new modes develop.

Personal mode

Julie starts to show expressive character in her songs, and later in her instrumental compositions. The character is most clearly seen through changes in dynamics and speed. A song about the sun shining gets louder and faster until Julie 'almost shines herself'.

Vernacular mode

As Julie starts to use repeated melodies and rhythmic patterns, her compositions become shorter and less apparently exploratory. Her composition appears more derivative.

Turn 3: form

Again, two new modes develop.

Speculative

Julie starts to use contrast in her compositions. A repeated rhythm will suddenly change to give a feeling of surprise. Gradually, her use of contrast and surprise becomes more polished.

Idiomatic

Julie works within a particular musical idiom. This may be pop or jazz, or if she has taken piano lessons she may start to compose piano pieces in a style similar to those she has been learning.

Turn 4: value

Now two final modes are added.

Symbolic

Julie investigates a wider range of styles.

Systematic

Julie develops a personal and distinctive style which draws on her work in various idioms, and which she may adapt for particular pieces.

The frame of reference of the spiral is the compositions of a group of children. Yet it seems also to explain some other musical behaviour. Swanwick (1988) applies it to the account of a teenager at his first sitar recital. After some minutes of incomprehension, the teenager becomes impressed by the sounds themselves (Turn 1), then the shapes and colours they imply (Turn 2), before getting inside the structure to the extent that he becomes susceptible to surprise (Turn 3).

This is an experience that many of us have had as we start to listen to music of a type with which we are unfamiliar. To begin with, the music seems without shape, meaningless. We might wonder if the choice of notes and timing is arbitrary. Gradually, we find something that we can hold onto, even if we cannot explain what that is. Finally, we feel inside the idiom. We know what is arbitrary, and what is not. We accept the idiom on its own terms. This is the process that I likened to acquiring suitable spectacles in Chapter 5 (see page 81).

We have to be careful not to generalize too far from this. A model that works well in one restricted situation, and seems to make sense in another, is not necessarily true of all musical activity. We do not know if it applies to the work of other teachers of composing, or to performing, or to all forms of listening. Neither do we know the extent to which it makes sense to superimpose composing, performing and listening spirals, for instance, and talk about a spiral of musical development.

Curriculum planning becomes less hassle-ridden when someone else has determined the aims of your curriculum. It can be tempting to cling to the spiral, to devise curricula intended solely to promote helical progression and to assess children mainly – or possibly only – in terms of where, spirally speaking, they are. But the evidence for the validity of the spiral in all these contexts is, as yet, slender. And some potential areas of application would appear to require development as well as evidence. The use of a spiral model for assessment is fraught with difficulty. If it is musical to revisit lower turns, for instance to absorb new musical experiences, then nobody can be assessed simply in terms of how high up the spiral he or she is.

While we wait for further evidence, we may wish to think of the spiral as we try to make sense of children's music making. But this should be critical thinking; we should be testing the spiral, not using it as a frame of reference. We should also be open to other ways of thinking about children's composing, performing and listening. The responsibility for curriculum planning, teaching and assessment must continue to rest with us. Being the best model around is not enough. If we don spiral-shaped blinkers, we may miss something even better.

CHILDREN'S DEVELOPMENT AS SONG COMPOSERS

Coral Davies's (1986) article, 'Say it till a song comes', offers an approach to thinking about a particular field of children's composing: song. Davies reflects on a collection of more than twenty songs composed by children aged three to thirteen. She seems not to be searching for a pattern of development so much as for a way of responding to the composition itself. Thus her approach is more reminiscent of that of Loane's (1984) work with secondary children than that of Swanwick and Tillman. Most of the children concerned were not learning to compose in any sustained way. Often, they produced their songs so that they could sing them in a play. Usually, they wrote the words first, and then repeated them rhythmically until a song emerged, repeating the song until it became stable. Davies's approach is descriptive rather than experimental, and the reader is left to come to her or his own conclusions. The main points I take away from her work are as follows.

The role of adaptation within composing

Many of Davies's composers base their songs on material they already know. This leads Davies to argue that a rich musical experience helps with composing. Some adaptation was explicit. For instance, a 3-year-old based her song on 'The Big Ship Sails Through the Alley-Alley-O'. In other cases, the influence was better integrated. Adaptation seems to be taking place earlier than would be predicted from the Swanwick/Tillman spiral (Vernacular mode). It is possible that children are more likely to adapt if they are not presented with an alternative model through being taught composing.

The differing needs of children as composers

Davies argues the impossibility of producing a single progressive music curriculum that will suit all children. Some children arrive at school already making up songs, whilst others need a rich diet of musical experience as raw material, and possibly also specific help.

Differing ways of assessing progress in composing

Progress may be evident in many ways, including:

> greater confidence in handling musical materials; an increase in melodic range, melodies which begin to open out rather than remain closed round the same few notes; a developing sense of shape and balance of phrases, or a more sustained, longer invention. It may be apparent in a more apt setting of words, use of more varied rhythm patterns, including syncopation, and a more imaginative turn of phrase in the words themselves.
>
> (Davies, 1986: 288)

Davies's approach complements that of Swanwick and Tillman. She stresses the need for open-mindedness, thinking about composers and compositions on their own merits and avoidance of prescriptive teaching. She comments on what is different, on what breaks the mould, whilst they look for what is common. The two approaches were developed in isolation; neither was a response to the other. They illustrate the differing ways in which researchers choose to make sense of what they see around them.

SINGING IN TUNE

Roger Buckton's (1988) study took place in New Zealand, but has implications of relevance to contemporary education in the UK. It consists of a survey of the singing accuracy of forty-nine classes of children aged approximately six: 1,135 children in all. It is difficult for a researcher to assess the individual singing accuracy of children without making them self-conscious, and consequently distressed and likely to underachieve. Buckton's approach was to devise a technique for measuring the children's singing accuracy in a situation close to a usual classroom setting. Individual children were assessed whilst singing, with their class and teacher, songs that they knew well. Personal microphones were distributed to ten children at a time. As everyone sang a song together, two microphones were switched on, with the result that two of the children were recorded individually using the two channels of a stereo tape recorder. At the end of a verse, a new pair of microphones was switched on. By the end of five verses, all ten children had been recorded. Further songs were chosen until all the children in the class had been recorded.

Buckton graded the children's singing on a seven-point scale, which ran from:

'7 – sung consistently with a high level of vocal accuracy',
through
'5 – occasionally vocally accurate, maintaining the general contour of the song, but singing incorrect intervals within that contour',
to
'2 – spoken, or unclear as to whether the child was speaking or singing'
and
'1 – invalid – no sound, indicating that the child was not singing, or a possible defect in recording.'

(Buckton, 1988: 59)

Those children who were graded 1 (forty-six in all) were excluded from further analysis.

Analysis of the data shows, as usual, that the boys are less able singers than the girls. But, more interestingly, Buckton also analysed the interaction between ethnic background (as stated by the teacher) and singing grade. He found that the mean grade of Polynesian children exceeded that of European children, and that the difference in the mean singing grade of boys and girls was less marked amongst Polynesians. The results of comparing the mean singing grade of classes classified according to whether they were predominantly Polynesian, predominantly European, or mixed, were dramatic. When the forty-nine classes were arranged in descending order according to their mean singing grade – that is, starting with the class with the highest mean singing grade – the six predominantly

Polynesian classes took first, second, third, fifth, ninth and seventeenth place. Only one of the thirty-two predominantly European classes appeared in the top nine.

Why is this? Were the Polynesian children receiving more systematic training in singing in tune in school? Quite the contrary. The more successful European classes *did* have systematic training. For instance, teachers provided children with opportunities to sing individually and kept records of their development. They took account of the need to find children's comfortable range, and develop confidence within this before working outwards. But Polynesian classes, though they sang a lot, did not have systematic training in singing in tune. Buckton came to the conclusion that his findings were the result of an interaction between cultural and educational factors. Singing is an integral part of Polynesian culture. Children sing with their families and in church from an early age. Fathers sing as much as mothers, so singing is probably less associated with females than it is in European culture. Children of European ethnic background, on the other hand, often arrive at school with little background in singing. Consequently, the educational needs of the two groups differ. The European children often need systematic help, whereas the Polynesian children just need practice.

What are the implications of Buckton's study for music education in the UK? It provides evidence that systematic singing tuition can help children learn to sing in tune earlier. But it also suggests that the system used needs to reflect the cultural and musical background of the children concerned. There is no way of teaching children to sing in tune, and methods imported from other situations may be of no help. We need to work out what children's problems are, and plan accordingly.

Generalizing from Buckton's investigation of singing, it would seem that matching of the task to the child is as important in music as in any other subject. We need a mixed-ability approach to music teaching. It is inappropriate to take some externally devised music scheme, apply it to all children, and hope for the best.

REFERENCES

Bentley, A. (1966) *Musical Ability in Children and its Measurement*, Harrap: London.

Bentley, A. (1968) *'Monotones' – a Comparison with 'Normal' Singers*, Novello: London.

Bridger, W. H. (1961) 'Sensory habituation and discrimination in the human neonate'. *American Journal of Psychiatry*, 117: 991–6.

Buckton, R. (1988) 'Vocal accuracy of young children – a New Zealand survey' in Kemp. A. (ed.) *Research in Music Education: A Festschrift for Arnold Bentley*, International Society for Music Education.

Bunting, R. (1977) 'The common language of music', *Music in the Secondary School Curriculum*, Working paper 6, Schools Council: York University.

Crowther, R. and Durkin, K. (1982) 'Research overview: language in music education', *Psychology of Music* 10 (1): 59–60.

Davies, C. (1986) 'Say it till a song comes (reflections on songs invented by children 3–13)', *British Journal of Music Education* 3 (3): 279–93.

Department of Education and Science (1985) *Curriculum Matters 4: Music from 5 to 16*, HMSO: London.

Loane, B. (1984) 'Thinking about children's composition', *British Journal of Music Education* 1 (3): 205–32.

Mills, J. (1984) 'The "Pitch" subtest of Bentley's "Measures of Musical Abilities": a test from the 1960s reconsidered in the 1980s', *Psychology of Music* 12 (2): 94–105.

———— (1988) *Group Tests of Musical Abilities: Teacher's Guide and Recorded Test*, NFER-Nelson: Windsor.

Moog H. (1976) *The Musical Experience of the Pre-School Child* (translated by Claudia Clarke), Schott: London.

Piaget, J. (1951) *Play, Dreams and Imitation in Childhood*, Routledge & Kegan Paul: London.

Ross, M. (1984) *The Aesthetic Impulse*, Pergamon Press: Oxford.

Seashore, C. E. (1938) *The Psychology of Music*, McGraw-Hill: London.

Shuter-Dyson, R. and Gabriel, C. (1981) *The Psychology of Musical Ability*, Methuen: London.

Swanwick, K. (1988) *Music, Mind, and Education*, Routledge: London.

Swanwick, K. and Tillman, J. (1986) 'The sequence of musical development: a study of children's composition', *British Journal of Music Education* 3 (3): 305–39.

Tillman, J. (1988) 'Music in the primary school and the national curriculum' in Salaman. W. and Mills, J. (eds) *Challenging Assumptions: New Perspectives in the Education of Music Teachers*, University of Exeter School of Education: Exeter.

Part III

Issues in music education

Chapter 9

Gender, musical meaning and education

Lucy Green

Like many adolescent girls in the 1960s to 1970s who played the piano and studied classical music at school, I was as much insecure as fascinated in the realm of rock music. I perceived my insecurity as the result of a split between classical and popular music, reflected in the parallel discrepancy between school and subculture: I had been classically trained at school, and this was why I could not understand the technicalities of rock. What I was unable to entertain was the additional possibility that my insecurity was a product of gender: that the problem was not so much to do with technical differences between classical and rock music themselves, as with the cultural ownership of rock by boys. I want to suggest that there is a peculiar difficulty about questioning one's own gender-position in relation to music, a difficulty which arises from a specifically musical factor: that we learn our gendered relationships with music, not only from wider historical, political and educational contexts, but also through musical experience itself. The operation of musical meaning as a gendered discourse occurs poignantly in the school classroom as a microcosm of the wider society.

I wish to sketch a theoretical distinction between two virtual aspects of musical meaning.[1] The first operates at the level of musical materials, the syntactical organization of which gives rise to the listener's sense of whole and part, opening and close, repetition, difference and all other pertinent functional relationships. I call this 'inherent meaning', not to indicate that there is anything essential or ahistorical about it, but rather that both the materials which form the signifying part of the process of identifying structures, and those which are being signified as structures in some way, are made up of musical materials: inherent, then, in the sense that they physically inhere. The materials of music are not just heard as random sounds, but they have relationships which can be perceived *as such*. These relationships can be said to have meaning in terms of each other, but without any symbolic content. Listeners' responses to and understanding of inherent meanings are dependent on the listeners' competence in relation to the style of the music. A piece of music whose materials are highly meaningful or very rewarding to you, might be relatively meaningless or lacking in interest to me.

This aspect of musical meaning is only partial, and can never exist on its own. We have become accustomed to the idea that the social or cultural images of performers make an important contribution to their commercial survival. It would be surprising, for example, to see a record cover of Schubert songs depicting the soprano Kiri Te Kanawa in bondage with purple hair; and if we see Madonna in a respectable suit we interpret this as postmodern dressing. But the manipulation of performers' images is not a mere marketing strategy, for clothes, hair styles or posturing on the sleeves of recordings are all details of a broader, necessary aspect of any music: its mediation as a cultural artefact within a social and historical context. This context is not merely an extra-musical appendage, but forms an intrinsic part of the music's meaning during the listening experience. Without some understandings of the fact that music is a social construction, we would ultimately be unable to recognize any particular collection of sounds as music at all. When we listen to music, we cannot separate our experience of its pre-symbolic, inherent meanings entirely from a greater or lesser awareness of the social context and symbolic content that accompany its production and reception. I will therefore suggest a second category of musical meaning, distinct from the first, and called 'delineated meaning'. By this expression I wish to convey the idea that music metaphorically sketches, or delineates, a plethora of contextualizing factors. As with inherent meaning, listeners construct the delineated meanings of music according to their subject-position in relation to the music's style. Delineated meanings are at some levels conventionally accepted, and at others, personal.

Whenever we hear music, we are affected to some extent by both types of meaning, and both must always be present in all musical experience. But each type of meaning operates very differently, each acting in various ways upon the other, to affect our total musical experience, our musical practices and the construction of our discourses on music. It is through the mutual interaction of the different aspects of musical meaning that we learn, among other things, our gendered relationships with music.[2]

I have used the examples of Kiri Te Kanawa and Madonna to indicate that the manipulation of their images contributes in part to the delineated meanings of the music they perform. I now want to suggest that, in much more complex ways than through clothes and hair styles, something fundamental about their femininity itself also forms a part of their music's delineated meanings. The female singer in a public arena performs on an instrument which *is* her body, without recourse to the manipulation of any palpable physical object in the world. She enacts a scenario which affirms an enduring patriarchal understanding of woman as both in tune with, and subject to, the natural givens of her body; while at the same time being alienated from, and needless of, technology. In this highlighting of the body away from technology, vocal performance is akin to a type of display, and indeed, the singing woman has been associated in most cultures with the sexual temptress or harlot.[3] But the woman singer not only appears sexually available, for in her private capacity she conjures up an inversion of this public image, that of the idealized mother singing to her baby. Pivoted upon the binary division between whore and madonna, harlot and virgin, the woman singer re-enacts some of the fundamental patriarchal defining characteristics of femininity. When we listen to a woman sing, we do not just listen to the inherent meanings of the music, but we are also aware of their position in this nexus of definition. Her femininity becomes a part of the music's delineations. This affirmation of femininity and its delineation in music is one of the reasons why, throughout the history of music, women have been more abundant and successful in singing than in any other single musical role.

In the case of instrumental performance, the presence and manipulation of the instrument itself to some extent interrupts the appearance of the woman's natural in-tuneness with and susceptibility to her body. The more unwieldy and loud the instrument and the more technologically demanding for the performer, the more problematic is the construction of an apparently feminine bodily display by the performer. The woman instrumentalist challenges the binary characterization of woman as either sexually available or maternally preoccupied.

> There was this young girl on stage, and this enormous drum kit. I couldn't believe that she was going to play it; but she walked across the stage and sat down behind it, and she did play it – and she played it well too!

These are the words of an astonished school caretaker at a recent concert. However familiar such incredulity is in so many walks of life, this should not distract us from the implications it raises for musical meaning. I would suggest that the idea of the girl's femininity had fleetingly become a part of the music's delineations in the experience of the caretaker. When he listened to the music, he was 'listening out' to discover whether she could play well. Not only for him, but for all of us, the gender of the female instrumental performer enters into delineated musical meaning, as an interruption to patriarchal definitions of femininity. This occurs to varying extents depending on the subject-position of the listener, the type of instrument, the musical style and the social context. The effects of this problematic relationship between femininity and instrumental performance are decipherable throughout the history of women's musical roles, which reveals the fact that unwieldiness, high volume or technological complexity tend to characterize those very instruments from which women have been most vehemently discouraged or banned.

Femininity also enters delineated meaning through the composer. Clearly there is no display of the composer's body, but composition requires a level of knowledge and control over technique, distinct from the physical motor-control of performance; and through this type of control, mind features in any composition-related delineations of music.[4] As we listen to music, one of the elements of which we are more or less aware, an element that we are prone to marvel at in our best musical experiences, is the mind behind the music. 'How *could* Beethoven have *conceived* of such a thing?' we are prone to say. While we listen, it is not just the inherent meanings that occupy our attention, but the idea of Beethoven's mind. When it is not Beethoven, but the woman composer Louise Adolpha Le Beau to whom we are listening, such a response is liable to be marked by an even greater level of incredulity than that of the school caretaker above.

> [The final variation] subsequently plunges passionately and boldly on and becomes so violent, that one has quite forgotten by the end that the composer is a woman; indeed, one could think that one were dealing with a capable man, who can truly strike earnestly and hard as here.
> (The words of a contemporary critic, concerning Le Beau's *Piano Variations, Op. 3.*)[5]

Like the display of body in performance, there is a metaphorical display of mind in composition, which becomes a part of the music's delineated meanings. When the composer is known to be a woman, the fact of her display of mind conflicts with her ideologically constructed natural submission to the body, going so far as to threaten patriarchal definitions of femininity. This is part of the explanation of why it is that women have throughout music history been even more vigorously discouraged from composition than from instrumental performance.

The discourses which surround different styles of music place various emphases upon the relative importance of delineated or inherent meanings. If the music is serious, classical, and purported to be autonomous, then any delineations are often altogether denied by listeners. In the case of such music, listeners are not supposed to be looking at the woman player, or disturbed by the femininity of the composer because they are not supposed to be paying attention to the delineated meanings at all. If the music is less autonomous, more commercial for example, as with certain categories of popular music, listeners very often take any display of femininity as a legitimate and pertinent part of the delineated meanings, which are themselves celebrated. The delineations of femininity, their capacity to affirm, interrupt or threaten patriarchal definitions, thus vary in degree like all musical meanings, according to the music's style, its historical context, and the subject-position of the listener. But even in the most supposedly autonomous music, the discourse surrounding which totally eschews the possibility of delineated meaning, femininity is none the less delineated to some extent. Otherwise, if I can put this in a nutshell, there would be no heat in the issue of women's musical roles, and the whole history of music would be different.[6]

I have suggested some ways in which the femininity of the performer or composer enters delineated musical meaning. Clearly, by my definition of inherent musical meaning as purely to do with musical materials, inherent meaning itself can have nothing to do with gender. But the gendered delineation of music does in fact not stop at delineation: it continues from its delineated position, to affect listeners' responses to and perceptions of inherent meaning. In the realm of performance, for example, if the delineation of a piece of music involves overt sexuality on the part of the female performer, we are disinclined to pay much attention to her manipulation of the inherent meanings. This disinclination surfaces in the visual culture of much popular music today, when in videos or television programmes, producers substitute the real performers by women whose main function is to display their bodies. The more attention is paid to bodily display by the performer in such a context, the less likely do we find it that the woman is actually playing the instrument, or even actually singing.[7] It is not only that a high degree of feminine display is in the delineations of the music, but that those delineations then cause us to hear and interpret the inherent meanings in a certain way.

In the case of composition also, once listeners are aware that the composer is a woman, a long history shows that they tend to perceive the inherent meanings of the music in terms of delineated femininity. For example, a Scandinavian music critic was in the habit of writing rave reviews about a particular composer. After many reviews, the critic found out that the composer was a woman. He carried on writing good reviews, but his language changed; his praise ceased to describe the music with words like 'strident', 'virile' or 'powerful', and began to include words like 'delicate' and 'sensitive'. What had happened was that his new knowledge that the composer was a woman, or in the terms I am suggesting, the delineation of the femininity of the composer affected the way that he also heard the inherent meanings. One cannot help wondering whether, had he known the composer's gender all along, he would have found any merit in the compositions to begin with. A great deal of music by women composers has been denigrated for its effeminacy; other music has been more favourably received as displaying positive feminine attributes such as delicacy or sensitivity; and a tiny amount of music by women has been incredulously hailed as equal to music by men. History gives us due cause to assume that the composer behind nearly all the music that most people hear, is a man; or to put this another way, part of all musical delineation contains the notion of a male mind. When we discover a woman's mind behind the music, her femininity then enters the delineations, from which position it acts to alter our perceptions, normally unchallenged in this regard, of the inherent meanings. The more that femininity is delineated, the less inclined are we to judge the inherent meanings as autonomous essences.

To summarize the argument so far, music delineates gender in a variety of ways, according to the gender of the performer and/or the composer, in combination with the music's style, its historical context and the subject-position of the listener. Musical delineations are not closed unto themselves, but they affect our perceptions of inherent meanings. When music delineates femininity through a female performer or composer, we are liable to also judge the handling of inherent meanings by that performer or composer in terms of our idea of their femininity. It is not that there is anything feminine about the inherent meanings, but that the idea of femininity filters our response to them.

I sent some questionnaires[8] to a selection of mixed secondary schools in different parts of England, which aimed to tap teachers' perceptions of boys' and girls' musical practices and aptitudes. It was no surprise to find that in almost every one of the seventy-eight schools, girls were reported to sing in abundance, often to the total exclusion of boys; that large numbers of girls played keyboard and traditional orchestral instruments enthusiastically, joining orchestras and bands and taking part in school concerts, whereas boys played mainly electric guitars, bass and drums. Overwhelmingly, teachers stated that girls are better at playing classical music than boys, giving the reason that girls are more persevering, hard-working and committed. It was interesting to discover something about teachers' views of pupils' proclivities in the realm of composition, a curriculum requirement which has only existed in any widespread sense in Britain over the last ten years or so. I found that in teachers' eyes and ears, girls are more conservative at composition, less imaginative, less innovative than boys, who are understood to have all the hallmarks of a sense of aesthetic adventure. In sum, musical girls are understood to be numerous, persevering, but ultimately conservative and mediocre; whereas musical boys are perceived as rare, creative and gifted.

Some of these perceptions, such as how many girls sing in the choir or play the piano, are easily empirically verifiable. In and across music classrooms there is a replication of the historical precedents that are part-cause and part-effect of gendered musical meanings, as girls and boys continue by their musical practices to reproduce the history of women's and men's musical roles. Others of the teachers' perceptions, such as how gifted girls and boys are at music and especially how creative they are at composition, are not empirically verifiable at all. Such impressions are based on aesthetic judgements about pupils' musical products. These judgements can be understood in terms of deeply embedded musical meanings handed down through history and like everyone else, teachers and pupils in schools respond to music in terms of musical meanings that are, among other things, gendered. This includes not only delineated meanings, but the effect of delineations upon our perceptions of inherent meanings. Thus, as with all listeners and critics, when teachers judge pupils' work, the gendered musical delineations, which cannot be avoided, also act to affect their perceptions of the music's inherent meanings. For pupils themselves, when they make choices about their musical practices and when they are working on performances or compositions, the delineated meanings of their chosen music and of their own work will come back at them and affect their perceptions of its inherent meanings.

Music's incorporation of gender does not reside hermetically in musical meaning, for gendered musical meanings affect our consciousness and experience, not only of music, but through music, of ourselves. Gendered musical meanings participate in the construction of our very notions of masculinity and femininity. This means, therefore, that we can use music to confirm and perpetuate our concepts of ourselves as gendered beings. Such a use of music lies behind many of the teachers' perceptions of girls' and boys' musical activities and abilities. Thus teachers may be right that girls are more interested in violins than drums, and they may be right that girls are conservative in composition. What is crucial, is that judgements themselves must be combined with the girls' own musical judgements and inclinations, all of which cannot be separated from the influence of gendered musical meanings. These meanings are not only handed down through history, nor do they only persist in the organization of musical production and reception in the society at large, but they are also re-enacted daily in the life of the music classroom as a microcosm of the wider society.

Musical meaning on the one hand, teachers' and pupils' practices and perceptions on the other – inseparably and complexly these combine in classrooms to make our musical, educational transactions far from innocent. This would therefore seem to be a very bleak outlook for the role of music education. If indeed stereotypical gendered musical meanings are impinging themselves in a way which reproduces the historical precedents of men's and women's musical practices, then there would not seem to be a great deal that the school can do to intervene. Any redefinition of roles and practices would seem to be blocked by the requirement of the redefinition of musical meaning itself. However the fact of this blockage does not make me despair.

The examples above suggest some ways in which pupils and teachers perpetuate gender stereotypes through their mainstream music educational practices. But it is also possible to resist through music. A group of girls in one Liverpool school got together with a youth leader[9] in the late 1980s to produce some rap, in which they played electric and percussion in-struments. They were at first aggressively ridiculed by boys, who referred to them as 'slags' and 'tarts', and to their music as 'rubbish', among other expressions. The girls persisted with their music-making on several afternoons when school was over, and eventually having finished a number, they relayed it in high volume down to the playground where a group of boys stood chiding. Now, the meaningful process such as I have been describing, whereby the feminine delineations of the music caused the boys to denigrate both the girls and the inherent meanings, acted in reverse: the confrontational political situation caused the boys to listen again to the inherent meanings. They found them convincing, and they then also changed their minds about the girls' aptitudes and intentions.

Such interventions are rare, not necessarily educative, and most probably short-lived. They do not require theoretical knowledge about musical meaning on the part of teachers, but political commitment. But if as a profession we do seek to harness such interventionary possibilities to the pursuit of our highest ideals, then it may be helpful to be aware of the complexity and depth-embeddedness of gendered musical meanings, not only in our educational structures but also in our musical experience.

NOTES

1 This theory is treated more fully, although without any reference to gender, in Lucy Green, *Music on Deaf Ears: Musical Meaning, Ideology and Education* (Manchester and New York: Manchester University Press, 1988).
2 Masculinity and femininity are only definable in relation to each other; therefore both must be equally relevant to music. Bearing this in mind, I concentrate in this chapter on femininity.
3 This is not merely idle speculation. See, for example, Ellen Koskoff, (ed.) *Women and Music in Cross-Cultural Perspective* (New York and London: Greenwood Press, 1987); or the growing bibliography on women in western music, of which four helpful starting points are Jane Bowers and Judith Tick, (eds) *Women Making Music: The Western Art Tradition, 1150–1950* (Urbana and Chicago: University of Illinois Press, 1987: 297); Linda Dahl, *Stormy Weather: The Music and Lives of a Century of Jazz Women* (London and New York: Quartet Books, 1984); Gillian Gaar, *She's A Rebel: The History of Women in Rock and Roll* (London: Blandford Press, 1993); Karin Pendle, (ed.) *Women and Music: A History* (Bloomington and Indianapolis: Indiana University Press, 1991).
4 Clearly in putting forward such an argument I am invoking a mind–body split; but this is not because I wish to claim the 'correctness' of such a split. On the contrary, it is because this split forms a definitive part of the very distinction between masculinity and femininity which I am to critique. See Charles Ford, *Cosi? Sexual Politics in Mozart's Operas* (Manchester and New York: Manchester University Press, 1991: 8–10 and passim), for a discussion of the Enlightenment roots of the construction of the male as reasoning and the female as tied to the body, with reference to music; Susan McClary, *Feminine Endings: Music, Gender and Sexuality* (Minnesota and Oxford: University of Minnesota Press, 1991: 17–18, 79, 151–1) for a discussion of mind and body regarding masculinity and feminity with relations to music, although I am not in line with her argument that music and woman are both associated with the body; and David Lidov, 'Mind and body in music', *Semiotica 66*, (1987: 69–97) for a characterization of performance as somatic, and composition as semiotic.
5 August Bungert, *Allgemeine Deutsche Musik-Zeitung* 3, 30 May 1876, 'Kritiken', 1,

no. 3; cited in Judith E. Olson, 'Luise Adolpha Le Beau: composer in late nineteenth-century Germany', in Bowers and Tick, *Women Making Music*.

6 The references in Note 3 would again provide a starting point for following up this claim.

7 See Barbara Bradby's sharp analysis of a legal case over the sampling of a woman's singing voice and the replacement of her body by that of another woman on the video: 'Sampling sexuality: gender, technology and the body in dance music', *Popular Music* 12 (2) (May 1993): 155–76. Sue Steward and Sheryl Garratt, *Signed, Sealed and Delivered: True Life Stories of Women in Pop* (London and Sydney: Pluto Press, 1984) cite evidence of bands in the 1980s, who took to hiring women to mime instrumental performance.

8 Lucy Green, 'Music, gender and education: a report on some exploratory research', *British Journal of Music Education* 10 (3) (Autumn 1993): 219–53.

9 Edwina Allcock, unpublished discussion presentation on panel 'Equal and unequal opportunities in popular music', Seminar on Popular Music and Social Policy, Institute of Popular Music, University of Liverpool, June 1989.

Chapter 10

Music with emotionally disturbed children

Yvonne Packer

THE STATUS OF MUSIC IN SPECIAL EDUCATION

> for children whose home background is not always as happy as might be desired, whose activities are necessarily limited, and whose friendships may not bring them complete fulfilment – pleasure in music-making with its accompanying sense of well-being and exhultation can do much to compensate for their lack of other opportunities.
>
> (Dobbs, 1966)

Compensatory education for the disadvantaged is, of necessity, one of the guiding principles in all special schools and those teachers who have experienced the effect of music on the lives of special needs children will surely appreciate the validity of Dobbs's statement and the potential power there is in music education to effect change and bring relief to damaged lives. Unfortunately, however, the situation at the present time is that if special schools are able to offer their children an adequate music education, they are exceptional.

The shortage of experienced music teachers in special education is a problem highlighted in Daphne Kennard's report for the Disabled Living Foundation (1979) in which reference is made to the lack of music provision in schools and attention drawn to the inadequacy of teacher training in this field. Recording that there was in the mid-1970s no college of higher education offering training in music and special education, Kennard expresses the hope that the training situation will not remain static in this pioneering field: but two decades later we seem to have moved hardly at all.

The expectation of those not actually working in special schools seems to be that teachers whose vocation is special needs work should first practice in mainstream schools for five years or so in order to equip themselves for transfer to special schools. I have rarely heard this view endorsed by special school teachers themselves and one wonders how much the principle is based on evidence that probationary teachers do benefit from being steered into the mainstream as a grounding for special education, or if it is rather an excuse disguising the fact that at the present time we seem unable to offer adequate training to those whose vocation is teaching music to children with special needs.

In those special schools where one is fortunate enough to be able to observe some ongoing music education, one finds more often than not that the teachers themselves are suffering from feelings of professional isolation and that, whatever their level of competence, they experience the resultant feelings of underconfidence and inadequacy.

Rather than allaying these feelings of isolation, it would appear that each new report relating to music in schools intensifies the problem if for no other reason than the sin of omission. Take, for example, *Music from 5 to 16* (DES, 1985) which supposedly refers to the needs of every child but makes no mention of the adaptations required to cater for special needs children, and demonstrates a total lack of awareness in the section relating to accommodation and equipment. A similar lack of awareness pervades the documentation on GCSE and the national curriculum, almost suggesting that special education is an embarrassment which no one is quite sure how to tackle. Inevitably, teachers are left feeling isolated, resentful and in limbo with regard to professional guidance on subject teaching.

COMPENSATORY/THERAPEUTIC EDUCATION IN EBD SCHOOLS

If there is a problem of music provision throughout special education, it is intensified in that area of special education relating to the child with emotional and behavioural difficulties (EBD).

The concept of compensatory education becomes more crucial in this area for:

> in work with other types of handicap, the teacher educates the child who nevertheless remains handicapped: the teacher cannot, for example, cure blindness or deafness. Teachers of maladjusted children, however, have a different role: by educating their pupils well, they reduce the handicap. Indeed it is largely by their success in doing this that their efforts are judged.
>
> (DES, 1965)

Yet it would appear to be the case that non music specialists working with disabled children or those with mild/severe learning difficulties are more likely to risk trying out some kind of musical activities than are those teachers working with maladjusted children. (The word *risk* is used advisedly and I will expand on this later.) Music festivals for combined special schools tend to reflect the alienation of EBD schools, and even those National Conferences which have been devoted to music in special education have so far overlooked the needs of maladjusted children.

The reason for this state of affairs may lie in the traditional attitude towards the education of the emotionally disturbed which used to be that these were sick children who had to be medically cured before their education could begin. In his *Pioneer Work with Maladjusted Children*, Bridgeland (1971) emphasizes the neglect of education in treatment but over the years, the emphasis has changed and now most schools have replaced the old medical model with an educational/psychological approach with which to meet the childrens' needs. In *Educating Maladjusted Chidren*, Laslett (1977) expands on the value of therapeutic education, a term which sounds somewhat nebulous when discussing music in view of the increasing general awareness of music therapy: but in fact there are distinct differences between the two disciplines and it would seem that the teaching model is the most suited to the requirements of EBD schools. However, one must consider that such literature as does currently exist documenting the effect of music on disturbed children relates almost exclusively to music therapy. The work of Nordoff and Robbins and other leading music therapists has brought to our attention the value of music when used as a tool to effect clinical cure in patients, and the potential force of this tool should be borne in mind when considering the musical education of maladjusted children even though they are not medically sick.

One should also bear in mind the claims of transference relating to music education based on Kodaly's principles as documented in Sandor's *Musical Education in Hungary* (1969), which suggests that music may stimulate the cortex and therefore result in improved performance intellectually, physically and in terms of social development. This would obviously be highly relevant in terms of the education of maladjusted children, though those who are sceptical of the Hungarian claims might prefer Dobbs's perception of transference, that being: 'on the success achieved in one activity and the confidence engendered by it, other successes, perhaps in the basic subjects, may be built'.

Dobbs's premise that this initial success may readily be achieved in music is borne out by my research in EBD schools and to a lesser extent, so is the theory that the sense of wellbeing brought about by this success leads to improvement in other areas. When one considers that 'any study of the maladjusted child is essentially a study in failure' (Shedden, 1984), the issue of providing success for the child becomes crucial, and one begins to realize the validity and enormity of the DES's assertion that teachers in EBD schools are working to reduce the handicapping condition of their pupils.

THE LACK OF MUSIC IN EBD SCHOOLS

The enormity of the problem is also one of numbers as the increased demand for educational provision for maladjusted children reflects that it is one of the two fastest growth areas in special education. In 1945, there was only one tutorial class in London for disturbed children but by 1983 there were 226 units in the ILEA offering places for disruptive children.

Disturbed and disruptive are obviously not tautological terms, but there has since 1945 been a great deal of confusion regarding precisely what sort of child the label 'maladjusted' refers to. In 1955, the Underwood Committee highlighted the symptoms which were indicative of maladjustment, they being – nervous behaviour, habit, psychotic and organic disorders, and educational and vocational difficulties. It is obviously a very mixed bag and though the emphasis is on *disturbed* behaviour, there is sufficient leeway amongst the categories to allow for *disruptive* behaviour to be included within the term maladjustment. As disruption and violence have been on the increase in schools, certainly since the raising of the school leaving age if not before, EBD schools now find themselves very often catering not only for genuinely disturbed children but also for those without emotional disorders but whose disruptive and deviant behaviour has made them difficult to contain in mainstream schools.

In their survey of the *Education of Disturbed Pupils* (1980), Wilson and Evans indicate that there are particular problems relating to the musical education of these children. Their difficulties concerning self-discipline, co-operation and concentration make composition, audition and performance extremely difficult to achieve and though Wilson and Evans record that teachers value the importance of creative work, music teaching was only infrequently observed by them. Apart from the nature of the children, one of the principle reasons for this was seen to be the scarcity of suitable teachers 'who are skilled in the use of the medium – and who are skilled in the management of disturbed pupils. Such people are naturally extremely rare'.

Because of the nature of the work it would be rare to find a music specialist working full-time in an EBD school but the lack of music in such schools is surely more of a reflection on the non-specialist teachers working in the field than the music specialists working elsewhere. Since most maladjusted schools conform to the primary model in the sense that class teachers are responsible for most of the subject teaching of their own children, one is led to ask why it is that teachers 'who happily tackle the teaching of mathematics, science, reading and other aspects of the school curriculum, shrink from organizing meaningful musical activities in their classrooms?' (Adams and Syers, 1983). It is a question which I put to seventy-seven teachers in special schools. All those questioned were currently offering a range of subjects to their pupils and in many cases the teachers were each responsible for the complete classroom education of their group of children. The teachers were asked: 'did your own higher education (teacher training/university course, etc.) equip you to offer some kind of music education to the children you are currently working with?'

and despite the fact that they were all teaching a wide cross-section of subjects – academic, recreational and practical – only five of the seventy-seven teachers replied 'yes' to the question and only three of the five were involved in music teaching at the time of answering.

Reporting on the *Music Consultancy in Berkshire Primary Schools*, Smith (1987) speaks of the 'deep-seated insecurity and lack of confidence' non-specialists feel about embarking on musical activities with their children. One may imagine how greatly intensified these feelings become when the children involved are disturbed, for Wilson and Evans observed how vulnerable music-making was in respect of its 'disruptability': which brings us back to the element of *risk* involved in such an undertaking. An integral part of the childrens' disruptive behaviour (whether intentional or not) is a consistent and systematic attempt to de-skill the teacher and this obviously is particularly pertinent to the non-specialist teacher attempting to introduce music into the curriculum. It means that, as well as coping with the childrens' problems of poor self-control, lack of concentrations, low motivation, retardation, etc. the teacher has to anticipate possible damage to him/herself both professionally and personally.

This issue was brought home to me during the course of an interview with a music therapist who had for many years been the headteacher of an EBD school. Though teacher-trained in the creative arts he had chosen *not* to teach music in his school because in his opinion:

> to teach music in this context one needs a cast-iron technique, clearly defined boundaries and sufficient maturity (or self-assurance) to cope with the children who seek to destroy it for you. You can't risk teaching something which is precious to you when you know that it will be ridiculed and denigrated.

He also felt that his pupils were very resistant to music education because of its 'exploratory nature which tends to frighten this type of child'.

This teacher believed that music education was threatening for the administrator principally because music appeals to a subliminal level which other subjects do not: but in fact it would appear that many teachers share the feeling that they are similarly threatened whatever subject they teach. Rather than being a music related issue it would seem that it is more to do with the children's efforts to de-skill and demoralize the teacher. The fact that music has the capacity to appeal to the subliminal nature of the child does, however, suggest that it has the capacity to cause damage if handled badly. Nordoff and Robbins acknowledge that certain aspects of their music-making with children were 'powerfully intrusive. If these facts were disregarded there could be the danger of placing insupportable stresses on a child and hence engendering confusion and instability' (1971).

Bearing in mind these points it perhaps becomes clear why there is so little music education happening in EBD schools, though in cases where teachers have observed it taking place their negative comments tend to centre on such issues as the noise factor and the problems arising from end of term concerts, etc. rather than psychological damage sustained by staff and pupils. One should not however underestimate music's potential and it would obviously be wrong for the layperson to attempt amateur music therapy, but it would seem from my experience in EBD schools that there is a place for music education and that it can successfully be promoted by the non-specialist teacher. The musical activities I have seen used success-fully with maladjusted children have largely been restricted to the type practised in junior or lower secondary classes which would in itself seem to be desirable at a time when we are urged to bear in mind the integration (or very often in this case the re-integration) of special needs children. Since there is a marked relationship between maladjustment and academic failure we need to ensure that EBD children are not further disadvantaged by our failure as teachers in providing them with such a restricted curriculum that they are unable to rejoin their mainstream classes largely because they have not followed the same course of work as their peers.

HOW MAY MUSIC BE SUSTAINED IN EBD SCHOOLS?

Despite their reservations about music in EBD schools and the limited amount of practice they were able to observe, Wilson and Evans argue for the inclusion of music and the other creative arts into the curriculum 'on the grounds that they may give pleasure, provide relief, facilitate communication or produce gratifying results'.

Unfortunately, there is to date very little written evidence endorsing their view, but one relevant article did appear in *Music Educators Journal* (1972) in which Price, Rast and Winterfeldt outlined their music programme with emotionally disturbed children and indicated its success not only in terms of the classroom experience, but also in terms of developing the childrens' social skills which were then transferred from the music room into other areas of the school.

We return then to the theme of therapeutic education but maybe this time we should approach it from a different angle. Overtones of music therapy are daunting to the music teacher and non-specialist alike, but it would seem that the latter rejects the idea of teaching music largely as a result of his/her inadequacy as a musician. The same teacher is, however, experienced in furthering the emotional, social and educational readjust-ment of his/her pupils, and it would therefore seem logical to assume that s/he would be able to utilize a new resource to the same effect if that resource were to be made 'user-friendly'.

The first priority must surely be to persuade non-specialists that teaching music is not dependent on being able to play the piano, nor do they necessarily need to have experience of playing any other instrument.

They should also be assured that teaching music does not automatically mean that they move into the impressario business in which they are required to churn out performers. Rather than aiming at musical excellence, the non-specialist should seek to use musical activities in the same way as s/he uses other activities first of all to engage the child, then to provide him/her with a satisfying experience and finally to cash in on this experience as a means of furthering the overall readjustment of the child. The last stage in this process will be the easiest for the EBD teacher (because that is what s/he is attempting to do all the time with the pupils) and the first stage probably the most difficult.

A guide to initial reading which gives an overview of music with special needs children is available from the Disabled Living Foundation. But the standard texts of Bentley, Salaman, Swanwick and Paynter are also relevant reading for, though they are specialist literature, we should aim to give maladjusted children as near normal an input as we are able. Non-specialists would be well advised therefore to consider all that is available and extract from it what they can confidently utilize though at the stage when non-specialists require advice on how to begin the actual teaching, guidelines in literature become more scarce. Though their work relates to primary schools, Jean Gilbert and Muriel Hart's suggested activities have starting points which are realistic for the non-specialist teacher in EBD schools and Storms's *Handbook of Music Games* is a useful resource. In addition, there is now available a compilation of musical activities which have been tried and tested in the EBD context (Packer, 1987).

The material contained in this pamphlet is not unusual in itself but the suggestions made regarding the manner of presentation indicate the significant differences between mainstream and special music education. There is, for example, no suggestion of a step-by-step continuous programme but rather a seemingly random selection of diverse activities from which to select in order to catch the child's fleeting moment of interest. Many of the activities are presented as games and they are complete in themselves designed to last no longer than twenty minutes, that being about the maximum time maladjusted children may be expected to engage in a single activity.

The overriding themes underlying the compilation are familiarity and instant success, components which may be desirable in mainstream education but are imperative in EBD schools. My own experience and that of colleagues has shown that to simultaneously ignore both of these ingredients is a recipe for disaster. This does not of course prohibit the introduction of new material but it does mean that in order to ensure some degree of successful integration, the teacher has to resort to devious tactics. Sometimes, an acceptable level of familiarity may be established by using new music as a background sound for other activities, but otherwise a workable system is:

(i)   Use familiar music when introducing a new activity to the child.

(ii) Establish the new activity so that it becomes familiar to the child.

(iii) Use the now familiar activity to introduce new music.

Though this appears to be a long-winded process, it is usually time- and labour-saving in the long run, for maladjusted children are notoriously resistant to change and if they feel in any way threatened by material which is unfamiliar, there is little chance that the teacher will be able to engage them in listening to or appreciating new music.

The need to provide instant success is also common to other subject areas in EBD education but it is perhaps more readily achieved in music because there is little need for verbal communication or academic ability. Because they have in the past consistently failed academically and socially, maladjusted children do not have the normal capacity for effort, endurance, optimism, etc. and they will therefore give up at the smallest stumbling block. Rehearsal is a skill which consequently evades them, but it is possible to develop this skill so long as the children have experienced the sweet smell of instant success as a regular part of their musical education. The activities recommended therefore in this compilation, together with the suggested manner of presentation, combine to ensure (as far as is possible) that success is within the children's grasp.

Since Packer's *Musical Activities for Children with Behavioural Problems* is designed for the use of those who are not music specialists, the activities included represent a somewhat skewed sample but it did provide much of the material for a day conference on music with maladjusted children. Held in July last year, the conference was the first of its kind to be held in this country and it brought together some of those currently involved with music education in EBD schools. The conference report (available from the Disabled Living Foundation) highlights the isolated and intermittent nature of this practice but also illustrates the success of that practice as observed by specialists and non-specialists alike. During the course of the day reference was frequently made to the alleviation of anger and depression (the two most dominant emotions experienced by maladjusted children) and the recurring theme was the compensatory and therapeutic value of music. Apparent in every anecdote and recording which was presented was the high level of enjoyment which the children were deriving from their music-making and which, it was suggested, was a level of enjoyment rarely experienced in other areas of the curriculum.

The results of a questionnaire put to other teachers using music in EBD schools reflected similar findings. Those engaged in music education spoke of their children gaining self-esteem and self-confidence through music-making, developing awareness and appreciation of others to the extent that they could play together (constructive play rather than the usual playground fights) and they also observed that in music lessons, children who were normally very tense were able to find relaxation.

These observations were in keeping with the comments of teachers involved in my own research. One teacher summarized the effect of music education on her children thus: 'the children are insecure and damaged. Within the context of music they are confident, happy, relaxed and eager to share: a rare thing for our children!'. Another observed that her class's response to singing and playing the instruments was 'spontaneous enjoyment which was for them quite rare. They could express themselves creatively and cooperatively in music lessons which they were unable to do in art, for example, as they found the latter more threatening and competitive. In music they experienced immediate success so it acted as a great boost to their confidence'.

Occasionally, class teachers' comments were something of a back-handed compliment, for example, 'I'm afraid you've got Duncan this afternoon but I should think he'll be okay. For some unknown reason he seems to enjoy his music lessons: a bit odd really because usually nothing in the world pleases him!' and on other occasions class teachers seemed to gain a new perspective on their children during the course of their music-making. One teacher was 'amazed' to see how one of her group, a normally extremely tense and anxious boy, joined in the music lesson enthusiastically and uninhibitedly, and she said with regard to the performance of another little boy that she had seen him behave as a child for the first time ever.

Such comments suggested that it would be interesting to keep a record of the childrens' overall performance in music lessons during the course of a term, and to compare this performance with the class teachers perception of the child's performance in other subjects, but the problem presented was, how could the non-specialist teacher be expected to measure performance in music? The solution was found in turning the focus of attention to the child's behaviour during the sessions since this could be easily correlated between different subjects and could also be taken to be a fair indication of the level of the child's involvement with the activities being taught.

Class teachers were therefore asked (in advance of the start of the music programme) to grade their children's average performance in the following areas.

During lessons, does this child usually:

- co-operate with staff;
- co-operate with peers;
- express satisfaction (or any substantiated negative reaction) to the activity;
- share positive comments on related issues;
- volunteer information or initiate any other positive contribution
- repeat or paraphrase information presented during the lesson?

Teachers were asked to grade the childrens' performance on a scale of 1–3 thus: (1) inappropriate/unacceptable; (2) inadequate/immature; (3) appropriate/acceptable, and to consider these terms in relation to the 'norm' for that child's chronological age.

None of the fifty-six children assessed were present for all the term's lessons but each child's individual total averaged out over the term showed that his/her performance during the music lessons was consistently and markedly higher than the class teacher's original prediction had been. The chart showing Uri and Nigel's performance shows that occasionally they fall back to the teacher's estimation, and also it coincidentally indicates the high level of absenteeism associated with this type of school for in the case of these two boys, they were only in school for four of the twelve lessons.

The first column shows the teacher's prediction before the music programme was started, and the following columns show the class teacher's grading of the child's performance during each of the music lessons attended.

Uri	Nigel
2 3 3 2 3	1 3 3 2 3
1 1 3 3 3	1 2 3 3 3
2 2 3 3 3	2 3 3 3 3
2 3 3 3 3	2 3 3 3 2
2 3 3 3 3	2 2 3 2 2
2 3 3 3 3	2 3 3 2 2

Rosemary was present for six of the twelve lessons and her chart shows a significant difference between the class teacher's original prediction and his actual observation of her performance during the music lessons.

Rosemary
1 3 3 3 2 3 3
1 3 3 3 2 3 3
1 3 3 3 3 3 3
1 3 3 3 3 3 3
1 3 3 3 3 3 3
1 3 3 3 3 3 3

One possible explanation for such an improved perception may be that during the course of these sessions two teachers were present, though one was cast as an observer rather than a teacher. There is, however, no evidence to suggest that improved staffing levels improve the performance of special needs pupils, in fact the research of McBrien and Weightman (1980) and Dalgleish and Matthews (1981) would seem to suggest the opposite, though their research does relate specifically to those with learning difficulties.

Another possible explanation is that the children would have naturally made this degree of progress during the course of a term and that it is therefore misguided to compare their ongoing performance with the teacher's original prediction (even though that prediction was in each case based on several years acquaintance with the child). Though this theory was not borne out by the subjective view of the teachers themselves, we are currently involved in further research which may give a different view, but at this stage it would seem that the results are fairly similar.

One is obviously reluctant to make grandiose claims about the therapeutic value of music education, but one begins to suspect that music can make a significant difference to the lives of some disturbed children and that it should therefore not be carelessly dismissed from the curriculum of EBD schools. It is, however, unreasonable to expect the non-music specialist to take the initiative and work in isolation to introduce music education for his/her pupils. The initiative must instead be taken by advisory music teachers and those in higher education to provide special school teachers with something along the lines of Reading University's Music Consultancy in Primary Schools (see Smith, 1987). Such a model (providing that the majority of the training could be done *in situ*) would surely be sufficient to inspire confidence in teachers and provide them with a dynamic resource with which to effect the emotional and social readjustment of their pupils.

REFERENCES

Adams, P. and Syers, A. (1984) *Music in the Primary School*, London: ILEA Music Centre.

Bridgeland, M. (1971) *Pioneer Work with Maladjusted Children*, St Albans: Staples Press.

Dalgleish, M. and Matthews, R. (1981) 'Some effects of the staffing levels and group size on the quality of daycare for severely mentally handicapped adults', *British Journal of Mental Subnormality* 27: 30–5.

DES (1965) *The Education of Maladjusted Children*, Education Pamphlet No. 47, London: HMSO.

DES (1985) *Music from 5 to 16*, Curriculum Matters 4, London: HMSO.

Dobbs, J. P. B. (1966) *The Slow Learner and Music*, London: Oxford University Press.

Gilbert, J. (1987) *Musical Starting Points with Young Children*, London: Ward Lock Educational.

Hart, M. (1974) *Music*, London: Heinemann Educational Books.

Kennard, D. J. (1979) *Access to Music for the Physically Handicapped Schoolchild and School Leaver*. London: Disabled Living Foundation.

Laslett, R. (1977) *Educating Maladjusted Children*, London: Crosby Lockwood Staples.

McBrien, J. and Weightman, J. (1980) 'The effect of room management procedures on the engagement of profoundly retarded children', *British Journal of Mental Subnormality* 26: 38–46.

Nordoff, P. and Robbins, C. (1971) *Therapy in Music for Handicapped Children*, London: Victor Gollancz.

Packer, Y. M. (1987) *Musical Activities for Children with Behavioural Problems*, London: Disabled Living Foundation.

Price, R., Rast, L. and Winterfeldt, C. (1972) 'Out of pandemonium music', *Music Educators' Journal* 58: 35–6.

Sandor, F. (ed.) (1969) *Musical Education in Hungary*, London: Boosey & Hawkes.

Smith, J. (1987) *Music Consultancy in Berkshire Primary Schools*, University of Reading, Berkshire: School of Music.

Shedden, J. A. (1984) 'Music and the Maladjusted Child', M.Ed. thesis, University of Newcastle upon Tyne.

Storms, G. (1981) *Handbook of Music Games*, London: Hutchinson.

Wilson, M. and Evans, M. (1980) *Education of Disturbed Pupils*, Schools Council Working Paper 65, London: Methuen Educational.

Chapter 11

Music education and a European dimension

Janet Hoskyns

WHAT IS MUSIC EDUCATION IN THEORY?

Music education is a process in which a human being becomes aware of and sensitive to music, develops an understanding of its function and meaning and enjoys being involved with it in a discriminating way. It is a process which should stimulate and encourage the development of the imagination as well as the emotions. It is not limited to any one mode of making music, performing music, listening to music, or knowing (in a sensory way) about music. Music is an art and education in the arts is a complex and unique process, being unlike other curriculum subjects in the ways it is experienced and understood. (see Gardner, 1986; Hargreaves, 1989). It may be helpful for the purpose of this paper to separate music education into three categories. These overlap to some extent, and together contain principle truths about the nature and delivery of music education: (1) music education; (2) musical education; (3) education through music.

1 Music education could be said to be the overarching member of the trio. It is the way an individual acquires an understanding of and about music. It may be a formal, institution-based process or an informal development in understanding of the nature and mechanisms of music: (2) and (3) are subsumed within it.

2 Musical education develops an understanding of music which is highly concentrated and professional. It may occur as a result of performing on an instrument or being involved in composing as an active pursuit. The results of a musical education should be a highly developed musical awareness and the potential to become a musician. It is also the main preserve of the Colleges, Music Conservatoires, *Musikhochschulen* and similar professional, vocational institutions.

3 Education through music refers to a process where music is used as the tool for educating, but the results of it may not be evident in a musical form. For example, individuals may experience a sense of personal well being or an interest in working in small social groups as a result of being educated through music. They may acquire a lifelong interest in and love of

music, but the principal aim of such an education would be the development of the individual as a socialized, well adjusted member of the society not as a professional musician. We may not know exactly what comprises 'a music education' in every case but using the three categories, we can identify an individual who has experienced such a thing.

Green (1988) defined music education as being a 'cultural mechanism designed to educate people about music'. While not being sure what is meant by 'about music' in this context, it is nevertheless important to define music education within the cultural mores in which it is experienced. The idea of a mechanism implies that an individual is being manipulated by the processes of a music education which, while being true of any kind of education to some degree, does not seem to be the whole of the story. In fact the notion appears somewhat mechanistic when described in these terms. Nevertheless, psychologists seem to be in some agreement about the culturally dependent nature of much music education although there seems to be some disagreement as to when cultural idioms start to dominate the process of musical development (see Hargreaves, 1989).

Education is often defined as a process of enculturation for an individual into a society. This view is reinforced by (Bullivant, 1981) defining a curriculum as a 'selection from a socio-cultural group's stock of valued traditional and current public knowledge, conceptions and experiences, usually purposefully organized in programmatic sequence by such institutional agencies of cultural transmission (enculturation) as schools'. As such, music education will normally reflect the place of music in that society via formal and informal education systems. Kabalevsky (1988) quotes Suchomlinsky as saying 'musical education is not the education of the musician, but above all the education of the human being'. In educating the human being in music, we attempt to promote the making sense of universal ideas through music itself. Swanwick (1988) says that music education in schools and colleges is 'a vital element of the cultural process . . . helping us and our cultures to become renewed, transformed'. Here again is a reference to culture, and clearly any music education will be culture bound to some extent. More pertinent is his view of the renewing and transforming influence music education can effect and the idea that culture is not static, but part of an eternally changing process. It is in this area that we may be able to begin the search for a European dimension. If music has a catalysing effect in cultural renewal and transformation, then presumably we can use it in the search for a pedagogy which educates the European and establishes some commonalities and differences amongst the nations, races and cultures which are Europe. But, in such circumstances it would seem that a philosophy of music education which does not place the dynamic relationship of a human being and the musical experience at its centre, would fail, to be a legitimate music education, whatever its cultural origins. We must look for those elements in music education which allow renewal and transformation, whilst not neglecting music of the past which may illuminate our search. The intercultural (or is it pluralist?) argument being developed by scholars involved with the European dimension in the UK and elsewhere attempts to provide a framework which will establish the entitlement of students to be aware of their own culture. (De Vreede, 1990). It is possible to outline the types of experience and development in music which could be said to constitute music education.

1.1 Active exposure to and involvement with music.
1.2 This could include listening to sounds in the environment or records, discs, tapes and live musical presentations.
1.3 It could involve music making, for example, singing, vocalizing, playing an instrument.
1.4 It might mean performing to others as an individual or a team.
1.5 It could include composing pieces of music for yourself or to be presented to others.

WHAT IS MUSIC EDUCATION IN PRACTICE?

In practice music education is not experienced by everyone. Despite the arrival in the UK of the National Curriculum, it is not yet a universal experience, in or out of school. In spite of declarations from EC bodies, there is as yet no entitlement to music education for all. Many (even most?) European citizens will be exposed to music in some form, but will they have experienced a music education? It is my suggestion that some will, but by no means all. Ardagh (1988) gives a devastating account of music rooms in Lycées and Collèges d'Enseignement Secondaires in France which are locked and unused as a result of the shortage of music teachers and the lack of a tradition of studying music as a school subject.

The changes in educational attitudes, methods and understandings over the last twenty years in western Europe seem to indicate a more child/ student centred view of learning. It is the learning needs that are highlighted rather than the taught content. Research carried out by Patricia Broadfoot and Marilyn Osborn at Bristol University would seem to indicate that as the National Curriculum causes British education to move towards an information-based curriculum model the French 'are recognizing its limitations and are moving to increase both personal and institutional autonomy within the education system' (Broadfoot and Osborn, 1990). So, music education should focus upon the development of musical experience and understanding, through activities. Engagement in any or all of the activities mentioned in the last section could result in an individual experiencing education in music. Too often in the past, music education has been a dry academic exercise concerned with the transfer of factual information. Activities, which avoid genuine involvement with sound and music should not be labelled music education.

Informal music education is probably responsible for much musical learning and development. That it doesn't take place in an institution does not invalidate its importance. It must be acknowledged and valued by those responsible for the music education of young children. It is difficult to quantify and to include in a study of music education. We can reasonably assume that most of western Europe is affected by the increasing amount of recorded music available both in the home and in public places. Many Europeans are subjected to music several times each day. We have difficulty in assessing the educative effect of such stimuli, but should be aware that they exist and teach pupils and students how best to respond to them.

HOW MIGHT MUSIC EDUCATION BE REGARDED WITHIN A EUROPEAN DIMENSION?

The 'Resolution on music education', adopted in May 1985 by the Standing Conference of European Ministers of Education and *Recommendation 929* (1981) on music for all by the Parliamentary Assembly of the Council of Europe should be considered alongside the 'Resolution' of the Council and Ministers of Education of 24 May 1988. The objective of the latter is, 'to improve the knowledge (of young people) of the Community and its Member States in their historical, cultural, economic and social aspects and bring home to them the significance of the co-operation of the Member States of the EC with other countries of Europe and the world'. *DES Circular 24/89* (1989) 6.4 directs institutions of teacher training to 'have regard to relevant European Community Resolutions and particularly those concerning the European Dimension in Education'.

The action which should be taken to achieve these objectives includes the following, which is to take effect in school programmes and teaching 'II.3 To include the European dimension explicitly in school curricula in all appropriate disciplines, for example literature, languages, history, geography and the arts' *Council and Ministers of Education* 88/C177/02 (1988). Since music is one of the arts, we must assume that it is intended that a European dimension will be explicitly included in all music teaching and learning, throughout the European community. Yet the evidence is that it receives less visible support than some more vocationally-orientated subjects.

'In the past, we have tended to try to give a European dimension to a few so-called "key-subjects", for example, history, geography, economics and modern languages. Has this led us to neglect the contribution which other subjects could make, for example, performing arts? Have these subjects in fact a special contribution to make?' (Peacock, 1982). Music is viewed as complementary to more vocationally-orientated curriculum areas, providing enrichment and often deep cultural understanding. Care must be taken to include and involve the arts in policy decisions at a European level and not to wait for their inclusion until other notionally important curriculum areas have evolved strategies for a European dimension. Depending upon the educational models and practices in different countries of Europe, the ways in which a European dimension might be viewed will vary. This need not be a problem, since diversity is at the heart of many of EC dicta. It is important that the European dimension is seen as a positive catalyst for co-operation and a means of ending the sometimes negative competitive view of music education. An example of the former might be the European Community Youth Orchestra, where students from all EC countries work together under one conductor.

It must not be allowed to become a vehicle for competitive nationalism – 'my music is better than your music'. For instance, some countries of the EC have much greater provision for tuition in some musical specialisms. It would be easy for students from (say) Denmark to believe that baroque fiddle playing, which scarcely exists in that country is not worthwhile. The European Community Baroque Orchestra attempts to overcome some of these problems but it can result in hostility or difficult decisions for some members. Taking a pupil-centred approach to learning, we may find it difficult to include an explicit European dimension, unless we can actively involve pupils/students in Europe and its music as part of their musical entitlement. This might take the form of making time for groups of pupils, students, teachers and musicians to get together to make music. This already happens to some extent, when twinned towns or schools share and exchange their musical groups. However, it is the exception rather than normal practice, and few children expect to have this as part of their school music education. It is clear that a policy which seems to promote one particular kind of culture – the European (if we can define it) – may inadvertently disadvantage others. Should not the European dimension in music education become a first stage towards an international dimension? With increased global communications and intercultural connections music doesn't fit easily into a 'European bag'. There are European elements in our musical heritage but as European music is subjected to influences from other musics it becomes harder to define what we mean by European music. Is it music made in the continent of Europe? Is it music composed by persons of European origin? Does it include folk, popular and classical music in their broadest sense? Music is not easily confined to the Europe of the member countries of the EC. (Having arranged for a group of London schoolchildren, steel band performers, to play at the UNESCO building in Paris, I am familiar with some of the cultural variations which may occur.) Music does not know national boundaries. The recently published *European Awareness Pilot Project*, striving towards a definition of the European dimension, suggests that it was concerned with the 'whole of Europe in its world context'. It suggests that this is in no way inconsistent with the 1988 'Resolution' nor with local authority policies on anti-racism and multi-cultural education. 'The importance of the European Community should not appear to ignore assertions of national identity or the needs of minorities' (Slater, 1990).

HOW MIGHT A EUROPEAN DIMENSION BE IMPOSED UPON MUSIC EDUCATION?

Some difficulties

The models for music education that exist in the countries of Europe and the EC give us some indications as to the diversity of delivery and relative importance of this subject in formal education. In some countries and regions music education is the concern of a ministry of culture; and in others it is organized by schools and an education ministry. In Germany, education is the responsibility of the *Länder* and the delivery of music varies from one *Land* to another. In EC countries there is a wide variety in the course content for prospective teachers of music. A common core appears to be the teaching of western European 'Classical' tradition from 1500 to 1900 and sometimes to 1991 (Oboussier and Swanwick, 1984). Could this be the Commission's European dimension in music? It could be a limiting and limited field, allowing a return to the delivery of information as opposed to active involvement in music. In 1984 only Germany, the UK, Denmark and France offered courses which included composing, ear training, singing, classroom percussion instruments, recorders and group rehearsals to trainee music teachers. Belgium and the Netherlands seem not to offer pop, rock, jazz or world musics and little evidence of the use of experimental or avant-garde techniques was available in Belgium, Eire, Greece, Luxembourg or the Netherlands. Italy did not train music teachers *per se* at all.

The teaching of specific musical instruments is not part of the school curriculum in most EC countries. In the UK, where it was to some extent the concern of schools and LEA's, changes in the recent Education Reform Act have meant that the provision is no longer as ubiquitous as it was.

Given this diversity, it is likely to be difficult to agree a uniform approach to the European dimension. The starting points are so many and varied. A measure of agreement at community level needs to be negotiated as well as some definitions of what constitutes music education and its purposes. ERASMUS and TEMPUS programmes offer some financial assistance, encouraging an increase in awareness amongst music educators, but we are at present a long way from agreement on matters of principle. In 1988 only three Higher Education Colleges in the UK appeared to offer Music as part of their European exchange programmes, and two of these were disguised in the form of Performing/Expressive arts. Since then the promotion by the Community of ERASMUS and other programmes has increased the number of exchanges.

It does appear that the language and accommodation difficulties these exchanges involve make music and the arts a relatively low priority. the LINGUA programmes do not allow students to develop an adequate grasp of any previously unknown language to survive lectures in aesthetics, musicology and the like. If EC countries were able to agree fundamentally what constitutes a music education and to resolve the specialist musicians' training versus the human being educated through music (among other things), then the European dimension might be easier to decide. Such agreement seems unlikely at present given existing bureaucracies and apparently differing aims for music education across Europe.

Some possible strategies

For the immediate future it is necessary to see where 'good practice' already exists and to monitor its progress. Existing ERASMUS schemes for University and Higher Education students already foster an interest in what is happening in other EC countries. School exchanges in music also are a good way to begin to develop a European view. These should be encouraged and expertise in organizing them shared.

Many of the schemes already running are linked with France and Germany, since these were logical neighbours even before the advent of 1992 and language teaching in the UK has traditionally concentrated on French and German. Different approaches may be necessary for different educational phases and institutions.

Perhaps as far as music education is concerned, exchanges and visits will be of two kinds: (i) those concerned with musical education, that is, orchestral, choral and instrumental groups; and (ii) those dedicated to education through music, that is, teachers of music in schools and their pupils.

The first will have experienced a relatively straightforward skills-based training in instrumental music, with the aim of becoming a performer, composer or very informed listener. The final part of such training might be of the kind provided by Conservatoires. The second group would be concerned with education through music, something we assume is necessary to become an educated member of the society in which we live. To include music education as part of the entitlement provision for all school-age children in Europe is in itself a radical proposal, with massive funding implications. Such a programme is implied by the reforms in Italy, where they are hoping to introduce music education to secondary schools following models developed in 'Federal' Germany. (Sperenzi, 1989). Whether or not the programme is implemented, its existence indicates a growing awareness of the potential value of music education for all in Europe.

It is our duty to ensure that music education remains on the agenda and that the European dimension includes wider access to music for all Europeans.

REFERENCES

Ardagh, J. (1988) *France Today*, London: Penguin.

Bullivant, B. M. (1981) *The Pluralist Dilemma in Education: Six Case Studies*, Sydney: George Allen & Unwin.

Council and Ministers of Education (1988) *Resolution 88/C177/02*, The European Dimension in Education, Brussels: Council of Europe.

Department of Education and Science, (DES) (1989) *Circular 24/89*, London: HMSO.

De Vreede, E. (1990) 'Guest editorial', *European Journal of Teacher Education* 13 (3): 111–12.

Gardner, H. (1986) *Frames of Mind*, London: Heinemann.

Green, L. (1988) *Music on Deaf Ears: Musical Meaning, Ideology and Education*, Manchester: Manchester University Press.

Hargreaves, D. J. (ed.) (1989) *Children and the Arts*, Milton Keynes: Open University Press.

Kabalevsky, D. B. (1988) *Music and Education: A Composer Writes About Musical Education*, London and Paris: Jessica Kingsley/Unesco.

Oboussier, P. and Swanwick, K. (1984) *The Training of Teachers of Music in The European Community*, London: University of London.

Peacock, D. (1982) *Europe in Secondary School Curricula*, (Symposium Report), Brussels: Council of Europe.

Slater, J. (1990) *European Awareness Pilot Project*, London: Central Bureau for Educational Visits and Exchanges.

Sperenzi, M. (1989) 'L'esperienza delle Scuole musicali in Italia ed in altri paesi europei', *BeQuadro* 33: 22–5.

Swanwick, K. (1988) *Music, Mind, And Education*, London and New York: Routledge.

Chapter 12

Concepts of world music and their integration within western secondary music education

Jonathan P. J. Stock

INTRODUCTION

Other than simply gaining the ability to disseminate a selection of inter-esting musical facts or combat the growth of one-sided, stereotypical views of different musical cultures, a primary benefit of acquiring familiarity with aspects of non-western musics is that doing so can lead us to see aspects of our own music, whether pop, traditional or classical, with new eyes or, perhaps more appropriately, to listen with new ears. Musical concepts and habits that we have acquired through the enculturation process, through being born and bred, within a particular culture, are sometimes overlooked; they become so 'natural' that we may no longer be able to perceive them. Studying a different musical culture brings these issues back to our atten-tion, and thereby encourages a deeper understanding of our own music. Studying musical activity from the perspective of concepts employed, in varying fashions, all over the world assists the western music teacher to teach music, rather than western music alone.

WHAT IS MUSIC?

The example below is a short transcription of two phrases of Koran recitation from Morocco. I have omitted the text to avoid the necessity of further introduction and contextual explanation. Sing or hum through the transcription, or listen to a recording of this type of material.

Example 1 Koran Recitation by El Hajj Mohamed al Hakim Bennani (Text Omitted). Transcribed, with permission, from *Musicaphon* BM 30 SL 2027 (n.d.)

Is this music? Certainly, it looks like music because it has been written down in musical notation. But does that mean that it *is* music? Perhaps the answer to this question, yes or no, will depend on our definition of music, the couching of which can be problematic. The *Macmillan Encyclopedia* says that music is '[t]he art of organizing sounds, which usually consist of sequences of tones of definite pitch, to produce melody, harmony, and rhythm . . . ' (Macmillan, 1988: 845).

If so, then example (1) is not music. There is a sequence of tones of differing rhythmic durations but there is no harmony. Indeed, solo pieces for many instruments or voice from the western classical tradition become non-music when this definition is strictly applied. Looking at an alternative definition, my paperback English dictionary describes music as 'the science or art of ordering tones or sounds in succession and combination to produce a composition having unity and continuity . . . ' (Penguin, 1986: 604). This seems quite a good definition at first, although it is also possible to arrange and combine successive sounds in unified and continuous ways that strike the listener as being not exactly musical.

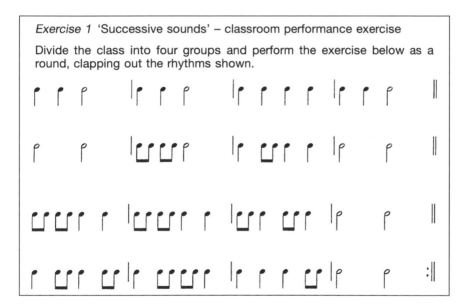

Exercise 1 'Successive sounds' – classroom performance exercise

Divide the class into four groups and perform the exercise below as a round, clapping out the rhythms shown.

Exercise (1) definitely satisfies the criteria of combined successive sounds ordered into a unified, albeit rather unimaginative, composition. But is it really what we mean by a musical composition? For one thing, there is no melody. At least example (1) seemed to have a tune. And returning to example (1), when the same definition is used to decide whether or not this is music, we run into a further problem: when listening to unfamiliar sound structures, how do we know if they are ordered and combined into a unified composition? This is one reason why we need to add the study of history and culture to that of another people's musical sounds.

In the case of example (1), the sounds are in fact carefully ordered and combined, but the man whose voice is transcribed above might as well be somewhat upset if we said his sounds were music. To the Moslem, the chanting of prayers and religious texts such as that in example (1) are not music but chant or poetry. *musiqa*, the Arabic equivalent of the English word 'music', refers only to secular, instrumental pieces. Performing non-religious music has been regarded in Moslem religious theory as dangerous, primarily because instrumental music was often heard in places like brothels and inns. Thus, by association, instrumental music is a potential threat to public morals, something that encourages and accompanies over-indulgence and intoxication. By defining secular instrumental pieces (music) on the one hand and religious vocal chant and sung poems (non-music) on the other as quite separate things, the typical Moslem has a quite different understanding of the concept of 'music' from that of the average European. This pattern is repeated all over the world. For example, people in some African cultures cannot conceive of music without dance. In other societies, there is no general term like our word 'music' at all, people merely talk of songs or poems, pieces or dances, rituals and hymns.

Taking this idea one step further, not only do people all over the world have their own, individual ways of defining and understanding music, but so do people of different times, different social classes and different educational levels, even within the same culture, something which may be overlooked when we study the music of our ancestors. Beethoven provides a good example of this. Today, many consider him a pre-eminent composer. Even those who do not especially care for his music would be unlikely to question whether it is music or not. But, in 1857 a well-educated music critic described one section of Beethoven's *Fifth Symphony* with the following words: 'I would say . . . that it does not belong at all to the art which I am in the habit of considering as music' (Bacharach and Pearce, 1977: 19). This critic was not joking, nor was he a philistine; the fact is that he and many of his contemporaries found this part of the piece difficult to accept, even fifty years after it was written. Since he did not understand what he heard, the critic questioned whether it was really 'music' at all. Many of us, when first exposed to something strange or different, may also think like this, and perhaps it is good to question what we hear, but we sometimes need to question our definitions of music as well. An extreme example of this is to notice how we divide up the sounds of the animal kingdom: birds sing, dolphins have language and dogs howl. Do we mean the first sounds like music to us while the second and third do not?

My intention, then, is not to propose a search for a 'better' definition of music. Instead, I have tried to show that our commonly-accepted definitions of music, like those quoted above, have their draw-backs. A definition of music that most westerners accepted might not necessarily be the best, most scientific or only definition of music in the world. It might be very useful for classical musicians in Europe and North America towards the end of the twentieth-century, but the further we move away from here, whether geographically or temporally, the less reliable it may become. In other words, to understand the music of a different culture or period, we have first to understand their conception of music. And as a prerequisite to this, we need to know about their social situations and cultural beliefs, their language, their instruments and much, much more.

If, in the end, there is no single, easy and convenient answer to the question, 'what is music?', this is something to celebrate not bemoan. Music would hold little fascination for us if it was so simply explained. Even questions that cannot be answered may be worth asking for the light that attempting to respond to them sheds on related issues. One such question is whether music is a language or not.

MUSIC AND LANGUAGE I

We often hear the phrase, 'music is a language'. Some might propose this as an answer to the previous question, 'what is music?' There are many similarities between music and language. For example, both are 'performed' through the dimension of time; both seem to have their own rules of structure and grammar; both can (in our culture) be written down using special signs and symbols; and both are essentially 'pan-human' activities that all normal people seem capable of taking part in and appreciating (Sloboda, 1985: 11–23).

But there are some important differences between music and language. For example, although music has phrases which are like those found in language, it is difficult to find a specific analogy in music to the lexical word. It would in many instances be impossible to communicate a detailed message musically. To be sure, within our own culture we can recognize music appropriate to a love scene, a dance type or funeral march, but, without any non-musical clues, we don't know who loves whom, where the dance is taking place or what the deceased died of. Any language can efficiently give us specific answers to all these questions, while music cannot. Likewise, although instrumental music can remind us of a conversation, it is hard to envisage a previously unthought-of, tangibly meaningful, two-way dialogue taking part in such a manner.

What music can do in many different cultures, is represent, describe or narrate by using sounds which, through habit, we have come to associate with certain events or emotions. The Kaluli people of New Guinea, for example, link different falling melodic patterns with the songs of different kinds of bird. Since they believe that people become birds when they die, the singing of songs based on these falling melodic patterns awakens in their mind all kinds of correlations: sorrow at the loss of dead relatives, loneliness and abandonment. So, although music is not a language, there is no doubt that it can embody certain extra-music associations or messages. And when we are given a programme, when we are told (in language) what a piece of music is about, then we can often detect quite detailed meanings in the sounds we hear. A short exercise should make this point clearer.

Exercise 2 Programme music – classroom listening exercise

The class listens once or twice to a short instrumental piece or excerpt in several contrasting sections such as the theme and first few variations from Brahms's *Variations on a Theme by Haydn*, Wagner's 'Prelude' to Act I of *Die Meistersinger von Nürnberg* or Debussy's 'Minstrels' (*Préludes* Book 1, No. 12). No information concerning the title, programme or composer of the music should be given. Each pupil sketches out a possible programme for the music. During the following lesson, a number of the most varied programmes can be read out and the music listened to again. Without some kind of linguistic clue like a title or programme, or some musical hint such as a theme we already know or an instrument we associate with a particular situation – the organ with Church music, say – even members of the same culture and age-group are likely to produce individual musical interpretations.

Because music can be meaningful, but isn't exactly the same as a language, it seems probable that we cannot always expect to be able to 'translate' music or musical meaning from one situation to another. This is another reason why we need to understand something about the culture of the people who have created the music we are listening to. If we wish to understand an unfamiliar form of music as one of its creators might, we have to be aware of any extra-musical associations that imbue the sounds with special meaning. Sometimes these can be quite the opposite of our own stereotypes. For example, in many western operas of the last two centuries, younger male roles have been acted by tenor singers, older men by basses. Similarly, lower-pitched instruments are often used to depict male characters in music. Which of us would say a bassoon, trombone or double bass was naturally lady-like? But, in at least one African culture, the higher-sounding of a set of drums or horns is believed to represent male characteristics. To us, the pitch of a low sound is similar to that of a grown man's voice; to them, the louder, more assertive sound of a higher instrument is like the stronger, more assertive speech of a man. Lower sounds, they say, are more like women murmuring softly in the background. Whether or not this is an accurate reflection of gender stereotyping in the culture in question, or a more theoretical abstraction used to explain musical practice would lead beyond the scope of this discussion. The point is that this isn't a case of one analogy being more fitting than the other: both systems have their own logic, and are decoded as such by accustomed listeners.

A second association many of us may share is that, in general, the busiest, more active instrumental parts are the most important. Instruments with slower-moving parts, often those lower in pitch, usually provide the accompaniment. So, in the symphony orchestra, the first violins more often play the tune above a slower-moving double bass accompaniment than the double basses perform with a violin accompaniment. This may seem perfectly obvious to us, but it is not a feature found in music all over the world. A well known exception is provided by Indonesian gamelan music. Gamelan is the name of many kinds of orchestra or ensemble made up principally of tuned metal chime bars and gongs. Very crudely speaking, the higher the pitch of the instrument, the more notes it plays. But every instrumentalist is deemed to be following the progress of a single underlying melody, and the lowest gong is the most important instrument in the ensemble. The occasional tones of the gong structure and underpin the whole performance. Players of the higher instruments decorate the underlying melody by embellishing each step with cleverly thought-out layers of interlocking patterns, and some of them may perform more than two-hundred different notes to each note of the lowest gong (Sorrell, 1990: 109–19). Listening to gamelan music as to symphonic music, or concentrating on the details of the fast-moving upper instruments, it would be easy to miss the melody at the performance's heart.

So far then, the necessarily inconclusive discussion of what music is, that is, different things to different people at different times, has led to the proposals that we cannot necessarily apply our own, familiar, definitions of music to foreign musical sounds, and that basic, fundamental principles which we take for granted in our own music may not be reflected in other kinds of music. Musical communication, it has been suggested, functions unlike linguistic communication. The agent which allows these perhaps uncomfortably negative discoveries to become aids to musical appraisal and understanding is the incorporation of cultural and historical material along with the musical sounds of foreign peoples. If we know what the members of a musical tradition themselves regard as important, what associations their music carries, how they define music, what their instruments are like and what function their music has, we have a better chance of making sense of the sounds we hear.

DOES MUSIC EVOLVE?

Having temporarily discarded the linguistic analogy, another explanation which is often put forward to account for musical diversity is that folk music and traditional musics from other parts of the world are simple or primitive, and that these kinds of musics are naturally evolving towards a music more like our own: music using twelve equal-tempered semitones, harmony and western instruments. But this view rests upon a number of misconceptions. Noting that another culture's music sounds different from ours, we may be tempted to see ours as somehow more valid, more natural or more fully developed than theirs. By doing so we are again setting up our own definition of music as a kind of universal yardstick against which all others must be measured. But what seems mature and fully developed to us today may just as reasonably be dismissed as childish or preliminary in a few centuries' time or in another part of the globe where the subtleties of our musical styles go unheeded. More importantly, this view suggests that 'music', itself an abstract concept, is somehow alive. Can 'music' develop in the general way which this view requires, and is there evidence of it having done so? Can something so abstract truly be mature or immature, natural or strange, right or wrong?

Music does not live on its own. Although musical ideas can be thought of and written down, they do not become music until, through some kind of physical behaviour, like singing or playing an instrument, they are actually performed to somebody. So, while it is true that styles of music come and go, and some do appear to influence others, what is really occurring is that composers and performers are being influenced by what they hear and by what they think their audiences expect to hear. The music that we perform today may not, therefore, be any 'better' than that performed in other times or places, it has just followed the changing preferences of the people who make and listen to music. Because people define music differently and use it for contrasting purposes at different times and in varying cultural contexts, it seems highly unlikely and somewhat ethnocentric to believe that all music in the world is developing from simple, unaccompanied melody along parallel tracks towards complicated, harmonic music. This is not to say that we are wrong to prefer our own kind of music-making; the point is to acknowledge that all humanity organizes its sounds with specific tasks in mind and within particular social systems. Unless we are aware of these tasks and systems, we may not be able to formulate a meaningful evaluation of the sounds in question.

Exercise 3 'Humanly organized sound – individual composition exercise

One very simple definition of music is: 'humanly organized sound' (Blacking, 1976: 3). Each pupil selects a number of different sounds, whether environmental, recorded or live. Using a graphic score, these sounds are organized into a short composition. The pupil explains what function the music is for (for example, entertainment, dance accompaniment, ritual) and then performs the piece.

MUSIC AND LANGUAGE II

Above, I criticized the oft-quoted statement, 'music is a language'. But it is true that music and language have much in common: they both need to be learnt through imitation, instruction and practice; in their most natural forms both typically rely upon the human voice and ear; and different cultures have tended to develop their own regional and local forms of both (Sloboda, 1985: 11–23). Both music and language involve the interlinked concepts of composition, improvisation, performance and appraisal, which I deal with below and, very often, music and language are combined in songs and chants.

Just as we often have different kinds of language for different occasions, so too we may use different kinds of music for different situations. The entertainment music of any culture may differ from that which supports ritual, although these two categories can also overlap, of course. Groups within a society may 'use' music to represent and present themselves, just as they employ particular styles of speech and clothing.

Exercise 4 Musical representation – homework sociology of music exercise

Using their peers, families and neighbours as subjects, students create a short multiple-choice questionnaire asking people questions such as their favourite kinds of music, their age group, their occupations, their normal styles of clothing on the occasions when they hear each kind of music and so on. The results of the questionnaires can then be totalled to see whether it is true that certain kinds of music appeal more to certain types of people than others.

Like speech, musical performances take place through time and are very often built up from 'phrases'. Moments of repose punctuate both speech and music. 'Cadences', 'pauses' or 'breaths' are found in many different styles of music-making. The organization and subdivision of performance time (tempo, rhythm and metre) are significant elements of many cultures' musical styles. We shall now look at these concepts in more detail.

The organization and subdivision of musical time

Tempo, or the speed at which a musical performance takes place, is an important feature in almost all music-making. In some cultures the speeds at which certain pieces can be performed is rigidly fixed, in others there is a certain amount of latitude. Some styles of music may be performed at what seems to us as a freely variable speed, getting faster or slower as the performer desires, other styles are more strictly interpreted. In some cultures musicians have created complex theories and terminology about tempo, in others they just have a feel for what is right and what is wrong.

In western classical music, the term 'rhythm' refers to the relative durations of different musical notes. The use of notes of varied durations is found in the great majority of other musical cultures as well, sometimes appearing in very complicated patterns. The term 'metre' describes how rhythmic patterns are organized into larger musical units. Although some music is not metrical, for instance certain operatic recitatives, a great deal of it is. Dance music, for example, is quite commonly organized into regular units which are repeated over and over. In western music it is the first beat of each unit which is considered the strongest, but in Indonesia gamelan music, for instance, the fourth beat of each unit is stronger. In much western music we subdivide each metrical unit into two, three, four or six beats, each of which is of the same duration and can again be divided into notes of half, a third or a quarter of a beat. In some other musical traditions, however, metrical units may have five, seven, ten or twelve beats, perhaps, and these beats need not necessarily be of the same duration each. We must be careful not to think of these as 'irregular' metres, since to their performers they may have very natural, logical patterns of rhythm, move-

Example 2 Music for *nay* (Arabic flute) and *tabla* (Indian drums). Transcribed, with permission, from *Saydisc* CSDL 387 (1991). Part for *saz* (Turkish long-necked lute) omitted.

ment and stress. Example (2) is an excerpt in $\frac{7}{8}$ metre from the Moroccan musician Hassan Erraji's composition entitled *Hiwar* (Dialogue). Note how every bar is regularly divided into two two-quaver beats and one three-quaver beat.

This example also reminds us that influence between different musics is an on-going process. Hassan Erraj's piece, recorded in Britain, is scored for two Middle Eastern instruments and the Indian drums known as the *tabla*, which, incidentally, are played on this recording by a Belgian musician.

Melody and musical space

One important aspect of music is that although its performance unfolds in time, it also unfolds in what we could call 'musical space'. By musical space I mean two things, first pitch, whether notes are high or low, and second, the musical roles of the performers, whether one group answers another or several people all play at once and so forth.

Many cultures have a concept of pitch. They may not, however, refer to notes as 'high' or 'low' as we do, an idea reinforced by our reliance on a system of notation in which 'high' notes appear graphically 'higher' (nearer the top of the page) than 'low' ones. Quite a number of cultures have names for the pitches they employ. These names may refer either to fixed, 'absolute' pitches (like our C, D, E, etc.) or transposable, 'relative' pitches (like our Sol-fa systems or tonic, supertonic, mediant, etc. terminology). Some cultures have both. In ancient China, for instance, each of the twelve semitones in an octave had its own name. A further name was given to each degree of the modes from which Chinese music was composed, and these modes could begin on any of the twelve semitones. Therefore, any note had two names, one which showed its absolute musical pitch and another which showed its relative position within the mode then under use.

The pitch-levels of individual musical notes are the building-blocks of melody, or the successive arrangement of musical notes. A concept of melody is common to many different musical cultures, although the exact definition of what makes a melody sound beautiful or apt may vary quite widely, and, as pointed out above, a melody is not always performed by the highest or fastest instruments in an ensemble.

There are several technical terms by which musicians refer to the way in which a melody is built up into a composition. When a melody is sung or played alone (whether by one performer or many), the music can be described as 'monophonic'. If, on the other hand, more than one melody is performed at the same time, then the term 'polyphony' is used. When all parts in a musical texture move with the same rhythm, the label 'homophony' is usually applied. Another kind of music is that in which the performers all produce the same tune together, but each present it in an individually decorated and adapted form. This kind of music is called 'heterophonic'. Finally, some music is 'antiphonal', which basically means that one part presents a melody and one or more parts then present an answer. Another term for this kind of performance is 'call and response'. Although these are western concepts and terms they are quite useful in helping us to recognize and classify different styles of music-making.

Exercise 5 The 'phonies' – classroom listening exercise

Pupils listen to a number of short musical extracts, deciding in each case whether the music they hear is monophonic, polyphonic, homophonic, heterophonic or antiphonal.

In most cultures certain of these ways of organizing musical space are more common than the others. For example, a large amount of African singing is antiphonal, while much Oriental ensemble music is heterophonic. Within some kinds of Christian church service, there may be antiphonal (call and response), homophonic (congregational hymns) and polyphonic (specialist choral) musical items.

Modes and scales

Musicians from many parts of the world choose the pitches they use in their music from sets of notes which we call modes. Most of us are familiar with scale, they are simply patterns by which all the notes in any musical 'key' are played or written one after the other, usually in ascending and then descending order. When composing 'in' a particular key, we typically choose our notes from those of its scale, although there are, of course, ways by which additional notes are introduced as well. Commonly, we start and finish with the first note of the scale, or key-note, as it is sometimes called. Example (3) shows two scales which are very commonly used in western music, C major and C minor.

C major   C minor

Example 3 Major and minor scales

'Mode' is often used to translate foreign terms similar in many ways to our words 'scale' and 'key'. However, in many cultures, specific modes may also call for the use of distinctive melodic progressions, patterns of ornamentation, intonation, instrumentation, cadential stress, register and performance techniques. In the Middle East or India, for instance, each mode provides the raw material from which an experienced musician can fashion a musical performance.

Needless to say, different sets of notes ('scales') and different ways of organizing them ('keys') are found all over the world. For example, in some parts of the world people make music from four-note modes (see Sachs, 1962: 65, 66, 68, 145–7). These four notes need not be the same as any of our twelve equal-tempered semitones, but even if they are, we should remember that the same rules as in our own scales and keys do not apply to their use.

Exercise 6 Dialogue – classroom composition exercise

Pupils choose four notes from which to create a short, antiphonal composition entitled *Dialogue*. Any four pitches may be chosen, not necessarily four consecutive notes like C, D, E and F. The composition should have six phrases (three sets of call and response), and the first and last phrase should end with the same note. The piece may be scored for instruments or voices, and may employ staff notation or simply numbers (for example, '1' for the first pitch, '2' for the second) with a key to explain which pitch each number denotes.

The 'lowest' pitch in a mode need not function the same way as our key-note, for instance. This is one point which can make listening to music from around the world difficult at first. Since the notes and mode used are different from ours, it can be hard to recognize the ends of musical phrases. The expectations with which we have been conditioned through years of listening to tonal music may hinder our appreciation of other kinds of music. But through becoming more conscious of our own conditioning, we acquire the opportunity to overcome its effects, and by, perhaps, transcribing and singing the pitches used in a foreign composition, we can begin to get more of a feel for the music itself.

Musical instruments

The great majority of civilizations have developed their own musical instruments, or adopted and adapted those of their neighbours. Several instruments well known to Europeans are believed to have been transmitted westwards from the Middle East. Others, especially certain types of drum, may have been introduced to Europe from Africa, possibly by way of the United States. Western instruments are now played in many nations all around the world. The use of musical instruments, whether to supplement or replace the human voice, is a feature found in many, many different cultures. The way a musical instrument is built and performed has a strong influence on the patterns of sound it can produce and the music which may be played upon it.

Classically-trained western musicians are familiar with the classification of instruments into the categories of strings, woodwind, brass and percussion. Although this division suits the tradition it was invented by very well, it is not entirely logical. Stringed instruments are named after the section of instrument which is sounded, while woodwind and brass are named after their traditional material of manufacture and percussion instruments after their most characteristic performance technique. Thus, certain scholars have proposed more scientific ways of dealing with musical instruments. One such method is the Hornbostel–Sachs classification, in which instruments are sorted into the following broad classes: idiophones, in which the body of the instrument itself provides the sound; membranophones, in which a tightly stretched membrane is sounded; chordophones, where strings are sounded; and aerophones, within which air is the principal substance of musical vibration. Examples of idiophones include such instruments as rattles and wood blocks, typical membranophones are drums, chordophones include fiddles and lutes, and aerophones many types of flute and reed instrument (see Hornbostel and Sachs, 1961; Myers, 1992: 444–61).

Other societies have their own ways of classifying musical instruments, some of which are quite complicated (see Kartomi, 1990). Cultures around the world also have their own ways of explaining, valuing and combining musical instruments. There may be legends of how specific instruments were created by culture heroes. Certain instruments may be reserved for particular classes of people, or for particular occasions. Musical instruments serve as cultural icons, as markers of identity. The study of attitudes toward musical instruments is as important as the study of their construction and performance techniques.

Process of music-making

Music-making world-wide can be divided into a number of activities: composition, improvisation, performance, reception and appraisal. Some of these activities overlap – for example, composition during performance can also be described as improvisation. Appraisal provides feedback to composers and performers, affecting the music they create on subsequent occasions. In some cultures these activities may have different forms from the shape they take in western society. For example, amongst the Blackfoot Indians of North America, the composition of new songs traditionally occurs during an individual's dreams (Nettl, 1983: 35). Some cultures do not use musical notations. In these traditions, which are often known as 'oral traditions', musicians have to rely solely upon their memories to remember and recreate music they have previously composed, learned, practised or rehearsed. Although it may be difficult for us to learn to compose in our sleep, we can enrich our own music-making by experimenting with, adapting and adopting many of the other techniques used in foreign processes of music-making. This is possible because even in our own score-centred tradition much of the learning process still takes place in an oral/aural context.

Musicians

There are musicians in every society, but the ways in which they are organized and create their music can differ quite markedly. Who the music-makers are in any culture is often a subject well worth investigating because it can explain much about the function and content of the music itself. Some societies rely on specialist musicians for their most important musical events. These specialists may be professionals, employed through a system of patronage or by payment for each performance. Others are semi-professional, devoting part of their time to musicianship and receiving some money or goods in return for their services. It is interesting to note that although music is often considered an important part of life, specialist musicians are frequently low in social status. In other societies there may be no musical specialists; everyone takes a theoretically equal part in all musical activities.

Within a culture, musical training, and the allocation of the roles of composer, performer or audience member can differ widely, depending on whether specialist or non-specialist musicians are involved. Some groups do not so much memorize and perform fixed compositions as know how to create a new one together during each fresh performance. Finally, within any one society there are likely to be many kinds of musical activity, from lullabies to hymns and from dance music to war songs. Those who bring the music to life in each case may be quite different groups of people.

CONCLUSION

Music means many different things to many different people. It is these differences which make music an interesting subject to study. But it does mean that when we listen to someone else's music, we shouldn't expect it to sound the same as ours. When comparing a new style of music with an old favourite it is important to recall that the new musicians may not be trying to do the same things as those we normally listen to. Only through acquiring some familiarity with the way in which a form of music is conceived, produced and received in its original setting can we begin to understand the sound structures themselves. None the less, we can also benefit from asking questions when listening to an unfamiliar musical style.

For instance, are there any rhythmic patterns that keep coming back, does the music often return to the same note, what kind of mode is used, how is the music organized metrically? Although musical sounds differ from one part of the globe to another, there are certain general similarities in the ways in which people think about, organize and create these sounds. Learning about these similarities is a good way to start the study of world music, and an excellent way by which to marry the study of world music to that of the western classical tradition.

APPENDIX 1 – SUPPLEMENTARY CLASS EXERCISES

1 In small groups pupils discuss and prepare their own definitions of music. These definitions can range from idiosyncratic to general, they can discuss what elements constitute music or what music means to its listeners. All the definitions are then read out to the class and compared.
2 As a homework assignment, students list all the similarities between music and language they can think of. They then prepare a list of differences.
3 In groups pupils compose a piece called *Birds of Paradise* in which a few simple melodic patterns, one representing each bird, are freely repeated above an accompaniment of rain forest sounds. These sounds could include the wind rustling in the leaves, rain drops falling to the ground and perhaps the occasional buzz and hum of small insects. One emotion could be attached to the call of each bird. In performance, these simple melodic patterns could become the basis for extemporization. Once the composition has been rehearsed, a programme could be decided upon and the whole piece performed to the remainder of the class.
4 Students compose a short melody for flute which uses a regularly subdivided $\frac{11}{8}$ metre. They must decide exactly how to subdivide each beat, and they emphasize this subdivision by adding a simple bass or rhythmic accompaniment.
5 Students listen to at least a dozen pop songs, counting how many beats per minute there are in each and deciding what metrical structure is used. Then they discuss whether or not a certain tempo range and metre seem to be preferred by composers of this kind of music. If composers of pop music do appear to concentrate upon songs of a certain speed and metrical organization, pupils suggest reasons why this might be the case.
6 Pupils look up and write short definitions of the following terms: accompaniment, improvisation, key, melody, metre, pitch and rhythm.
7 Students research the early history of the following musical instruments: guitar, lute, viol, mouth organ, oboe and timpani.

APPENDIX 2 – CROSS-REFERENCES AND POSSIBILITIES FOR EXPANSION

Possibilities for further expansion in the classroom of some of the ideas discussed above include continuing with more work on the subject of programme music and the introduction of *musique concrète*. The latter would be particularly appropriate if tape-recorded sounds are integrated into Exercise (3). Definitions of music could lead to a discussion of the innovative work of John Cage. The third class exercise could lead to the appraisal of Western pieces with avian themes, such as Respighi's

The Birds or various compositions by Messaien. For a more thorough criticism of the idea of musical progress from simple, primitive music to advanced Western compositions see Sachs (1962: 210–22).

Mention and discussion of metre could lead to an examination of the varied metrical patterns employed by Stravinsky in the *Rite of Spring* or by Bartók in his 'Six Dances in Bulgarian Rhythm' (*Mikrokosmos* Vol. VI, Nos. 148–53). One step further removed, Bernstein's 'America' from *West Side Story* makes interesting use of alternating metrical subdivisions (Bowman, 1992: 20–1), while many Baroque compositions include the somewhat similar hemiola effect. Much music theory, particularly that concerned with tonality, could be introduced or reinforced with the very brief mention of scales and keys given above, while advanced groups could become acquainted with the European church modes as well. The subject of musical organization and training is further discussed in Booth and Kuhn (1990). Although their categorization of folk, art and popular musics is rather simplistic, it none the less contains many stimulating points which advanced pupils would be able to comprehend.

ACKNOWLEDGEMENT

I am grateful to Joo-Lee Stock for trying out preliminary versions of exercises proposed in this article with classes at Lagan College, Belfast and Grangefield School, Stockton-on-Tees.

REFERENCES

Bacharach, A. L. and Pearce, J. R. (eds) (1977) *The Musical Companion*, revd edn, London: Pan.

Blacking, J. (1976) *How Musical is Man?*, London: Faber and Faber.

Booth, G. D. and Kuhn, T. L. (1990) 'Economic and transmission factors as essential elements in the definition of folk art and pop music', *The Musical Quarterly* 74(3): 411–38.

Bowman, D. (1992) 'GCSE Analysis: Songs from West Side Story', *Music Teacher*, 71(7), 20–5.

Feld, S. (1982) *Sound and Sentiment: Birds, Weeping, Poetics, and Song in Kaluli Expression*, Philadelphia: University of Pennsylvania Press.

Hornbostel, E. M. von and Sachs, C. (1961) 'Classification of Musical Instruments', translated from the original German by A. Baines & K. P. Wachsmann, *Galpin Society Journal*, 14, 3–29.

Isaacs, Alan (ed.) (1988) *The Macmillan Encyclopedia*, London: Guild Publishing.

Kartomi, M. (1990) *On Concepts and Classifications of Musical Instruments*, Chicago: University of Chicago Press.

Myers, H. ed. (1992) *Ethnomusicology: An Introduction*, New Grove Handbooks of Music, London: Macmillan.

Nettl, B. (1983) *The Study of Ethnomusicology: Twenty-nine Issues and Concepts*, Urbana: University of Illinois Press.

Penguin (1986) *The New Penguin English Dictionary*, Harmondsworth, Middlesex: Penguin.

Sachs, C. (1962) *The Wellsprings of Music*, J. Kunst, ed., The Hague: Martinus Nijhoff.

Sloboda, J. A. (1985) *The Musical Mind: The Cognitive Psychology of Music* (Oxford Psychology Series, No. 5), Oxford: Oxford University Press.

Sorrell, N. (1990) *A Guide to the Gamelan*, London: Faber and Faber.

Chapter 13

Assessment in the arts
Issues of objectivity

Gary Spruce

INTRODUCTION

In general terms, what are the characteristics that underpin an effective assessment model? Harlen *et al.* (1994) proposes three roles for assessment: first that it should provide feedback about the on-going process of education (Formative); second that it should communicate the level and nature of a pupils' experience (Summative); and third that it should summarize for the purpose of selection. Harlen goes on to say that underpinning these roles are a number of key principles which should characterize the assessment model. These are that the assessment model should match the purpose for which it is intended, be integral to the teaching process, reflect the full range of the things that have been taught, be communicable to outside bodies, indicative of an institution's effectiveness and contribute to a national perspective.

Sally Brown (1994) advances a number of propositions about assessment which develop the ideas propounded by Harlen, giving them a qualitative context and relating them explicity to teaching and learning. She argues that assessment should be broad-based and be seen to be 'fulfilling multiple purposes' – including fostering learning, improving teaching, providing valid information and enabling pupils and others to make choices; that there should be 'an increase in the range of qualities assessed and the context in which that assessment takes place'; that 'descriptive assessment' – a description of what the child has achieved – should replace a bland listing of marks and grades; that assessment should be devolved to 'schools, teachers, work-experience employers and young people themselves'; and finally, that there should be greater access to certification, 'certification should be available to a much greater proportion of the population of young people'. These, then, are the basic principles that must lie at the heart of any assessment model.

OBJECTIVITY

Two particularly prevalent ways of thinking about assessment – one generic and one specific to the arts – can militate against the formulation of a successful assessment model. The first is that all assessment should be demonstrably objective and the second, at first sight mutually exclusive view, is that the particular nature of the arts render them unsuitable for any kind of external evaluation. Although neither position is entirely unsustainable, and elements of both perceptions may well contribute to an ideal assessment model for the arts, when applied in an inflexible and doctrinaire fashion, each has the potential to cause damage. This danger was acknowledged by HMI in their document *Music from 5–16* (1985).

> There has been a long-standing controversy about the feasibility and even the desirability of assessing progress in aesthetic subjects. Opponents of the idea cannot see any way of evaluating development which intimately involves human feelings and emotions; proponents contend that the effectiveness of all forms of educational provision should be subject to regular assessment. Ironically, certain aspects of musical progress have been more thoroughly assessed (via graded examinations) than almost any other area of the curriculum. Unfortunately, such examinations do not always identify such elusive qualities as musicianship and creativity, sometimes valuing technical accomplishment above musical understanding.
>
> (DES, 1985: 18)

The significance attached to demonstrable objectivity in the formulation of assessment models is rooted in two diametrically opposed ways of perceiving the function of education and the nature of intelligence. The first derives from the highly stratified and essentially conservative nature of post-war English education, and the second from the comprehensivisation of the nation's schools that took place during the ostensibly more liberal 1960s and early 1970s. It may be, as Gipps (1994) says, that: 'over the last twenty-five years, assessment has been undergoing a paradigm shift from psychometrics to a broader model of educational assessment, from a testing and examination culture to an assessment culture', but the requirement that assessment models should be as objective as possible has remained a common feature. Their validity has depended upon them being perceived as such.

In the context of the selective nature of post-war education, the importance of demonstrable objectivity in assessment is understandable. It proceeded from a perception of the purpose of education and the nature of intelligence which perfectly concorded with the prevailing philosophy. Intelligence was perceived as being inherited and fixed (much in the same way as is the colour of one's eyes) and could, through assessment, be demonstrated and quantified. Education was essentially a utilitarian process, the success of which was measured by summative assessment. The results of such assessment could then be norm-referenced and used as the basis for selection to type of school or as the means of access to higher education, job or career. Education and assessment were 'about sorting people into social roles for society' (Brown 1993: 227). It therefore follows that assessment was perceived as being primarily judgemental and its fairness had to be seen to be beyond reproach. This was achieved through the demonstrable objectivity of the assessment model.

The main criticism of demonstrable objectivity (and the key word here is *demonstrable*) is that, in the formulation of the assessment model, the need to demonstrate objectivity is frequently of such overriding concern that it is applied to the detriment of all other considerations. Such is the importance attached to demonstrability, that the assessment model is designed not with the primary aim of exhibiting a child's 'best performance' but rather to exhibit its objectivity. This is achieved by removing from the assessment model (where possible) all variables associated with subjective judgement. Consequently, the test model acquires a highly controlled context: timed tasks (almost always written) which assesses the ability to memorize, retain and repeat bodies of prescribed information. Therefore, whereas it may have been an appropriate form of assessment for the stratified system of education that prevailed in England from the end of the second world war through to the end of the 1980s, it was a singularly inappropriate one for a comprehensive system whose fundamental philosophical basis was a belief in the value of education for its own sake and the educability of all children. How then did the primacy of objectivity maintain its grip on the education system?

The answer I believe lies in the nature of the public service ethos of the 1960s and 1970s. Stewart Ranson (1992), in an analysis of the public service models of the period defines two types: the 'Professional Service Management' model, and the 'Corporate Management' model. Both, although essentially liberal in design, perceived their function as delivering services to the community without involving the community in defining what those services should be. They believed in: 'the essential atomism of society composed of private and self-sufficient individuals . . . thus the welfare state identified with and served the needs of individual clients rather than enabling the development of whole communities' (Ranson, 1992). In the early 1970s some progress was made towards involving the communities in defining their own needs. However, few authorities fully took on board the recommendations of the Bains Report (1972) that local government should not limit its perspective to the narrow provision of a series of services but should have, 'within its purview the overall economic, cultural and physical well-being of that community'. In education, the omniscient style of local government became manifest through the 'professional domination' of the service provided: 'an educated public was to be delivered by specialists rather than lived and created by citizens with the support of professionals' (Ranson, 1992). The rationale for such a system was that decisions made on behalf of the community were informed by professional, detached objectivity. Objectivity and hence neutrality were justifications for a monopoly of power over the decision-making process. Therefore involvement in anything that could be construed as involving value judgements was, where possible, avoided.

Education became inextricably linked with this non-value laden – and hence frequently non-judgemental – philosophy. Assessment was applied in as objective a manner as possible and value judgements were eschewed. The impression to be given to the student was that a qualitative decision had been made through the mechanistic application of clear criteria. (This was the era of the multi-choice examination.) Thus it was that the continued adherence to the rigid application of objective criteria-based assessment and a resistance to the very notion of assessment other than that which could be applied empirically, derived from the same philosophical stable.

The non-judgemental approach to education became particularly manifest in the arts. For, whereas objective assessment could easily be applied to maths and the sciences it was possible to argue that the arts were purely concerned with feelings rather than with cognitive development, and therefore assessment was both inappropriate and impracticable. It proceeded as David Best says, 'from the misguided assumption that emotional feelings in general and the kinds of feelings most centrally involved in the creation and appreciation of arts are purely subjective and therefore not open to objective evaluation' (Best, 1992). This view received widespread support amongst arts teachers during the late 1970s and early 1980s. It was perceived as being what gave the arts their uniqueness and therefore a justification for their place on the curriculum.

However, as both Best (1992: 96) and Swanwick (1979: 149) point out such an attitude is politically unwise and educationally unsound. For, unless arts educators can demonstrate that learning takes place within what *they* define as being the *raison d'être* of the arts – the realm of the creative imagination and the development of the artistic and aesthetic – then the existence of the arts on the curriculum cannot be justified. The case for the arts is best articulated by demonstrating that they have a unique contribution to make to what is the main function of schools – teaching and learning. For, 'unless artistic experience is answerable to cognition and reason, there can be no reason for including the arts in our educational institutions' (Best 1992: 29). It is only through assessment that we can confirm that this is so. What the arts require is an assessment model that has legitimacy in a whole-education context and also serves the specific needs of the curriculum area.

ARTS VS. SCIENCE: A FALSE DICHOTOMY?

The assessment philosophy of post-war British education was therefore driven by the need to objectively evaluate. Consequently, as the sciences and humanities were more amenable to objective assessment than were the arts, their status increased accordingly.

Distinguishing the arts from the sciences along the lines of their relative objectivity is, however, a philosophy rooted in the nineteenth century. The Victorian desire to define their existence in terms of verifiable facts – epitomized by the character of Gradgrind in Charles Dickens's novel *Hard Times*: 'Facts are all that are needed in Life' – inevitably marginalized the arts. The arts were perceived in terms of sensate experience and having little to do with cognition. They were seen either as being pleasantly irrational or as deeply concerned with emotions – or most often as somewhere on the continuum between those two points. As Wittgenstein (1921) said, 'people nowadays think that scientists exist to instruct them whilst poets and musicians exist to give them pleasure. The idea that the latter have something to teach them, that does not occur to them'. The detachment of the arts from their social context was further increased by the changing perception of the nature of the artist in society:

> For the first time the musician was conceived of as an artist, a term that was beginning to take on a deeper meaning . . . Bach and Mozart never considered themselves as artists; they were very much functional and well-integrated members of their societies, achieving modest worldly success by virtue of their abilities. Yet in the emerging Romantic art cult, the composer was thought of as a solitary individual, ruled by wayward passions, in fundamental opposition to a philistine society. The artist existed on a more exalted plane than the workaday world of his audience; he breathed a rarefied ether and consorted with those sublime Intelligences that had once been charged with turning the crystal spheres.
>
> (James, 1995: 194)

In such a way was accomplished the exclusion of arts and artists from the functioning of society. Science and art were considered to be separate and mutually exclusive. Society had lost its ancient belief in the 'serene order' of the universe, in which the arts and sciences were united in a quest to discover the key to eternal truths.

Yet, as Best and others have pointed out, there is an essentially false dichotomy here. Science has frequently required a creative impulse to effect the cognitive leap required for the greatest of its discoveries. Copernicus postulated the idea that the earth travels around the sun whilst it was left to Galileo, born twenty years after Copernicus's death, to mathematically verify the concept. Furthermore, objectivism is only contemporary – fit for the time – and is not in itself a demonstration of absolute and eternal proof. For as the philosopher Karl Popper points out, we can never know for certain that a scientific statement is objectively true. For what we have observed in the past, and observe now, cannot be guaranteed to occur in the future.

Furthermore, the idea that the arts are exclusively concerned with feelings and emotions and have no basis in cognitive experience is equally ill-founded. As the composer Schoenberg says: 'music is not merely another kind of amusement but a musical thinkers representation of musical ideas; and these ideas must respond to the laws of human logic'. Thomas Mann writes: 'her strictness, or whatever you like to call the moralism of her form, must stand for an excuse for the ravishments of her actual sounds' (Leverkuhn, *Dr Faustus* (1947)). Thus the arts *are* about cognitive development and the sciences *do* require creative input. The dichotomy is essentially false and we must therefore look to renew the links between the two disciplines.

New insights into the nature of human perception and intelligence, and developments in philosophy of the sciences and of the arts have begun to dissolve these dichotomies and to re-establish the relationships between artistic, scientific and other modes of understanding. The sciences have many characteristics that have come to be almost exclusively associated with the arts and vice versa. The processes of scientific enquiry draw deeply on the scientists' powers of creativity and personal judgement. . . . Equally work in the arts shares some of the recognized characteristics of the sciences. If the arts require creative imagination and aesthetic judgement, they also call on painstaking discipline in the acquisition and application of skills and intellectual rigour in the pursuit of formal and conceptual solutions. These affinities between different modes of understanding are significant both for the planning and practice of education.

(NCC, 1990: para. 50)

THE PRIMACY OF THE SENSATE

Some arts educators have attempted to turn to their advantage the non-cognitive view of the arts by espousing the notion of the primacy of the sensate. This is essentially a retreat from the cognitive argument by justifying the existence of the curriculum area in other terms. The 'primacy of the sensate' argument therefore tends either to be dismissive of the role of cognitive development in arts education or seeks to reinterpret it in terms of sensate experience. It is an attitude which whilst purporting to be radical and progressive is, as I indicated earlier, firmly rooted in the nineteenth century: 'The first concept is always the best and most natural. The intellect can err, the sentiment – never' (Schumann).

Ross and Mitchell (1993) articulate a persuasive case for the 'sensate' perspective, basing their argument on a distinction between two types of sensate experience: *sensate surface* and *sensate resonance*. Sensate surface includes 'every appeal to sensory apprehension offered by the work – everything we see touch or hear that constitutes the body of the piece', while sensate resonance is:

> the operation of those self-same structures to evoke a sense of order feeling and imagination. . . . If surface delights us, resonance is what moves us . . . we must hold to the primacy of perception of the sensate dimension. It is only and exactly upon the sensate dimension that aesthetic understanding operates. Every art work is constrained by its sensate parameters.
>
> (Ross and Mitchell, 1993)

For Ross, arts education is about the enabling of personal expression. He considers the arts as being a subjective dream world, 'the realm of mood character, symbol metaphor'. Children's education is about enculturation as a means towards a developed personal expression.

> Feelings arise in a cultural context. They find expression and realization in ways and by means available in and acceptable (meaningful) to that culture. We appropriate the conventions available within our culture for the expression of personal feeling, for the transaction and communication of personal meaning. It is clearly of the utmost importance that children should be skilled in such forms, customs conventions and practices as will permit and facilitate the legitimate expression of feeling. . . . Children should be given the opportunity to appropriate the expressive forms they need from the full range now available in the modern world, both contemporary and traditional and to convert them into personal style or autograph.
>
> (Ross and Mitchell, 1993)

From this perspective they propound an assessment ideal that is process-based and legitimate only in as much as it is negotiated through dialogue with the child. They argue that the essential purpose of assessment is to engage with the part of the child's creative process that results in the artefact, not to assess the artefact itself. Ross and Mitchell believe that to do the latter would be to work against the 'non-judgemental environment [which is] of the essence'. However, the aim of any process – and particularly a creative process – is the production of an artefact, and it is arguably naive to attempt to remove this from the assessment equation. Furthermore, it seems to me that there are inherent dangers in giving absolute primacy to the child's inner world and/or in excluding external intervention. As Gardner says:

> if the creator is too removed from the domain, too much in his or her own world, . . . there will not be any rules by which to operate, and those knowledgeable about the domain will be unable to relate to the work produced. . . . In the absence of knowledgeable others, who can apprehend and judge what one has created, one's work is consigned to a kind of limbo.
>
> (Gardner, 1995: 15)

OBJECTIVITY AND CRITERIA-RELATED ASSESSMENT

It is of critical importance that an assessment model should be seen to have legitimacy by all of those involved with it. A central precept of this legitimacy is the perception that the evaluation process is objective. This is most frequently achieved by formulating assessment models in terms of clearly defined criteria which are strictly applied in controlled contexts. However there are dangers associated with criteria-led assessment, particularly in the way in which it connects with, and impacts upon, objectivity.

An attempt to achieve objectivity through laying down strict criteria can inhibit the educational experience by allowing into the subject area only that which can be objectively assessed: 'it is a generally held perception that formal assessment has hindered and distorted work in the secondary classroom through laying too much emphasis on what is easily examinable, regardless of its relevance as musical experience' (Aspin, 1986). Thus there is a danger that the criteria might look not to the subject area and the children for its point of reference but to the assessment model itself. If this occurs, then the whole educational process becomes distorted: '[the] artistic endeavours of children are frequently assessed examined according to externally pre-determined sets of criteria and standards that "measure the measurable" often at the expense of those qualities arts education professes to develop'. (Cartwright, 1989: 283).

Furthermore, Margaret Brown (1991) has shown how strict criteria related assessment can lead back to norm-referencing behind what Drever *et al* (1983) (quoted in Brown) describes as 'a smoke screen of pseudo criteria'.

However, the main danger of an assessment model that is too rigidly criteria-related, is that the process will become fragmented. This is particularly true of the assessment of musical performance, where there can be great temptation to separate music into its component parts of rhythm, pitch, etc. – assess these separately and then aggregate them for a summative mark. A number of exam boards adopted such a model in the early years of GCSE. This was a typical example of the need to demonstrate objectivity taking precedence over higher educational – and in this case artistic – ideals. No doubt adopting this system meant that every mark could be justified, but at the cost of missing the point of the musical exercise: the performance a a whole. For, as Suzanne Langer says:

> The first principle in music hearing, is not, as many people presume, the ability to distinguish the separate elements in a composition and recognize its devices, but to experience the primary illusion, to feel the consistent movement and recognize at once the commanding form which makes this piece *an inviolable whole.*
>
> (Langer, 1953; emphasis added)

Furthermore, simply because an assessment model can demonstrate high objectivity this does not in itself imply reliability. Janet Mills (1991) refers to a study carried out by Fiske (1977) which in fact demonstrated that holistic assessment resulted in a greater consensus of opinion than did assessment which was fragmented. Thus the theory that strictly applied criteria necessarily equals absolute objectivity was shown to be deeply flawed. Mills suggests two reasons why this might be so:

> 1 Overall performance is real. In other words, all the judges hear the same performance. If we are to assess a component of the performance, such as rhythm, on the other hand, we must partial out much of the other material. Our ability to do this, or our technique of doing this, will vary. Thus our perceptions of the rhythmic element of a performance may differ. Abstracting rhythm from melody is not a conceptually simple matter like filtering out impurities from a sample of rain water, or absorbing light rays within some defined frequency range: melody consist of a dynamic relationship between rhythm, pitch and a host of other variables. It is not clear what the expression 'the rhythm of a performance' means.
> 2 We are practised in the assessment of overall performance. Every time we listen to TV jingle, a pop song, a Brahms symphony, or a passing ice-cream van, we have the opportunity to make judgements about what we hear. On the other hand, we are less frequently presented with examples of pure rhythm or intonation, or whatever this means, to assess.
>
> (Mills, 1991)

Mills is writing here particularly about the summative assessment of musical performance. However, it seems to me that her point applies equally to formative evaluation. Her arguments are not designed to prevent the assessor from judging a performance holistically and then analysing the component parts in order to formatively feed back to the student. What must be avoided however, is the adoption of an assessment model which loses sight of the whole through assessing the parts – not seeing the wood for the trees. As Goldman says:

Dissecting a work analytically may alienate the analyst from the work's expressive effects, especially from the expressive tone of the whole. This is not to dismiss the value of critical scrutiny or of its communication in educational settings; it is only to call into question the location of that value. . . .

(Goldman, 1990)

The important thing with criteria statements is, as Denis Lawton says, to avoid being so 'general that they become untestable' or so specific that 'they become trivial and atomistic'. However, as he somewhat gloomily concludes, 'this problem has not been solved' (Lawton, 1994).

CONSTRUCTING AN ASSESSMENT MODEL

In addition to being perceived as having validity by all those involved with it, an assessment system should provide 'good quality information about pupils' performance without distorting good teaching practice and therefore learning' (Gipps, 1994). Furthermore, it should be aware of the uniquely personal nature of creativity, recognizing that creativity is not only integral to the arts but is central to the entire educational process.

It seems to me that in constructing such an assessment model we are required to redefine our perception of the nature of intelligence and our concept of what constitutes objectivity. Having done this we can then proceed to devise a model which adopts a more holistic view of the assessment process and therefore a more appropriate one for the arts.

The perception that the arts are unconcerned with cognitive experience is based on the idea of intelligence as a unitary and fixed function. However over the last decade there has developed the idea of the arts as constituting a distinct and unique 'way of knowing'. The arts as a way of knowing has become something of a clarion call for arts educators. Essentially it is a means whereby the terms of reference of much of education can be redefined in favour of the establishment of a coherent arts curriculum. It has been interpreted in different ways by a number of arts educators – particularly Abbs (1985), Best (1992), Ross and Mitchell (1993). However, I wish to consider it, perhaps somewhat tangentially, from the perspective of two particular publications: Howard Gardner's *Frames of Mind* (1984) and the Gulbenkian Report, *The Arts in Schools* (1982). Gardner, whose book is subtitled *The Theory of Multiple Intelligences*, argues for the existence of a number of intelligences: linguistic, musical, logical-mathematical, spatial, bodily-kinaesthetic and personal intelligence. Having defined this multiplicity of intelligences, he draws attention to the fact that only two are developed to any degree during formal schooling: the linguistic and the logical-mathematical. Gardner is therefore suggesting that much of a child's cognitive potential remains unexploited and particularly that which relates to the artistic and aesthetic. Perhaps then, as Peter Abbs suggests, the educational debate should centre around this failure rather than 'the present massive and barbaric retreat into "basics"' (Abbs, 1985).

Gardner's particular way of thinking about intelligence obviously has great significance for assessment in arts education. For if one accepts his theory of multiple intelligences, then it follows that there must be an equal multiplicity of ways of assessing cognitive development. It is no longer satisfactory to apply the psychometric model to learning irrespective of its appropriateness to the learning model. This was clearly the view of the Gulbenkian Report, which said:

> Like others before us, we reject the view that the only valid kinds of knowledge are those that are open to deductive reasoning and empirical tests. The ways of getting knowledge are not limited to the intellectual, book learning or scientific kind. The aesthetic the religious and the moral are quite as these others at conveying knowledge. In our view, public education has been too devoted to particular kinds of knowledge at the expense of others *which are of equal importance.*
> (Gulbenkian Report, 1982: para 24; emphasis added)

Furthermore, what follows naturally from this, is a redefinition of what we mean by objectivity. The first misconception we must dispense with is the idea that objectivity and subjectivity are mutually exclusive and that in matters other than of concrete fact it is possible for an assessor to be totally objective:

> rather than treating subjectivity and objectivity as exclusive alternatives, we should think of them rather as two poles of a spectrum. . . . At one end we might find entirely subjective remarks . . . such as "I like strawberries". This it is said makes no claims about the qualities of strawberries but merely reports how I, a subject, respond to them. At the other end of the spectrum there will be judgements which will be thought to be entirely objective: the judgement that triangles have three sides, perhaps. But for most of us, a large percentage of our judgements . . . will be more or less objective (or subjective). My judgement of *Othello* may be objective to the point that it avoids haste, prejudice, ignorance and the like, but my response may also be dependent on things which are part of my personal life history. The point I wish to make is that the fact that my judgement is for these latter reasons not entirely objective (since I cannot assume that we all have the same sort of psychology or cultural background) does not make it entirely subjective.
> (Lyas, 1992: 377)

Gipps (1994) expands on the relationship between objectivity and the assessor, further arguing that absolute objectivity is simply not possible:

The modernist view is that it is possible to be a disinterested observer while the post-modern view is that such detachment is not possible: we are social beings who construe the world according to our values and perceptions, our biographies are central to what we see and how we interpret it . . . reality is constructed by the observer and there are multiple constructions of reality.

(Gipps, 1994: 288)

Having therefore established that we need to redefine our perception of what intelligence is and having ceased worshipping at the temple of objectivity, we can proceed to develop an assessment model which is much less content-orientated and much more holistic in approach.

The nature of holistic assessment is that it should attempt to elicit 'best' rather than 'typical' performance and that it should be aware of factors external to the content of the test: specifically context and the relationship between assessor and assessed. As part of a definition of what characterizes good assessment, the late Desmond Nuttall in his classic paper 'The Validity of Assessments' draws attention to how assessment draws inferences from a sample of behaviour: 'every assessment is based on a sample of behaviour in which we are interested; we tend to generalize from the particular sample of behaviour we observe to the universe of that behaviour' (Nuttall, 1987). Gipps, in an analysis of Nuttall's article, expands on these points, emphasizing that the quality and range of cognisance of the assessment model is of crucial importance to the delivery of an accurate sample of behaviour:

Significantly what the paper brings into the definition of the universe of behaviour is the 'conditions and occasions' of assessment as well as the content (Nuttall, p. 110). We know that the content, context mode of the assessment will affect pupil performance; we have to distinguish 'between competence (the basic ability to perform) and performance (the demonstration of the competence on a particular occasion or under particular circumstances) . . .' (op. cit., p. 112). What marks out educational assessment from psychometrics is a different view of the learner, and a different relationship between pupil and assessor. At the heart of this lies an understanding that performance is affected by context including the relationship between pupil and assessor, the pupil's motivational state and the characteristics of the assessment task.

(Gipps, 1994: 286)

A successful relationship between pupil and teacher, which is so necessary to the successful functioning of holistic assessment, is founded upon a number of 'pupil awarenesses': first, that absolute objectivity is not possible and that what is being brought to bear is informed subjectivity; second, that the acquisition of informed subjectivity is one of the aims of arts education;

and finally that although some assessment is, in the final analysis, judgemental, the process is essentially a collaborative seeking after 'best performance'.

Gipps considers the key aspects in eliciting best performance are:

- a range of activities, offering a wide opportunity to perform;
- match to classroom practice;
- extended interaction between pupil and teacher to explain the task;
- normal classroom setting, which is therefore not unduly threatening;
- a range of response modes other than written.

The appropriateness of these aspects to arts education and their importance as the foundation stones of any arts-based assessment model is manifestly obvious. They have the virtue of being applicable to all areas of the curriculum whilst being particularly relevant to arts subjects, and they entirely dispense with the psychometric model of assessment which has so distorted arts education. The notion of holistic assessment therefore provides a philosophical basis for assessment which not only serves the arts well but also, of perhaps greater importance, is of equal applicability to other curriculum areas. To achieve a universal assessment model would be to bring together hitherto disparate curriculum areas in a unity of educational purpose.

In conclusion, I wish to consider once more the conflicting perspectives of those who believe in the necessity of assessment in the arts – either from a political and/or educational viewpoint – and those who are essentially opposed to it on philosophical and/or practical grounds. Possibly there is no way of reconciling such divergent views. However, I believe Gardner comes closest to proposing an ideal accommodation. He rejects the idea of a non-judgemental approach whilst emphasizing the difficulties inherent in assessing in the arts. In doing so, he provides what I believe to be not only a framework for assessment, but also a philosophical framework for the teaching of the arts:

> The future creator must evolve into a certain type of person. He or she cannot be too ready to please, too influenced by the surrounds, too upset by critical feedback. Here is where shrewd parenting and teaching come in. It is equally damaging to tell the youngster that everything that she fashions is great, as it is to rip everything that she does to shreds. The educator of the future creator needs to walk a fine line – always encouraging the youngster to stretch, praising her where she succeeds, but equally important providing support and a non-condemnatory *interpretative* [my emphasis] framework when things do not go well . . . when the most demanding creative work is being tackled, it is important to have at one's side some other person who can provide sustenance . . . by later childhood, it is not inappropriate to introduce the standards of

the domain and allow the student to see how judgements of quality are made. The field is not always correct; indeed the history of creativity is the history of judgements that were initially off the mark. But the point is one simply cannot do without some kind of evaluative feedback.

(Gardner, 1995)

REFERENCES

Abbs, P. (1985) 'Art as a way of knowing: notes towards a more formal aesthetics', in A. Bloomfield (ed.) *Creative and Aesthetic Education*, Hull: The University of Hull.

Aspin, D. (1986) *Assessment and Progression in Music Education*, Music Advisers' National Association.

Best, D. (1992) *The Rationality of Feeling: Understanding the Arts in Education*, London: The Falmer Press.

Brown, M. (1991) 'Problematic issues in national assessment', *Cambridge Journal of Education* 21(2).

Brown, S. (1994) 'Assessment: a changing practice', in B. Moon and A. Shelton Mayes (eds) (1994) *Teaching and Learning in the Secondary School*, London: Routledge.

Cartwright, P. (1989) 'Assessment and examination in arts education', in Ross, M. (ed.) *The Claims of Feeling*, London: Falmer Press.

DES (1985) *Music from 5-16*, London: HMSO.

Drever, E. *et al.* (1983) 'A framework for decision – or 'business as usual'?' *Scottish Educational Review* 15(2).

Fiske, H. E. (1977) 'Relationship of selected factors in trumpet performance adjudication reliability'. *Journal of Research in Music Education* 25(4).

Gardner, H. (1984) *Frames of Mind: The Theory of Multiple Intelligences*, London: Heinemann.

Gardner, H. (1995) 'Creating creativity', *The Times Educational Supplement*. 6 January 1995.

Gipps, C. (1994) 'Developments in educational assessment: what makes a good test?' *Assessment in Education*, 1(3).

Goldman, A. II. (1990) 'The education of taste', *British Journal of Aesthetics*, 30(2).

Gulbenkian Report (1982) *The Arts in Schools*, London: Calouste Gulbenkian.

Harlen, W., Gipps, C., Broadfoot, P., Nutall, D. (1994) 'Assessment and the Improvement of Education', in B. Moon and A. Shelton Mayes (eds) (1994) *Teaching and Learning in the Secondary School*, London: Routledge.

HMSO (1972) *Bains Report*, London: HMSO.

James, J. (1995) *The Music of the Spheres*, London: Little, Brown & Co.

Langer, S. (1953) *Feeling and Form: A Theory of Art Developed from Philosophy in a New Key*, London: Routledge & Kegan Paul.

Lawton, D. (1994) 'The National Curriculum and its Assessment', *Forum* 6(4).

Lyas, C. (1992) 'The Evaluation of Art', in O. Hanfling (ed.) *Philosophical Aesthetics: An Introduction*. Milton Keynes: Open University Press.

Mills, J. (1991) 'Assessing musical performance musically', *Educational Studies*, 17(2).

National Curriculum Council (NCC), Arts in Schools Project (1990) *The Arts 5–16*, London: Oliver and Boyd.

Nuttall, D. (1987) 'The validity of assessments', *European Journal of Psychology of Education* 2(2).

Ranson, S. (1992) 'Towards the learning society', *Education Management and Administration* 20(2).
Ross, M. and Mitchell, S. (1993) 'Assessing achievement in the arts', *British Journal of Aesthetics* 33(2).
Swanwick, K. (1979) *A Basis for Music Education*, London: National Federation for Educational Research.

Part IV

Music education and the classroom

Chapter 14

Music education as I see it

A report of an interview with a seventeen-year-old student concerning his music education

George Odam

The following monologue is based on a conversation which took place at Broadoak School, Weston-Super-Mare, England, between John Brock, Specialist Music Teacher and Danny Farrant of the Upper Sixth form and leader of the 'Burning Hearts' Rock Group. Danny Farrant went on to enter a music conservatoire as a percussionist.

'I remember singing in Primary school most. My parents started me with piano lessons and promised to buy me a drum set for Christmas if I worked at it. When I had my drums I would play them in Assembly at school. I did learn to play the recorder for a while but my friends thought it a bit cissy. I used to be noticed by other children because I sang in tune.

The first three years of my secondary schooling (11–14) were of no use. I used to think "What am I learning? This isn't really useful". It was too geared towards classical music and was quite boring.

I appreciated the work far more when I started studying for the 16+ examination at the age of 15. Now I am working for my Advanced Level Examination (18+) I find that what I do outside school (playing in various groups) is amplified by work in school. It gives me a general overview. Working "academically" makes you think more and think out problems when you are playing. I appreciate the music that I play much more.

I think that the approach to harmony should be much more creative than the approach through stylistic writing. I don't equate the work I do in school harmony with the harmony of my own songs. It's totally irrelevant to the songs I'm writing. I don't feel that my harmonies or melodies are comparable to those of Schumann or Schubert. I'd rather write from my head than from the rules. When we write Schubert stuff we have to write from the rules. I don't like doing that. I wish I could *feel* what is right. It's not very musical. When I write my own songs I'll mess around on the piano and pick up on a chord sequence I like or maybe in the day I'll be singing some riff or melody and then I'll sit down at the piano and find what chords fit to it or I'll have a chord sequence worked out in my head already.

I sit down at the piano and just do it. I use a greater amount of chords in my pop music than I've ever used in my Bach Chorales. I'm really scared of using a III or a VI, but I know I use them in my pop music all the time – and I know that they sound good. I'm scared of using them for examination work.

I use a lot of seconds in my chords as well – take a chord of C and I'll have C, D, E, G – which goes with whatever I'm playing or I'll have an added sixth which you don't ever use in chorales. You never add a second except as a suspension. If I feel parallel fifths fit I'll use them, although I must admit I don't like the sound of fifths too much.

I know I have to work for my examinations and they are helping me get into higher education so they have been important to me. Studying a piece of music gives you a different kind of appreciation – chords and rhythms and that sort of thing. I enjoy finding out about the composers and why the pieces were written.

There are very few people I know who compose music now – especially classical music - or "serious" music. No. I don't like to call it "serious" music because my pop music is pretty serious.

The music that most kids are doing today is not being taught in schools. My musical experience has been largely outside school although perhaps my introduction to music was first from inside school. If pop music in school was only used for listening to, the kids would take no notice. It has to be practical. But most teachers have gone through the old system. They don't listen to pop music or understand it. Schools haven't got the right equipment or the right sort of rooms to work in.

Rock musicians should be brought into schools to run workshops. They could help people learn about the different styles like Rock and Roll and Swing. I want to learn about all kinds of music in school. The options should be open to allow all young people to have as wide an appreciation of music as possible. I hope that more young people will get involved in music – not necessarily writing it but appreciating it. I'd like to see more people appreciating classical music. They don't know what they are missing. They think it's all Mozart and nothing else. If they only sat down and listened to Shostakovich I reckon they'd love it. I'm not saying that pop music is worse and that people should only listen to classical music. They should listen to what they enjoy. More people should have the chance to listen widely. Pop music is simple. I like to listen to a pop LP and think of it as something like a symphony. There are some Rock musicians – Gabriel for example – where the whole LP merges into a single statement. It sums up the mood of thought of the moment. It's well thought out.

The present classical composers I know of are Peter Maxwell Davies, Giles Swayne, Nigel Osborne, Luciano Berio, Anthony Payne and Penderecki. Music of our time should be given more importance in school rather than listening to Haydn and Mozart all the time. Minimal music seems out now – Philip Glass and Steve Reich. Although some people say so, they are not really using Rock material in their music. For instance we saw Jonathan Harvey's piece on television. The sounds there were nothing like Rock sounds. They were still intellectually worked out – I'm not meaning to sound snobby – but they were sort of meant to last. Pop music isn't like that. If it *does* last that's great. It will always react to fashion.

To include pop music in the curriculum for 11–18 would be much more relevant to the average student. If it was a basis from which to start a broadening study it would benefit more people. It is important that we should have knowledge of as many kinds of music as possible including the music of other ethnic groups. Rock musicians study it and it affects their music. I used to think that Asian music was rubbish until I went to the Steve Reich workshop day and heard about the techniques of *tabla* playing. Those of us who are already "on the music bandwagon" so to speak, will always go off on our own and pursue our own interests anyway, so it is more important to pay attention to what everyone receives in their music education. Everyone should have as broad an education as possible and choose which way they want to go at the end of it.'

Chapter 15

Classroom management for beginning music educators

Margaret Merrion

'Are the kids like this all of the time?' asks a junior practicum student in disbelief.

'How do you get the class to listen?' asks a senior starting her student teaching.

'How can I maintain better discipline?' worries another student teacher at midterm.

'I'm not sure I want to teach!'

As a supervising teacher of music, I had such questions posed and thoughts shared with me on countless occasions by students in our college of education, who undergo three phases of practicum experiences. Phase one and two experiences entail a number of hours of classroom observation, tutoring, and small- and large-group teaching in preparation for phase three – student teaching. These future teachers essentially share one major concern – classroom discipline, more fashionably termed 'classroom management'. Not surprisingly, this concern is also the number one dissatisfaction among many parents of school children.

It seems to me that our teacher-training institutions are more competent than ever in instilling the basics of educational psychology. Practicum students have no difficulty in understanding reinforcement schedules, theories of motivation, concept formation, and even behaviour modification. Further, music education students are often fairly well skilled in music reading and performing skills. The instructional management phase of teaching thus offers little threat to most beginning teachers. The most frightening of all first-day jitters concern the task of classroom management.

Fortunately or unfortunately, the issue of classroom management within music instruction poses unique problems due to the aesthetic nature of the arts. To maintain a learning environment free enough to permit personal and individual responses, improvisation, and creativity while providing a structure in which all students can collectively remain on-task and actively involved seems impossible. Just how *does* one manage classroom behaviour?

PREVENTIVE DISCIPLINE

I would like to propose a few preventive discipline measures. They are by no means the most essential strategies but rather a few techniques especially pertinent to music educators. No discipline strategy can compare, of course, with the sense of credibility teachers must establish once they are on the job. Of paramount importance is one's genuine interest in and respect for children. There are, however, a number of factors the teacher can directly prepare for and can control through advance planning.

Even though times may change, certain classroom management practices should remain constant. Two of these policies are fairness and consistency. When fairness and consistency prevail, a certain sense of security exists within the classroom. Fairness also builds trust, the foundation of any good relationship. A child's perception of a teacher's authority rests on the fairness and consistency with which the teacher manages. Children then have a better understanding of what behaviours are appropriate and what measures will be taken should behaviours deviate.

A gentle and sensitive teacher I encountered during my student-teaching period offered a third procedure for preventive discipline: 'come into the classroom with an iron fist; later, you will find you can put on a velvet glove'. In this era of permissiveness, I find few who advocate such apparently strict firmness. But this advice does not relate to corporal punishment or 'never smile before Christmas' practices. Rather, it is meant to address the attitude a teacher conveys. The expectations that an educator sets as appropriate classroom behaviour must be highest at the beginning of the school year. If the expectations are low or even mediocre, students will merely conform to those second-rate levels. Another important consideration music educators must take into account is that they generally teach a child for more than one school year. It is therefore crucial to begin the school year with a structured, well-conceived management plan that can operate throughout the school year as well as the ensuing years.

We know that three types of learning are operative at all times: cognitive, motor-skill, and affective. In music education, teachers must be committed to the priority of the affective goal and never shortchange that aim. Regardless of the type of learning experience, students and teachers of music must not compromise any aesthetic end for a cognitive or motor-skill learning. This fourth aspect of preventive discipline is of central importance.

I once observed a high school choral director spend close to an hour rehearsing several opening measures of one selection from a musical. The precision with which the students sharpened their dramatic and musical skills in that single rehearsal was a remarkable indication that exceptional educational success can be achieved in performing-orientated experiences. The personal and collective rewards were not necessarily reaped on opening night of the musical, but during these moments when each member of the group began to feel the proper vocal balance and gestures. Because music educators often spend the majority of their instructional hours in process, it is in their favour that aesthetic rewards be realized in the process of learning fine music literature and not just in the final product of public performance. Selecting music experiences capable of strong and rewarding aesthetic outcomes not only ensures on-task behaviours but eliminates distractive and disruptive behaviours by virtue of increased student involvement.

TEACHER PRESENCE

A fifth preventive discipline measure has to do with a teacher's physical image. The saying 'never judge a book by its cover' is a lesson one *learns*; one's natural inclination is to judge books, people, or places by their outward appearance. My observations of elementary school children reinforce this suspicion: books and materials often are selected by children for their visually attractive colours, drawings, sizes, or shapes. Similarly, children may also judge teachers by their physical appearance.

Research discussed in *The Master Teacher* indicated that not only the style but even the colour of clothing has a direct effect on children.[1] Although it is not possible to compile lists of what a teacher should or should not wear in the classroom, one can confidently assure practising teachers that T-shirts and blue jeans only reinforce an overly casual relationship with children. Ask yourself: if you were seated in a room with a number of other adults, would a child approach you for information, suspecting you were a teacher by your dress?

The matter of image and presence is not easy to document. Yet numerous administrators instinctively search out this trait during the hiring process. It is a characteristic that often indicates competence and ability to manage learning and behaviour. Children meet teachers visually before they meet them aurally. That ever-so-slight advantage of sight before sound can help or hinder the establishment of respect.

Other facets of teacher presence include the pitch and tempo of one's speaking voice (when instructing, when disciplining, when talking on a one-to-one basis); facial expressions of approval and disapproval; teaching postures; and frequency of posture changes. These behaviours need forethought and practice before actual teaching contact. Decide how long you will remain seated at the piano; experiment with your facial expressions in the mirror; record your voice and check it for clarity, sincerity, and direction.

The effectiveness of these aspects of teacher presence, of course, depends upon two conditions. The first is the degree of their compatibility with the teacher's personality. A second consideration is the nature of one's student clientele, including the size of the group and the ages, learning styles, abilities, and handicaps of the children.

SHARING AGENDAS

A final effective strategy I have used in general music is what I call 'sharing the agenda'. Because the general music class provides opportunities for children to engage in a diverse variety of activities, students often can come into the classroom curious, anxious and even overmotivated. One key to effective management of these energies is to share the agenda for that period with the children as soon as they arrive.

When my daughter was five years old, she accompanied me on a number of errands with the understanding that there would be a long-awaited stop for ice cream. I explained to her that our agenda would include a number of stops. First we needed to stop at the dry cleaners, then walk to the post office. Next we would drive to the chemist, go on to shop, and finally stop at the petrol station. I found that this method of sharing the agenda was quite helpful in organizing and directing our errands, especially if we were delayed by traffic. My daughter was assured we would proceed to each destination regardless of minor interruptions. Knowing the plan facilitated the flow of events.

Similarly, if a music teacher has only four Autoharps and twenty-four students who each want to perform a solo, sharing the agenda can assist in managing behaviour throughout the class period. The children are secure with the expectation of their eventual turn on the Autoharp.

Sharing agendas also serves as a cognitive framework for music experiences. For example, in teaching the concept of melodic direction, one might open the class period by explaining that the plan will include discussion; singing songs with different melodic directions; playing directions on bells; listening for direction of melodies on recordings; moving in different directions; and reading melodies of various directions. One might begin with the children giving directions for getting to the library from the classroom. Following that discussion, the children can explore road signs that give directions. After they have convinced the teacher that they know what 'direction' is, it is the teacher's turn on the agenda to tell what he or she knows about direction. When children understand that the teaching/learning process relies on two-way communication, they are more responsive to listening when it is their turn.

A student teacher under my supervision once had an uncomfortable delay in finding a particular piano selection in a large anthology. Her annoyance with herself was pleasantly counteracted by the patient and co-operative spirit of the students, who obviously realized that she was organized but momentarily delayed in facilitating the next learning experience. It clearly was not a let-me-see-what-shall-we-do-next pause. Children who are not sure of the conceptual and behavioural bearings of a music class may misconstrue such delays. Often they will use that time for undesirable classroom behaviours.

In music methods courses I have taught, I always have required students to demonstrate/teach a segment of a lesson. Even though college students serve as an unrealistic learning audience, the skill of conceiving a lesson plan and executing it with a comfortable pace and flow is an attainable goal within an artificial setting. It is my hope that once student teachers are in their practicum experiences, their instructional skills will be secure and time then can be appropriated for classroom management.

Much of the art and many of the skills of effective teaching can be learned in a variety of settings. Some students are able to learn vicariously via astute observation. Others may sharpen their skills in parenting. If one is committed to the joyous and rewarding ends of music education, each learning experience must be facilitated effectively. Few of us would question the necessity of instructional planning (lesson plans, advance selection and study of repertory, organization of learning outcomes). With classroom behaviour management, similar preventive planning can reduce the anxiety and probability of disenchanting experiences while enhancing the positiveness of effective teaching and learning.

NOTE

1 Robert L. DeBruyn, 'Dress for respect'. *The Master Teacher* 9 (19 November, 1978): 1.

Chapter 16

RX for technophobia

Kirk Kassner

Have you embraced the blessings of electronic technology, or have you developed symptoms of confusion and fear when the subject of computers or electronic instruments comes up? You may be suffering from the latest epidemic of 'technophobia'. This unreasonable fear of using computers and electronic technology to teach music is not fatal, but it can prevent you from helping your students reach their full potential as makers and appreciators of music. If you have a touch of technophobia, don't despair: The suggestions in this chapter can help you diagnose and cure it.

FEAR OF THE UNKNOWN

Technological jargon consists of terms for concepts that music teachers and musicians use every day. For example, a voltage-controlled oscillator (VCO) is the electronic equivalent of the vocal cords or a clarinet reed. A VCO is simply a source of vibration, a component of sound. An ADSR (attack, decay, sustain, release) or envelope generator is analogous to the musician's concept of articulation. 'Data base' is simply a system for organizing facts and ideas, much like a file-card system. There are only about two dozen electronic terms we really need to know, and many people get by with even fewer than that.

FEAR OF HIGH PERSONAL COSTS

Although it is important to keep learning (because technology itself is changing rapidly), very little time, money, or effort is needed to learn to use technology effectively and efficiently in the classroom. Universities and colleges offer many fine classes in which people can quickly learn the fundamentals of electronic technology. Often one workshop can provide enough training to get started with confidence.

Books, articles and free workshops are also available to help teachers get started. Software reviews in various magazines can give teachers an idea of what different packages can do for them. Almost every music educators' conference held recently has offered workshops in computers and electronic technology, and many school districts have sponsored in-service workshops. In addition, many music stores allow their customers to preview music software.

FEAR OF FAILURE

All of us have undoubtedly been successful and feel comfortable with the 'old' ways, and some may be reluctant to take the chance of failing by using unfamiliar equipment, especially around evaluation time. But it is perfectly acceptable *not* to know everything. Keep in mind that we must equip our students to be musical in both the present and in a future where technology will play an increasingly important role. Many students already know a great deal about new technology because they or their parents have invested in computers, electronic keyboards, or other electronic equipment at home. Invite people who are 'community resources' (including students) to share their knowledge with your classes and thereby help your students heighten their musical understanding while you learn more about the available technology.

FEAR OF UNEMPLOYMENT

Reports of robotic automation in the automobile industry and stories of entire studio orchestras being replaced by one or two people on electronic instruments seem too close to home for music educators to ignore. By extension, they wonder whether the voice and traditional acoustic instruments will be used in the future and whether music teaching will be taken over by machines, leaving them without jobs. Change has been and will continue to be inevitable. Music educators, like everyone else, must adapt to changes to survive. Belief that one can stop change by refusing to acknowledge it will contribute to unemployment much more than computers and electronic technology ever could.

Although many teachers have tenure, programme cuts can mean that continued employment is not ensured. Given our society's taste for technology, music programmes that include the latest technology will be less vulnerable to cutbacks. Those who fear becoming unemployed need to take steps now to keep up with new developments. The administrator of the future, given the choice of two otherwise similarly skilled music teachers, will certainly hire and retain the most technologically literate one.

FEAR OF COMPUTERIZED TEACHING

Computers and electronic technology have been widely discussed in recent education literature and at conferences. At a recent conference, Sandy

Feldstein, immediate past-president of the Music Industry Conference, stated:

> Technology, like the record player, Kodály, (or) Orff, is not the saviour of music education. We must not throw out what we are now doing, but add technology to it as another tool. Computers can do some things better than we can: guided home study, time-intensive drills, individually paced learning, immediate reinforcement – and do all these things with sound.

His comments are in agreement with many other reasoned opinions voiced among music educators: technology should be a tool, not a major part of the curriculum. The software that is currently available cannot provide a total music education; rather, it is a supplementary aid. Programmes must be used for the right reasons in the proper settings. It is important to sequence and integrate programmes into the entire music curriculum. We need to have a sense of balance and perspective and knowledge about 'what works best' when using technology.

FEAR OF LIMITED BUDGETS

Money is often easily available *outside* the music budget. Schools realize that today's children need to be prepared to live and work in a world of high technology, and they are making funds available for computers and software even when other programmes are being cut back. Music educators need to 'get smart' and tap into these funds, which can, in effect, augment their music budgets.

What do you say to convince the 'money people' in your school? Remind them that, just as in other subjects, computers can provide music students with self-paced, individualized learning. Computer lessons are structured and sequential, and they provide unlimited drills to increase students' music skills without tying up teacher time. Computer lessons allow teachers to serve diverse groups of students having widely varying skill levels and interests. Computer lessons give students control of their learning situations and keep them on task through a modern, exciting mode of learning that reacts immediately to their input.

If your money people need even more convincing, remind them that the ability to use computers is an important life skill and that the students get positive feedback from music software, which helps them enjoy and become comfortable using computers. Remind them that many other schools are providing opportunities for their students and that your school needs to take immediate measures to catch up with the leaders.

Providing high-quality education helps get budgets passed, even if it costs more initially to provide the latest equipment. There may be enough computer hardware in your building already, and all you may need is an administrative decision to allocate computers to the music room and to purchase several pieces of software.

Even within the music budget, however, investing in technology is a wise decision. Skilful use of technology can strengthen existing programmes far more efficiently than almost any other conceivable expenditure. Convinced of this, some music educators have raised the money themselves through fundraising activities or by obtaining grants from outside groups.

FEAR OF WASTING TIME

Because classroom time is limited, music teachers may fear that time spent on computers is wasted and that other worthwhile music activities will be sacrificed if computers are introduced into their curricula. On the surface, this fear seems justified: teachers rarely have enough contact time with students. But, as always, careful planning is the key to good use of music instruction time. Judicious use of technology can help students learn more efficiently; in fact, technology use can mean that some types of information that require many repetitions by the learner can be taught and mastered faster with the help of a computer. This allows *more* time for learning about the aesthetic facets of music.

I grappled with the problem of limited time and devised two related plans:

1 I examined the music curriculum and decided which teaching methods were best suited for presenting each concept or skill to be taught. The approaches and resources included Kodály, Orff, Froseth-Weikart, Manhattanville Music Curriculum Project, computer software, and key-boards. Then I organized these decisions into a six-year plan that included weekly goals and a suggested method for achieving each goal.

2 Having planned when technology would not be used in the classroom, I then launched a computer home study (CHS) programme in which students spent time outside the class learning music. The students and parents enthusiastically embraced the CHS programme. Parents often reported that they (and sometimes grandparents and neighbours) spent as much time using the software as their children did. Each student used the software for an average of eight hours per week. Thus, instead of taking up music instruction time, technology expanded it. By using the speed and individually–paced learning options that the computer provided, I was able to offer more instruction using such personal teaching methods as Kodály and Orff. Student music performances were better than ever.

FEAR OF POOR MATERIALS

Although it is true that there are a number of software programmes on the market that provide little opportunity for actual learning, there are also traditional education tools (music compositions, musical plays and films) that are silly and trivial. Music educators do not have to buy or use 'cute' programmes or music. They need to keep in mind, however, that what children find fascinating, adults often find boring and vice versa. Good programmes, like the best music, can and should be both educationally sound and emotionally satisfying. Computers, coupled with good software, MIDI technology, keyboards, synthesizers and other tools, can provide a wide range of interesting graphics, tone colours, melodies, rhythms and harmonies that can help deepen students' music understanding and enjoyment. The cure for this fear is becoming informed about a wide variety of technological offerings and using them appropriately.

FEAR OF RANDOM SOUNDS

The fear that technology encourages students to produce sounds without understanding what they are doing is not limited to electronic technology. Computers and electronic keyboards do indeed encourage students to produce sounds: students are fascinated with them. Isn't a fascination with sound an interest that music teachers want to encourage? Students will probably not fully comprehend what they are doing in any medium unless music educators help them understand sound in all its variations, components, subtleties and structures. If students fail to grasp what they are doing, the fault is not with technology but with teachers who have not used each student's interest in technology to further his or her understanding of music.

FEAR OF LOSING AESTHETICS

Will aesthetic understanding and expression, creativity and imagination, individuality, social interaction and ensemble experience, and the 'joy' of music be lost if technology is substituted for human teaching? The evidence is clearly otherwise. There are many teachers who are enhancing the achievement of all these ideals through technology. Fundamentally, electronic media fulfill the same function as our current acoustic media (such as pianos, clarinets, and violins): They provide alternative means for human expressiveness and interaction. The difference is that electronic media involve many 'hi-tech' features that most people do not understand and consequently consider foreign to aesthetic values.

Teachers do not need to understand the engineering complexities of the computer or synthesizer to enhance student learning any more than they need to know how to build an acoustically accurate viola, flute, or record player. We already use many things we do not understand technically to further music education; using electronic media is the next logical step in this development.

FEAR OF LIMITED LEARNING

Do students sit alone, mesmerized and unresponsive, while the computer grinds mechanically through its programmes? Nothing could be further from the truth. All the processes involved in music understanding – listening, moving, singing, playing, describing, composing and judging what is aesthetically valuable – can be learned through technology.

The real power of technology is the increased amount and speed of interaction between student and teacher: students are constantly guided to listen, press buttons or keys, sing, or play and they receive immediate feedback on their actions and decisions. Several years ago much of the available music software was written to teach lower level cognitive skills, such as identifying pitch names or naming rhythm symbols, and provided opportunities for only limited responses. This has changed, however, as newer and more sophisticated programmes and equipment (especially those with MIDI capability) have been developed.

FEAR OF LIMITED TRANSFER

Will learning through technology transfer to performance? Transfer does not seem to depend on whether concepts and skills are taught by means of the voice, Orff instruments, recorders, guitars, band instruments, computers, or synthesizers. The significant advantage that computers and electronic instruments have over other media is that the electronic instruments participate in the learning process by responding to student input and by structuring learning. The instruments do more than provide a mechanism for sound production.

The fight against technophobia goes on. Although no vaccine has as yet been developed, this 'disease' can be beaten. Do not be embarrassed if you have technological fears, but do get treatment immediately. Technophobia will not just go away by itself: summon your courage, and call your local technophile for an introductory look at what electronics can do for you. Preview software, investigate hardware, and read reviews. Your teaching will be stronger, and your students will love music even more for your efforts.

Chapter 17

MIDI-assisted composing in your classroom

Sam Reese

A walk through the halls of the music department at Lincoln Junior High School in Park Ridge, Illinois, exposes the passerby to a startling array of sounds. A wide assortment of synthesizer, drum machine, and keyboard sounds squeeze through doors and walls as students experiment with various instruments to produce original compositions and recordings.

The students creating these sounds are enrolled in an elective course called Contemporary Composing. It is a twelve-week class that meets for forty minutes each school day and is open to any student, regardless of that individual's level of musical experience. The course focuses on helping students think and create in some of the same ways that many popular-music composers do today.

For young music students, MIDI technologies can reduce the need for advanced performance skills and higher-level use of staff notation. As a result, larger numbers of students are now able to experience the initial stages of composing original, popular-style music. The emphasis of the Contemporary Composing class is on the creation, development, and extension of musical ideas into complete pieces of music and not on learning music fundamentals, music theory, music performance, or synthesizer programming skills.

The goals of the course include an increased understanding and perceptiveness of the expressive elements of music – melody, harmony, rhythm, form and tone colour – by experimenting with and controlling these elements to produce whole works. This is an approach to learning about the expressive effects of music elements 'from the inside out'. It is an integrative, synthesizing method of working with the elements of music rather than a more analytical process, wherein students study one element of music at a time. We try to assist learners in actively constructing their own understanding, relating new information and concepts to what they already know, and working collaboratively with others.

MIDI AS A MEANS

MIDI technologies are used as a means to develop music understanding, music sensitivity and compositional skills; these technologies are not studied for their own sake. Consequently, we spend very little time teaching students how MIDI systems operate technically.

Since the Contemporary Composing class includes sixteen to twenty students, it is necessary to have multiple small MIDI workstations. We set up five mobile MIDI workstations, each of which includes a computer, a MIDI keyboard, a multi-timbral synthesizer sound module (a stand-alone unit that contains all the sound-producing components of a synthesizer without the keyboard), a drum machine, and a powered speaker (a speaker that has an amplifier built into it so that no other amplification is needed). All of the hardware for a workstation is positioned on a typical classroom computer cart. This makes it possible to easily move the workstations into nearby practice rooms and classrooms so that several groups can work simultaneously without disrupting other groups.

All composing projects are small-group, collaborative projects with three or four students per group. The major means of composing has been multitrack MIDI recording (sequencing) and the loop recording mode of drum machines.

A central theme of the course is that composers often work by creating relatively short musical ideas – motives and phrases – and then develop and extend these ideas into complete musical pieces. These ideas include rhythm patterns, melodic motives or phrases, chord progressions, or simply intriguing tone colours. Thus, we introduce students to skills they need to create musical fragments. Then they alter and manipulate these fragments into longer and more complete phrases and sections.

Within the twelve-week period, students generally have been able to complete three or four composing projects. The typical process for carrying out a project has been an alternation between demonstrations or explanations for the whole class and small-group work to carry out specific tasks at the workstations. It has been challenging but important to divide the process into small enough steps so students can get sufficient hands-on time soon after a new workstation technique or composing concept is introduced. Adolescents are definitely not receptive to long lectures or demonstrations.

KEEP IT SIMPLE

The first project is the creation of an original arrangement of 'Heart and soul' – the piece that most music teachers wish they never had to hear again! The reason for beginning with it is that almost all students have played at least a portion of 'Heart and soul' on the piano before. This makes it possible for them to experience some immediate success by recording parts directly into the sequencer from the keyboard.

The purpose of the project is to develop and extend the musical ideas of 'Heart and soul' in the same way as an arranger would. In addition, the project introduces an initial set of workstation skills to the students. The assignment is to record an arrangement with a bass part, chords, melody and an improvised solo. The form of the piece is assigned and includes an introduction, one play-through of the melody, an improvised solo, a second playing of the melody and a short ending.

Students are taught how to record tracks on the sequencer, how to change MIDI channel settings to select different instrument parts (or tone colours), how to use tape-recorder-style controls, and how to change tempos. Decreasing the tempo of a piece while recording a track, and then playing it back at faster tempo is one important way to reduce the technical demands of playing parts on the keyboard. Students learn to use the 'copy' and 'paste' functions of the sequencer to manipulate, move and alter musical material. This process also reduces the amount of repetitive playing required for inexperienced students to record the parts.

Students develop the musical elements of 'Heart and soul' by creating their own rhythms for the bass and chord parts, by improvising a melody for the second time through, and by creating an original way to end the piece.

The overall reaction of most students was satisfaction with arranging and recording a complete piece of music on their own. I will often hear 'I can't believe we did all of that ourselves'. The students then were motivated to create more original works of increasing complexity.

LAYERED COMPOSITION

The purpose of a second project is to create original patterns or phrases that can be layered together and repeated to create a full texture. An original bass pattern, chord pattern, and melody pattern must be created to fit together rhythmically and harmonically. Although students find it difficult to create longer original phrases or sections, they can successfully create patterns (ostinatos) based on scales or simple chords. This project gives students the opportunity to create original music, but in small amounts at a time. When the patterns are layered together, a complete musical texture is created. More advanced students use these patterns or phrases as motives, which they develop into simple variations as the composition proceeds.

During the project, students learn about a number of music concepts and practice several skills. They work with the concept of a scale by creating a pattern based on the Mixolydian mode, which is often used by rock musicians. They manipulate rhythm by improvising rhythm patterns for their bass, chord and melody parts that match the rhythmic style of a drum-machine pattern. Harmony concepts are studied by learning four basic rock chords (I, IV, V^7, and lowered VII) based on the Mixolydian scale and by creating an original pattern that uses these chords. A bass pattern must also be created that fits the harmonic pattern of the chords. Students experiment with tone colour by selecting synthesizer sounds that complement the overall character or style of their piece.

MIDI workstation skills are enhanced by more extensive use of cut-and-paste functions, by introducing step recording as a way of creating a rapid sixteenth-note ostinato, and by using markers to indicate at which measure the different patterns enter. (Step recording involves recording notes one at a time, while shaping each note as to duration, timbre, loudness, and so forth. If the student does not change the durational parameter, all the notes played will be of the same length – such as sixteenth notes.)

The procedure includes (i) teaching the notes of the Mixolydian scale and the I, IV, V^7, and lowered VII chords and (ii) giving students the time to improvise a variety of bass, chord and melody patterns based on this scale and these chords. After improvising, students select the patterns they believe are most successful. Next, they select a drum-machine pattern and begin to record their bass, chord and melody patterns on separate tracks. Copy-and-paste functions are used to create a number of repetitions of each pattern. A typical form is to gradually introduce the patterns to thicken the texture – first drums, then bass, then chords, then melody – although the students create a number of variations on this plan. The step-recording procedure is used with a percussive sound to add another rhythmic effect that adds additional energy to the expressive quality. The final challenge is to create a satisfactory ending to the piece. The students often do their most creative work in developing their ending section. Although each group is following a similar plan and using related melodic and harmonic material, each composition is unique.

Explanations are extended and enhanced by listening to compositions that use related techniques. 'Piece for synthesizer', a recording that accompanies the *World of Music, Grade 7* general music textbook published by Silver, Burdett & Ginn, is a clear example of the layered form. There are baroque forms such as pasacaglias and chaconnes that make use of repeating phrases within pieces. A popular example is the 'Canon in D' by Pachelbel. Carl Orff's *Carmina Burana* also has a number of sections in which repeating patterns and phrases are layered together to create an exciting, rhythmically charged quality.

BLUES

A third project is the composition of an original blues melody and accompaniment. This project requires students to create longer melodic phrases and assemble them into a typical three-phrase melody that follows the traditional blues chord progression. Students learn melodic concepts of the blues scale, rhythmic and melodic motives, the harmonic progression of the blues based upon primary chords, and reading and playing of syncopated rhythms. In addition, they gain improvisation experience with a blues scale. The MIDI workstation skills students use while doing this project are similar to those used in the layered composition project.

After related study of the history of the blues and listening to several examples of blues pieces, students learn the blues scale and blues chord progression by playing these on song bells or keyboards. We also do beginning improvising with the blues scale. Following this introduction, each student composes his or her own blues melody. Students are expected to be able to play this melody on an instrument and notate it sufficiently so that it can be played in the same way in repeated playings.

Students choose from among six drum-machine songs that the music teacher has prerecorded in different rhythmic styles: jazz, hard rock, rock 'n' roll, electronic pop, Latin and funk. The workstations are used to record a bass part, which is improvised to fit the chords or follows a traditional boogie-woogie bass line.

Chords are recorded with students improvising the rhythm of the chords to fit with the overall rhythmic style of the piece. Finally, an original melody of one member of the group is recorded. This is followed by an improvised solo, and then by a replaying of the melody. Copy-and-paste is again used to reduce the need for repetitive playing of patterns.

RAP COMPOSITION

A final project focuses on rhythm by introducing students to programming original drum-machine patterns and songs. The rhythmic drum-machine parts that students have already created are then used as an accompaniment to an original rap. Students review reading and playing of basic rhythm values and learn the usual role that instruments of the drum set, such as bass drum, snare and hi-hat, play within rhythm patterns. They also learn the different functions and sounds of basic time patterns, fill patterns and ending patterns. They experiment and make decisions about the organization of rhythm patterns into phrases and sections.

After listening to and reading notation for a number of drum-set patterns in a variety of styles, students learn to use the loop recording mode of drum machines. They improvise until they determine rhythm parts that work well together to form a drum-set style rhythm pattern. These are recorded by playing the pads of the machine, and this activity requires rhythmic steadiness and accuracy. Typical fill patterns are studied, improvised and recorded. When several basic time patterns, fill patterns and ending patterns are successfully recorded, a drum-machine 'song' (series of patterns) is recorded. This obliges students to organize their patterns into phrases and sections that fit with the words of their rap they have written earlier. Some groups use the sequencer to record a rhythmic bass part or repetitive chord pattern to add to the texture of the accompaniment. The raps are performed by the students and recorded along with the drum-machine and synthesizer parts on to cassette tape.

All compositions are recorded on to cassette tape and all members of the class receive a cassette of all of the compositions produced during the class. A cassette label is printed with a laser printer, giving the end product a professional appearance. This helps make the outcomes of the class more tangible to students. After all, music isn't 'real' in the eyes of adolescents until it's on a tape.

EVALUATION AND UNDERSTANDING

All compositions are evaluated by all members of the class during group listenings and discussions. Through discussion, two criteria were chosen for judging the success of the pieces: originality and technical skill. Compositions are rated on these criteria by each student, and then the extent of agreement within the class is checked. Discussions focus on the strengths and weaknesses of each composition.

The evaluations by class members are reviewed by the teacher. These evaluations, along with the evaluations of the teacher, are used as the basis for assigning grades for the students.

This approach to developing music understanding and sensitivity is consistent with much of current research on learning that has been carried out by cognitive scientists and psychologists.[1] It emphasizes the need for learners to be active participants in constructing their understanding (by working with the materials of the subject), in relating new knowledge to existing knowledge and in learning from others and helping others learn during collaborative work. The act of composing involves students in these types of learning experiences.

Composing offers students and teachers a powerful way to study how music works, that is, how the elements of music interact to create expressive results. MIDI technologies provide students with tools that enable them to actively engage in the process of musical thinking and creating. Less-experienced students are able to participate in composition because these technologies remove some of the barriers that can be posed by the need for performance skills and staff notation. As we continue to develop MIDI-assisted programmes, we must avoid the temptation to concern ourselves only with producing a pleasing final product through a pre-scribed, step-by-step process that does not involve students in thoughtful reflection and musical problem solving.

SOME MIDI TERMINOLOGY

Drum machine: an instrument that stores drum and other percussion sounds electronically and permits the user to record them in various rhythms, patterns and combinations. The player usually creates the sounds on one or more of a half-dozen 'touch pads' using the fingers or drumsticks. Players can create combinations of multiple percussion sounds by modifying what has been recorded.

Powered speaker: a speaker that has an amplifier built into it so that no other amplification is needed.

Sound module: a stand-alone unit that contains all the sound-producing components of a synthesizer without the keyboard. A sound module may be connected to a keyboard or a computer with a cable.

Step recording: the recording of sounds one note at a time, in which the musician specifies the duration, timbre, loudness and so forth of each note. If a single durational parameter is set, all the notes played will be of the same length, such as a sixteenth note.

NOTE

1 Some current research on learning can be found in the work of Howard Gardner, *The Unschooled Mind* (New York: Basic Books, 1991), and that of Lauren Resnick, *Toward the Thinking Curriculum: Current Cognitive Research* (Alexandria, VA: Association for Supervision and Curriculum Development, 1989).

Chapter 18

Putting listening first
A case of priorities

Philip Priest

Within every view of musicianship we will find those perceptions, skills and responses that we refer to as 'aural'. The need for a label is the result of music having become a subject, an activity to be trained in. For it is only because we refer to printed scores, because we can study music silently, that the need is felt to stress the fundamental and over-riding place of the ear in music. The totally aural tradition of most musics of the world means that they would have no need of the arguments reviewed here, though we can learn much from them. Even for formally-educated, British musicians, the idea of listening as 'the normal mode of all musical experience', is surely undeniable, though Brian Loane's argument (1984) that 'listening is the whole of music education' may be too strong for some.

George Pratt (1990) has challenged the common practice understood by 'aural training' with ideas, developed from a research programme, which broaden and perhaps deepen our understanding of the term. We must all develop a better understanding of what is meant by 'aural' in music education. The use of the term is odd, despite its familiarity to music teachers. Programmes of study in music, particularly those leading to examinations at GCSE or A level or instrumental grades, are broken up according to a syllabus and one section is allocated to aural. Imagine periods of 'visual' training in art education, or 'visual' tests appended to drawing examinations. We have aural culture, aural training, aural skills and, of course, aural tests. The word is used as a noun – even a plural noun, and has developed an organic life of its own. Here are a few reactions by PGCE students to the aural lessons they received in schools, colleges and universities:

'The aural that we were subjected to was either too difficult or too easy.'
'I had no idea how inflexible the teaching of aural would be . . . limited to trying to write down rhythms, melodies and chord progressions as required by exam boards.'
'As soon as they say aural I go deaf . . . notes swim about in my head.'

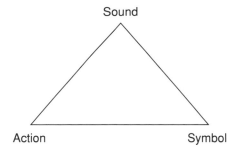

Figure 18.1

The dissection of aural acuity in music into rhythm, pitch, amplitude and so on, in the 1930s, while helpful in an academic sense, has held sway ever since in the form of compartmentalized testing. Worse still, the emphasis on tests has been tied inextricably to notation. 'Aural' has usually meant writing. An assumption of literacy skills is always present, with 'co-ordination of ear and eye' given as the most useful skill of a musician. This link between aural and literacy is strong: it is said that the 'aural mental-image' gives the power to 'hear' printed music silently; and that sound or action can be enough to recall the symbol (Fig. 18.1).

This view of 'aural' forms the basis of books of 'aural method', examination syllabuses and common practice in schools and colleges. The fact that young instrumentalists can read is taken for granted; that many of them seem to have difficulty in hearing is merely regretted; and individual response to music as art does not feature generally in work under the 'aural' heading. As another student said about his aural class at a conservatoire: 'it seemed ridiculous to have a music college full of people who thought they couldn't hear very much'.

To be able to write what is heard accurately enough for another performance is of course a useful skill. But to see aural development in music education in this limited way not only ignores the musician who does not read and music which has not been written; it also means that the concentration on accuracy of pitch and rhythm marginalizes any other quality of music. Yet the idea persists. Of course it is important to encourage children to develop their 'inner ear', as it is called – the ability to recall in silence music that has been heard previously; but the idea that true understanding of music is reserved exclusively for those who can read notation is preposterous. (For those who need reassurance about the value of non-literate intelligence I recommend Howard Gardner's *Frames of Mind*, especially the chapters on 'Music' and 'Kinaesthetic intelligence'.)

Even the widely-used tests of musical ability have been seen as subtly assuming a knowledge of notation, whilst one of the standard aural tests of the examining boards demands an oral description of notation. Small wonder that so many parents and other adults consider themselves to be non-musicians, or even unmusical, because they cannot read.

Notation implies conscious analysis and can lead to an assumption that memory depends on this. This is not true. Tunes we know are not 'coded in memory' by differences in pitches and rhythm alone, and are not recognized like this either. Memory and recognition are complete experiences: the meaning of music is conveyed by the interaction of its parts. By Swanwick's (1979) use of the terms 'materials' and 'elements' of music, we may recognize the familiar problem of students battling with traditional aural testing; not being able to see the wood for the trees, and oblivious to the beauty of either.

Some music educators, trying to move away from a dependence on reading when discussing hearing, acknowledge the fundamental place of aural ability, referring to it as 'thinking in sounds'. They imply that literacy may not be involved at all, but regret that this would make an incomplete musician. Others have been well aware of the need to develop perception and imagery and 'auditory feeling' in order to avoid a mechanical approach to reading. If musical understanding is the objective, different from 'knowing about music', then the ability to use operations in music is clearly more important than knowing the formal names for them; terms such as 'dominant', 'perfect cadence', 'legato', or the note names of pitch or rhythm. All of these familiar materials of music can be understood, and are used, by musicians who do not know these names. There are musical operations which do not have adequate terminology or signs, which cannot be expressed adequately in words. These are much more interesting and challenging because they represent much less secure territory in formal teaching.

Confusion has always been apparent between aural awareness of music as an expressive power and notation and names. Three hundred years ago Christopher Simpson was baffled by 'hard words and obscure terms' and how these related to the 'tuning of a song' (Lawrence, 1978). And Carl Seashore (1938/67), who writes of sensing and imaging sounds and of 'sustained thinking' in them, is very blunt about so-called musicians who cannot do this: 'some musicians are not musical' he writes.

Fifty years ago, writers on music education in this country and in America were enthusing about the need for ear-training to aim for a grasp of phrase and tonality rather than a sort of drill with tests of separated aspects of sound. Yet the response by teachers to the aural tests of examining boards is so often a form of drill: coaching for particular tests; dealing in materials rather than elements, for the most part unrelated to the pupils' instrumental playing and to music they know; and using only the piano. A former student, recalling her first experience of an ABRSM aural test for a grade exam, said, 'It didn't sound like any other music I knew'. The task of practice in these tests is in some cases left to someone-anyone else:

> 'I couldn't do aural, there wasn't a piano.'
> 'I don't deal with aural – I leave that to your class teacher.'
> 'I had heard other people talking about aural but I had never really understood what it was. When I asked my teacher whether we would be doing some she said: "Oh no, we don't need to do any because you are not taking any exams yet".'

'Aural', in the experience of those we teach, should be concerned with sounds in the head and responding to them practically. These can be remembered sound patterns or new, imagined ones. We might depend on some prop or mental reference point which could be aided by notation, but need not be. If such imaging of sounds is considered to be an essential part of behaving like a musician, it should be integrated with other aspects. Then the aural experience would be seen and felt to be at the heart of musicianship, at the heart of performance, at the heart of composition and at the heart of listening, rather than the appendage it sometimes is when the following of notation is insisted on, and for many absorbs all their attention.

Some teachers' work is as soundly based as this; but what is equally true is that children are still emerging from the formal education system as musicians lacking skills and perceptions identified as essential for musicianship. Included among these children are some who became teachers, primary and secondary, class and instrumental. And so the system can so easily perpetuate a cycle of deprivation among formally-taught musicians.

Aurally-based methods do exist in the UK and are used widely; commonly, of course, by musicians learning outside the formal education system. They are used too by those teachers fostering jazz- and rock-inspired groups in schools, by Suzuki teachers for certain instruments, by many of those who train steel bands and by many vocal groups. All of these, however, lean towards the learning of a fixed or teacher-chosen repertoire by rote, with less attention, or perhaps none, given to imaginative exploration of sound; using your instrument to make your own music. Now that such exploration is considered to be an essential feature of the curriculum, we should ask whether this is fostered best by aurally-based methods, and whether it may be frustrated by the habit of using notation.

The influence of reading on the development of skills and musical understanding is very strong. To many, reading notation is such a basic part of musicianship that it hardly needs to be mentioned. Can you imagine the art of choreography developing in the way that musical notation has, to the extent that literacy in it takes over in dance in formal education? In order to learn to dance at school you must read the notation.

Some class teachers believe that literacy skills have been overstressed in the past, but among instrumental teachers there seems to be no choice for those they teach *but* to read. If children who learn instruments, and their teachers, are never seen to operate without reading, a strong impression is given to all other children.

Research studies highlighting the negative aspects of an insistence on musical literacy have been ignored. Many students wishing to pursue music at degree level, and graduates applying to become teachers, view with suspicion and alarm the idea that they should play at all without notation. This is regrettable, but it can be overcome. The effect on those children still struggling with basic technique who are expected always to read while playing is even more unfortunate, for they may be discouraged and give up. In the classroom, the eighth year pupil trying to learn two or three chord shapes on keyboard would become fluent in them much more quickly without books or work sheets to decipher. And in the practice room, pupil and teacher of cornet or clarinet could more usefully have their eyes free for each other rather than fixed constantly at the tutor-book.

Materials for use in school have been criticized for the imbalance shown between the over-stressed learning of symbols and the more necessary aural discrimination. 'Sound before the sign' seems to be interpreted by some as 'sound illustration before the inevitable and obligatory sign'. The intention is surely that sounds should be enjoyed, worked with, chosen and arranged independently of any signs, until the children feel the need to fix their musical ideas graphically. And when they do, increasingly there is available a machine that will do it for them. As a breed, we music teachers are slow to help children realize the inadequacy of musical notation to convey the essentials of music – anything beyond the nuts and bolts. The very basic sheet music produced for chart songs may be an acknowledgement that, since one cannot convey the original in print, a sort of blueprint is best; a ground plan on which to build.

Arguments for the importance of music literacy include the claim for the 'social discipline' of reading and playing a part in ensemble. But this is too often practised at the expense of listening, which tends to be hindered or even obscured completely – especially by the habitual concentration on counting rests. In any case, literacy is only necessary for certain groups playing certain kinds of music.

Before moving on to consider how teaching and learning can take place without omnipresent notation, it may be useful to glimpse how music is taught and caught in some other societies, and to see what can be learned from them.

In Afghanistan there is a form of oral notation, with names for pitch and rhythm, but it is known and used by only professional musicians (Baily, 1979). It is part of the secret science of music, kept secret because it is not written down. The children of professionals are encouraged to observe, learn and join in as soon as possible with their parents' public performances. Amateur music-making is done in private, for the performer's own enjoyment. A more accurate translation of the word for amateur is 'enthusiast'. Children are actively discouraged from wanting to play. A determined teenager has to learn by stealth, creeping out after dark, watching other players from a distance, even denying that s/he has learned in this way, and practising secretly. Do we distinguish between intending amateurs and intending professionals? Should we? Who is more enthusiastic? Do we offer too much instruction? Should public performance be the goal for all?

The music of the Japanese puppet theatre has been systematized for over two hundred years, but apparently without recourse to standardized notation (Motegi, 1984). Traditionally, aural methods are used, based on listening, watching and imitating; though some teachers or schools have developed their own system of notation as an *aide-mémoire,* scribbled in the margin of the script. For performance, however, both libretto and cues must be memorized. It is claimed for these methods that they develop a clear understanding of the music's structure, foster musical imagination, and allow – even demand – freedom of interpretation. Recent attempts to revive wider interest in the genre have been on different lines, resulting in uniformity through the use of tapes and notation from the outset. Pupils who learn by this modern method can perform more quickly, it is acknowledged, but they are said to 'master the form' without being able to 'express the content'. Are these musicians in our schools who have 'mastered the form' but fail to 'express the content'? We refer to such playing as 'unmusical' (or 'playing without the music', as Busoni wrote, in contrast to 'playing without the copy'). Would we be willing, as teachers, to marginalize notation?

A similar form of rudimentary notation was discovered by Colin McPhee for the Balinese gamelan. It was never intended to be read in performance, serving mainly as a reminder of the 'nuclear tones' for specialists. Traditional music was – is – kept alive by group-memory, and new compositions are taught direct to the players by the composer. In McPhee's colourful account some methods of teaching are described, including the singing of tunes before playing them, all depending on acute listening and copying someone else – the teacher or a more advanced player. 'The teacher explains nothing, since for him there is nothing to explain' (McPhee, 1955). Yet the music is not simple – nothing like as simple as some parts our children play in brass and wind band marches, or 'Tunes for strings', which have to be read. Every rehearsal had the pitched instruments accompanied by the 'exuberant' rhythmic drive of the gongs and cymbals. McPhee says he thought it was this background that gave impetus, 'that made these rehearsals go, made these children coherent from the very start'. Have we anything to learn? Music literacy serves music teachers well in so many ways. We may deny that it hinders our own aural awareness at all, and this may be the case. But the argument here is made from the perception of what music is to those who do not read, and to some – the majority – who never will.

Peter Ustinov tells how, on a train journey, he was reading the newspaper, looking across occasionally at a man sitting opposite who was reading an Eulenburg miniature score. The man smiled from time to time and even chuckled with delight as he turned a page. Ustinov says he never felt more inferior in all his life.

Yet if we are to encourage music teachers to downgrade the importance of notation, to defer its introduction, even to do without it or at least put it in its place and concentrate on aural awareness and still to pursue children's development through performance and composition, then some will feel a prop has been removed. It is a useful prop. The trouble is we tend to rely on it too much, because we can, and maybe to insist on it because we know it and they don't. What else do we put in its place? How else can we refer to music? What is there of substance children can learn and be seen – and heard – to learn?

How do trombonists know how far to move the slide? How is it that pianists seem to know where to put their fingers? How do kit drummers become so well co-ordinated with hands and feet? These are the questions in the minds of children, sometimes put to teachers, and the answers all have to do with the psychomotor element in the process of playing a musical instrument, which has been undervalued by teachers.

Kemp (1990), writing on kinaesthesia in music, reminds us that we are dealing with both the sense of touch and of movement; with both the physical feeling – through fingers, mouth or feet – of an instrument, poised to produce a certain known sound, and with the movement of various parts of the body to change this sound – its duration, timbre, dynamic or pitch. The distinction is between the tactile and the kinaesthetic.

Analyses attach much importance to 'mechanized processes' in the development of musical skills on instruments (Priest, 1989). These are developed through repetition, with 'each isolated action in the series becoming a stimulus to the next'. There is general agreement among psychologists that musical performance must be based on the 'mechanization of the sound–action relationship' (Mainwaring, 1951). Some music teachers might react to the use of the term 'mechanized' and confuse it with 'mechanical' performance. 'Mechanized' refers to the way in which basic common patterns of sound (for example, scale passages, chords) are produced on instruments – how they are learned and how executed. The player is still free subtly to change the way they are played – in tempo, gradation of tone, or in any other way. The point is that s/he is not having to concentrate on the basic action of fingers, arms and mouth, but on the sound and its effect. If a player's conscious mind is to be on the aesthetic aspect of the music then there must be a large degree of 'automatic

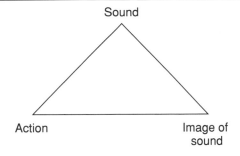

Figure 18.2

performance'. In the early stages of learning, both teacher and learner must consciously attend to physical skills. Physicians, particularly neurologists, give very detailed accounts of the fine changes in all forms of physical movement and sensation in singing and playing that must be experienced and learned (Phillips, 1977).

In most analyses the eye is involved, responding to notation. But there is a suggestion that the aural image of the sound might be enough to stimulate the action, once learned. Now, if this image of a sound can be experienced without a visual (notation) symbol, either real or imagined, and if this is sufficient to be able to reproduce that sound on an instrument, then we seem to have a different triangle. We now have a similar link between an aural image, the action to produce it and the sound itself – playing by ear (Fig. 18.2).

But how can we best develop in young beginners this familiarity with the instrument; this concentration on sound shapes rather than on their graphic representation, on the thing itself rather than pictures of it? By acknowledging ways of learning kinaesthetically.

Among others (see Kemp, 1990), here are two. First, by valuing experiment. Interest in soundmaking activities through experiment is often thought of in connection with very young children, but such interest can be observed in people of any age; and perhaps could be allowed, or encouraged, more by music teachers, because the feedback of the sound produced by the action is the greatest aid. Once a sequence of movements, different in some degree from our previous attempt, produces a sound that pleases us, our classmates or our teachers, then we can repeat it, return to it and remember it like Skinner's pigeons.

Second, by accepting the importance of the 'image of an action' (Priest, 1989). This can include all forms of pretend or imaginary action springing from musical performance – voluntary or involuntary. One example is the extrovert members of a seventh year class miming the action of a trombone as soon as it is mentioned. Another is the silent 'bowing' (arm movements) that usually accompanies the marking of string parts. It is the common experience of instrumentalists, when listening to others play, to 'feel' the actions of the players, to share the sensation of playing. In its most gross form this might include very definite movements of limbs and digits, clearly perceptible and even disturbing to others. Usually there will be only tiny muscular changes to various parts of the body, involving the diaphragm and the larynx, even though they need not result in a sound. Instrumental teachers may recognize in this the way they are ready for action as a pupil plays – breathing with the phrases even with stringed instruments, ready to burst into a vocal version of the music being attempted. The teacher's 'ghosting' action is supposed to encourage the player.

But a fundamental point has been made about imaging the action: 'the instrumentalist is apt to use fingers, etc. in cognizing music' (Vernon, 1933). Or to use Kemp's words, 'knowing through whole-body experience' (Kemp, 1990). Here we have the idea of cognition that comes from practical action associated with sound but independent of signs and labels. 'Doing is active, analytic, critical and objective'. Kinaesthesis is valuable 'in drumming fingers on thighs with, say, trumpet fingering, or forming the shape of chords for an imaginary keyboard on the table, as an aid – tactile or kinaesthetic – in the same way that a visual cue is an aid. And by 'visual cue' in this context, we should think not of notation or other written instructions, but of seeing the teacher or another player. The learner sees an action which produces a sound – a hand position, arm movement or inclination of the head – and imitates it, hoping for the same result. Aural, visual, kinaesthetic and tactile senses operate together, and an attempt can be made to produce a similar sound to the teacher's model. The development or growth in skill and powers of expression through experience will be with the continued aid of a model, usually the teacher. Close imitation of the action of others is a common trait, forming the basis of the work of mimics, actors and dancers. Kinaesthesis has been described as the 'sixth sense': 'the capacity to act gracefully, to apprehend directly the actions or the dynamic abilities of other people and objects' (Gardner, 1983).

All musical performance, then, has an important psychomotor element. Playing without notation, in its many forms, is likely to be especially dependent on this element. The action of playing is real, and needs no intermediary between it and the aural image. The sounds themselves, and the means to produce them, form the only substance necessary to play. Even if the name and sign are known, still the physical means to produce the sounds might give a stronger identity to that sound for some players. The *feel* of playing low F on trombone, or of grabbing a diminished seventh chord on a keyboard, is important to the player. For some it may be the strongest image of the sound, or even the only one. The image of the action can conjure up the image of the sound. The skill of playing is acquired, at least in part, experimentally and in imitation of a model. But however important the psychomotor element, the aural image comes first. If a child is about to play a tune or chord sequence from memory, s/he might go through the note-names, or might rely on 'motor memory'; but the most important thing is that s/he should recall the sound of the tune.

REFERENCES

Baily, J. (1979) 'Professional and amateur musicians in Afghanistan', *World of Music* 212.

Gardner, H. (1983) *Frames of Mind*, Heinemann.

Kemp, A. (1990) 'Kinaesthesia in music and its implications for developments in microtechnology'. *British Journal of Music Education* 7(3).

Lawrence, I. (1978) *Composers and Music Education*, Scholar Press.

Loane, B. (1984) 'On "listening" in music education', *British Journal of Music Education* 1(1).

McPhee, C. (1955) 'Children and music in Bali', in Meade and Wolferson (eds) *Childhood and Contemporary Cultures*, University of Chicago Press.

Mainwaring, J. (1951) 'Psychological factors in the teaching of music', *British Journal of Educational Psychology* XXI,Part II.

Motegi, K. (1984) 'Aural learning in Gidayu-bushi music of the Japanese puppet theatre', *Yearbook for Traditional Music* 16.

Phillips, C. (1977) 'Brains and hands', in Critchley and Henson (eds) *Music and the Brain*, Heinemann.

Pratt, G. (1990) *Aural Awareness*, Open University Press.

Priest, P. (1989) 'Playing by ear: its nature and application to instrumental teaching', *British Journal of Music Education* 6(2).

Seashore, C. (1938/67) *Psychology of Music*, McGraw Hill/Dover.

Swanwick, K. (1979) *A Basis for Music Education*, NFER-Nelson.

Vernon, P. (1933) 'The apprehension and cognition of music', *Proceedings of the Music Society.*

Chapter 19

Designing a teaching model for popular music

Peter Dunbar-Hall

THE NEED FOR A TEACHING MODEL FOR POPULAR MUSIC

Popular music, despite its existence on syllabuses in various forms, is still a problem area for many music teachers. This is due to a number of factors: both the study of popular music styles and methods for teaching them are missing from many tertiary courses; the mainly art music backgrounds of many music teachers act against an understanding of popular music; there is a shortage of critical material in this area to which music teachers can refer; and an accepted model for teaching popular music has not yet developed. It is the lack of a teaching model that is the concern of this article.

A teaching model is a framework of ideas about a subject through which that subject can be taught. Such models are often derived from implicit ideas about the subject. In music, these may include beliefs about what music is acceptable for study or is culturally appropriate, ways that music can be analysed, and definitions of music itself. A teaching model usually precedes day-to-day curriculum planning and in this way influences teaching methods and the selection of content. Because it is based on the nature of its subject, a teaching model also expresses values about and attitudes to that subject through the process known as a 'hidden curriculum'.

The problem of a teaching model for popular music is partly due to the fact that music teachers from art music backgrounds automatically know how music of the western tonal tradition is taught, but lack the same instinctive teaching knowledge for popular music. This is because the study and teaching of western tonal music have been their method of training as teachers and, even before that, a daily activity through the learning of an instrument. In this way an understanding of western art music can be seen as a type of cultural heritage for such teachers. This cultural heritage precludes understanding of the ways popular music might be taught.

These are basic differences between art music and popular music which make the ways of studying the former unsuitable for the latter. Analyses of tonal plans typical of the study of art music are a good example of this. In this type of analysis, key and modulation are related to formal plans, and melodic development is seen as a way of expressing harmony. In such analyses the elements of melody and harmony are usually studied at the expense of rhythm. These analytical assumptions cannot be made for popular music. Popular music does not rely on the establishment, movement away from and return of a key that is the basis of much tonal art music. Popular music can require a greater understanding of rhythm and texture, rather than of melody and harmony. Processes that are not prominent in much art music, for example, improvisation and repetition, become important in popular music and need to be studied. In addition the underlying difference between art music and popular music which can be seen in their respective philosophical bases make the methods of studying art music unsuitable for popular music. Art music is created and notated regardless of whether it is ever performed; popular music usually exists in performance and is not primarily a notated music. This short list of simple differences between art and popular music demonstrates that the analytical methods suitable for one are not necessarily applicable to the other and that there is a need for alternative ways to study popular music. Because ways of studying music depend on the prior construction of a teaching model, it is necessary to construct models through which popular music can be taught. One suitable way of designing a teaching model for popular music is through consideration of its etic and emic characteristics.

ETIC AND EMIC PROPERTIES OF MUSIC

At least since the time of Plato two ways of perceiving music have been discussed by numerous writers in an attempt to define music's meaning. In the first of these, music is studied as a collection of elements (pitch, duration, timbre) and how these have been handled to make pieces of music. In the second, the emotional meaning given to music by its creators and listeners is considered. Even though the terminology of writers differs, there is agreement that music involves both objective fact and subjective response. Mayer explains that 'music . . . is said to communicate emotional and aesthetic meanings as well as purely intellectual ones . . . [and is] a puzzling combination of abstractness with concrete emotional experience' (1956: vii). Lippman discusses what he calls the 'familiar referential aspects of musical meaning, and . . . form or structure' (1981: 184). While Doubravova describes the two sides of music as 'meanings of natural and anthropological nature' (1984: 33). Middleton uses the terms 'etic' ('objective and autonomous') (1990: 175) and 'emic' ('the product of cultural knowledge') (*ibid.*) to refer to these ways of defining music. What is clear is that to all these writers music can be discussed both as a set of universal elements, and also as a symbolic object that carries meaning dependent on cultural interpretation. The former of these approaches is etic, the latter, emic.

The use of the terms 'etic' and 'emic' comes to music from anthropology (for example, Geertz, 1973; Levi-Strauss, 1964), and originates in the linguistic concepts of phonetic (the study of sounds) and phonemic (the study of meaning). The idea that music could be taught through consideration of both its etic and emic levels is found in the literature of music education where it is referred to as the study of inherent (etic) and idiomatic (emic) musical concepts. For example:

> if music education began with inherent concepts which pertain to all music . . . students would not make . . . value judgements which apply only to some music (*idiomatic concepts*) . . . but would be able to consider all music without bias.
>
> (Choksy *et al.*, 1986: 16f)

The etic approach to music is found in many syllabuses in which music is studied through consideration of its elements. The current importance of this type of study dates from changes in educational thinking that took place in the 1960s. The most important of these changes was the replacement of content specific syllabuses with ones that focus on processes. In music, this involved the switch from syllabuses which were designed around the study of selected pieces of music, to ones that encouraged the study of any music that could teach how music worked. This change in direction led to a broadening of the ways music is studied and taught. It challenges the hold of traditional analysis on music education, replacing music as a collection of historical repertoires with music as examples of how music works. Because this later view of music education studies the question 'how does this piece function?' instead of the former 'who wrote this, and why is it great?' it represents a paradigm shift in music education for many teachers. Because it focuses on music, and not the people who wrote it, it also allows any music to be used as the basis of study: early music, music of non-western origin, and popular music.

The emic, or interpretative, way of studying music provides a way of understanding what music means to its creators and listeners. This is based on the assumption that different types of music are perceived by their listeners as having national, religious or cultural meanings. This can be broken down into two areas: generally, music as ideology, and specifically, how ideologies are expressed through musical styles. The idea that music can be seen as ideology is expressed by Wolff when she states that:

> works of art . . . are not closed, self-contained and transcendent entities, but are the product of specific historical practices on the part of identifiable social groups in given conditions, and therefore bear the

imprint of the ideas, values and conditions of existence of those groups and their representatives in particular artists.

(Wolff, 1981: 49)

An example of this approach is the common academic pursuit of studying popular music as the means of expressing political messages (see Frith, 1981; Street, 1986; Denselow, 1989; Szatmary, 1991).

Popular music exists as a set of related musical styles, for example, punk rock, ska, heavy metal, thrash, folk rock, jazz rock, reggae and funk (Dunbar-Hall and Hodge, 1989; Charlton, 1990). To some writers, these styles of popular music are representative of sub-cultural lifestyles and their associated beliefs. Hebdige (1979), for example, analyses the importance of music styles of punk rock and reggae to skinhead culture and Rastafarians respectively. As has been discussed elsewhere (Dunbar-Hall, 1992) this can be shown by a diagram in which a style of music represents a lifestyle, and this lifestyle, in its turn, represents a set of beliefs or a philosophy:

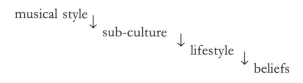

The combination of the etic and emic approaches to music can provide a model for teaching popular music for a number of reasons. First, the etic level provides musicological information, something lacking in the literature on popular music. Frith's comment that 'rock, despite the millions of words devoted to it, is still seldom subject to musical analysis' (1998: 176) is echoed as recently as 1990 by Middleton: 'musicology, "the scientific study of music", . . . should study popular music. . . . With a few exceptions . . . it has not done so' (1990: 103).

Second, a combination of etic and emic studies of popular music sets up a disciplined approach that follows a standard procedure of analysis and data collection, followed by interpretation and comment. In this way the teaching of popular music is given an academic framework in which to work. Third, if music is defined as the combination of three factors: creation (composition); works of art (pieces of music); and reception (listening and interpretation) – between them the etic and emic studies of popular music can cover all three areas. The etic level concerns examples of music for their musical construction. The emic levels can show how music's meaning is interpreted by its creators and listeners:

creation . . . . . the work of art . . . . . reception.
(emic)   (etic)   (emic)

APPLICATION

An example of the combination of etic and emic studies of popular music can demonstrate how a teaching model based on them can be designed.

1 Etic

The song 'Exodus', by Bob Marley and the Wailers, is performed by Bob Marley and a vocal backing group. Accompaniment is provided by a lineup of electric guitars, drumkit, a brass section, electronic organ, and extra percussion (including congas and tambourine). The song has a rhythmic profile that includes a bass guitar ostinato,

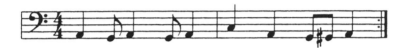

Figure 19.1   Bass ostinato

which also appears on the lead guitar and in the brass instruments. A 'one drop' (a single note on snare and bass drum on the third beat of the bar) noticeable at the beginning of the song,

Figure 19.2   Bass drum rhythm

the repeated tambourine rhythm,

Figure 19.3   Tambourine rhythm

and layers of rhythms on congas, hi-hat, and snare drum all add to the song's rhythms.

Melodically, the song uses a hookline,

Ex - o- dus.   Move- ment   of   Jah peo - ple

Figure 19.4 Hookline

which is employed to mark the beginnings of the song's three vocal sections. Each of these sections is made up of the hookline followed by four call and response lines between Marley and the backing vocalists. The responses are all versions of the motive,

Figure 19.5 Response motive

depending on the amount of syllables that have to be fitted in. Two examples are:

and look   with - in

and

we're   go - ing   to   our   fath - er's   land

Figure 19.6 Two responses

while two responses (repeats of the same line) add the note 'd'.

with the life you're li - ving

Figure 19.7 Responses with 'd'

Marley's calls use five melodic shapes:

(a)   men and peo-ple will   fight you down

(b)   let me tell you, if   you're not   wrong

(c)   so we're go - nna   walk

(d)   we the gen - er - a - tion

(e)   op - en your eyes

Figure 19.8 Marley's five call shapes

of which (a), (b) and (c) each occur once, the song becoming alternations of versions of (d) and (e).

Harmonically, the song is static, consisting only of an A minor chord resulting from the ostinato and the build up of layers of melodic material. In this way, 'Exodus' can be analysed to show the use of limited melodic material over a rhythmic accompaniment. Processes of repetition, alternation between soloist and backing group, and voices and instruments, and the use of motivic development are essential characteristics of the song.

2 Emic

The emic considerations of this song cover two areas: the creation of style, and the sub-cultural implications of that style.

1 Style: The musical characteristics of this song are typical of reggae. Reggae is a style of Jamaican popular music that developed from a combination of Caribbean, African and American musics in the 1960s. The prominence of the bass guitar ostinato, its contrasting syncopated and non-syncopated rhythms, the use of a one drop on the bass drum, the build up of layers of rhythm on both melodic and percussion instruments and the use of a rock style lineup of bass and lead guitar and drumkit supplemented by a brass section, electronic organ and extra percussion instruments (especially congas) are traits of reggae style (see Bergman, 1985; Davis and Simon, 1983). The half-speed feel created by the one drop, which gives the effect of a rhythmically augmented backbeat, is also typical of reggae.

2 Sub-cultural implications: Reggae assumes meaning for its Jamaican listeners as one of the musical styles associated with the Rastafarian religion. Rastafarianism is a black consciousness religion that deifies the late Ethiopian emperor, Hailie Selassie, from whose African title, Ras Tafari, it takes its name. The perception of Africa as the original and ultimate home of black peoples is a fundamental Rastafarian belief. Musical clues to these beliefs are embedded in reggae.

The lyrics of 'Exodus' include the following: 'Exodus, movement of Jah people', 'we're leaving Babylon, we're going to our father's land (Our Father's Land?)'. The word 'exodus' recalls the use of Biblical reference to the same idea (freedom) in Negro spirituals. In Rastafarian terms, 'Babylon' refers to the poor living conditions of Jamaicans of African descent (slavery, white domination). 'Jah' is the Rastafarian word for God; 'Jah people' are the Rastafarians. The song expresses a wish for movement from present conditions to better ones through the analogy of Africa as a desired home.

References to Africa are echoed in reggae through musical means. In this song this includes the contrasting syncopation and non-syncopation of the bass ostinato, and the use of layers of rhythms to build up a complex texture. The alternation of solo and group in 'call and response' type patterns and the pentatonic nature of the song (the 'b' of Marley's third motive appearing only once in the vocal parts) could also be interpreted as deriving from African music. To Rastafarians, reggae is a form of religious music that refers to Africa both in its lyrics and through their accompanying music.

After its local Jamaican success, reggae was introduced to world-wide audiences in the mid-1970s. Its subsequent spread was along two separate paths. First, reggae's links to black consciousness led to the style being taken up by other black, but non-Jamaican, musicians in songs that express black/white political ideas. Examples of this are Stevie Wonder ('Happy Birthday', 'Master Blaster'), New Zealand Maori groups (for example, Herbs), and some Australian Aboriginal rock groups (for example, Coloured Stone, No Fixed Address) (see Breen, 1989). This is an emic use of reggae style. Second, the musical style of reggae was imitated by white musicians; reggae copied in this way had become another commercial style of popular music open to use by anyone. Examples of this etic use of the style are Blondi's 'The Tide is High', and Sting's 'Roxanne'.

The etic and emic characteristics of this song can be made into a model for the teaching of popular music in the following way. The etic and emic sides of the song have become two parallel streams running through the model. The places in the model where these two streams coincide and can

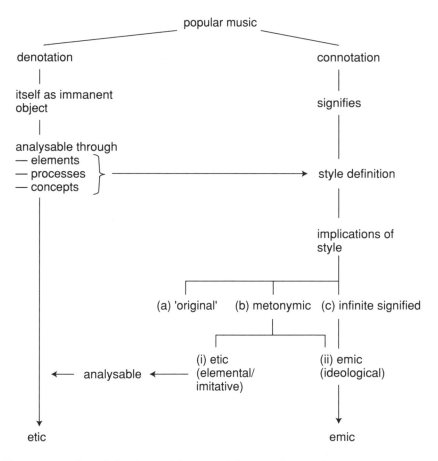

Figure 19.9 An etic/emic teaching model for popular music

be linked in teaching are shown by horizontal arrows. Notice should be made of the division of 'implications of style' into three areas: (i) original; (ii) imitated; and (iii) unlimited. The 'original' implications of style are those that belong to the originators of the style, its first creators and listeners. The 'imitated' implications are those that follow when the style is copied, both by musicians that agree with the music's original meanings and also by those that use the style commercially (without ideological implications). The 'unlimited' implications consist of any other meanings that a listener cares to give the music. The interaction of the etic and emic levels as a teaching model for popular music can be shown in Figure 19.9.

CONCLUSION

As long as a lack of developed teaching models for popular music exists, popular music's place in music education, despite popular music's appeal to students and richness as a source of teaching material, will stagnate. Because it is based on the recognition of music's two-sided character as the combination of analysable facts and interpreted meanings, a teaching model based on the etic and emic characteristics of popular music includes consideration of the range of qualities that make up any piece of music. The comprehensiveness of this method could benefit both the teaching of popular music, and its standing as an area of research.

REFERENCES

Bergman, B. (1085) *Reggae and Latin Pop*, Poole, Dorset: Blandford.

Breen, M. (1989) *Our Place: Our Music*, Canberra: Aboriginal Studies Press.

Charlton, K. (1990) *Rock Music Styles: A History*, Dubuque: Brown.

Choksy, L. R., Abramson. R., Gillespie, A. and Woods, D. (1986) *Teaching Music in the Twentieth Century*, Englewood Cliffs NJ: Prentice-Hall.

Davis, S. and Simon, P. (1983) *Reggae International*, London: Thames & Hudson.

Denselow, R. (1989) *When the Music's Over: The Story of Political Pop*, London: Faber & Faber.

Doubravova, J. (1984) 'Musical semiotics in Czechoslovakia and an interpersonal hypothesis of music', *International Review of the Aesthetics and Sociology of Music* 15(1) 31–8.

Dunbar-Hall, P. (1992) 'Semiotics as a method for the study of popular music', *International Review of the Aesthetics and Sociology of Music* 22(2): 119–25.

Dunbar-Hall, P. and Hodge, G. (1989) *A Guide to Rock and Pop*, Sydney: Science Press.

Frith, S. (1978) *The Sociology of Rock*, London: Constable.

Frith, S. (1981) *Sound Effects: Youth, Leisure and the Politics of Rock 'n' Roll*, New York: Pantheon.

Geertz, C. (1973) *The Interpretation of Cultures*, New York: Basic Books.

Hebdige, D. (1979) *Subculture: The Meaning of Style*, London: Methuen.

Levi-Strauss, C. (1964) *The Raw and the Cooked*, New York: Peregrine.

Lippman, E. (1981) 'The Dilemma of Musical Meaning', *International Review of the Aesthetics and Sociology of Music* 12(2): 181–202.

Meyer, L. (1956) *Emotion and Meaning in Music*, Chicago: University of Chicago Press.

Middleton, R. (1990) *Studying Popular Music*, Ballmoor: Open University Press.

Street, J. (1986) *Rebel Rock: The Politics of Popular Music*, Oxford: Blackwells.

Szatmary, D. (1991) *Rockin' in Time: A Social History of Rock and Roll*, Englewood Cliffs NJ: Prentice-Hall.

Wolff, J. (1981) *The Social Production of Art*, London: Macmillan.

DISCOGRAPHY

Legend: The Best of Bob Marley and the Wailers, (1984), Island Records RML 52042.

Chapter 20

Classroom improvisation

Derek Bailey

Adapting the only proven effective way of teaching improvisation, the traditional way as exemplified by the Indian method, to teaching in a classroom raises many problems: maintaining the necessary degree of empiricism; maintaining the non-documentary, purely practical character of the activity; avoiding the establishment of a set of generalized rules; and always allowing an individual approach to develop – these are essentials which, in a classroom situation with, perhaps, a large group of people, are in danger of being lost. And the only places where, to my knowledge, improvisation is successfully taught in the classroom is in those classes conducted by practising improvisers.

In England the first musician to run an improvising class was John Stevens. Stevens has always been a teacher. From the time in the middle 1960s when he emerged as the leading organizer of free music in London, having an idea, for Stevens, has been only a prelude to persuading his friends and colleagues to adopt it. Not surprisingly, his improvisation classes have been successful. Many people who subsequently became regular players have at one time or another attended his classes, many of them meeting each other, and free improvisation, for the first time through him.

He described to me how he came to be teaching improvisation.

I don't know where it started. Something that I often found myself doing long before I started playing free music or almost any music was grabbing people to play, I remember getting together with a brass band cornet player in the army. There was no one else in the block at that time and I said to him 'come in here and play' and he said 'what shall I play then?' and I said 'play anything you like and I'll drum with it'. He said 'but I can't do that'. And I said 'but you can – just blow a note – any note– and I'll play this and you play that'. And so that was a sort of beginning. And when I teach now it's not that different.

You know I've always been interested in large ensembles. Well, quite often, in order to get one together it would be necessary to have people in the ensemble who, although they were open to playing the sort of music we were playing, would also be professional musicians. I mean that in the bad sense. When somebody is a professional musician it often means that their involvement is a bit limited. So, I turned more towards people who were actually getting off on the music but not necessarily playing it. People who were excited by the fact that there was a group of people who were struggling towards some sort of group experience within a free improvisation. These were the listeners and what was required of them would be a real feeling for what was going on. And quite often there were people who were more spirited – more involved in the activity – off the stand than some of those who were on it. There were always people such as the regular members of the Spontaneous Music Ensemble who were totally involved but there might be people playing with us who were less involved.

I remember once in the Little Theatre Club suggesting to the audience that if they wanted to take part there was something they could do in relation to us that was simple and which would create a collective experience within the club. And they did it – and it was a nice experi-ence and some of them, because of hearing us play and because of that experience, started taking up instruments. Their approach to taking up instruments was based on their having listened to us and the way we were playing our instruments so that was the beginning. It was the beginning of people asking me questions and the beginning of me getting involved with people other than developed musicians. Up to then it had always been people like yourself or Evan, developed musicians, people who had gone through other music.

So it started really with the audience at the Theatre Club which actually developed into a group. And because it varied from people who had just started playing to people who had been playing a little longer, then what I would do is get them to do something like – say – inhale deeply, play a long note, as evenly as possible, and get into a collective continuum as a group. Initially, what everyone is looking for is comfort. So if they start on one note and it provides difficulties, they change to something more comfortable. Once they are comfortable with this process of inhaling, exhaling and blowing a note, then they can allow the note to change in sympathy with the group. So that is simple enough for anyone to do. And that includes people using penny whistles, or if they have no instruments, their voices. Another thing that I see as important, in relation to working with groups of people, is staying in touch with the whole group of people all the time. Keeping watch for the equivalent of the little kid at school who is shy – who feels the more things are going on the more he is excluded. And the way I would set up something would always be in direct relationship with that person feeling comfortable. That's a priority. So the method, or process, that you are teaching has to be simple enough to communicate easily to the group as a whole, and for all of them to be able to do it. But it also has to be demanding enough of concentration to satisfy those who are more developed musicians. So, for instance, in the continuum exercise, the long note thing, the breathing is one part that any musician can concentrate on and find useful.

Another thing I would use is something else which is basic to people, like numbers. Just counting numbers or using words. Say, for instance, the use of words. A phrase. We'll use the phrase 'a phrase' as an example. If you are going to say 'a phrase' and repeat it, you are going to say it in your own way and it's not so far removed from singing. You're not actually singing, you are saying the words, but in a musical context that can be very close. And because it's simple, when somebody repeats it they realize how close they are to taking part in music. So if you say 'a phrase', accenting the 'a', you have already provided at least a rhythmic element. And that might seem better, more complete, if you say 'a phrase is'. In which case you've improvised.

This thing is so wide and over the years I've developed what you might call pieces and exercises, which do actually work. I don't know how many there are, but it's a lot. They are not written down. I carry them in my head. They are just things that I can use. They are my tools, shall we say. Some of them deal with rhythm, others deal with group involvement and spontaneity. By that I mean moment by moment involvement. The piece will be designed to require a moment by moment involvement and you are trapped into that. It gives them an experience of how quickly they can relate to each other and forces them to keep their ears open to the rest of the group. So the pieces come out of a need to want to get across a certain experience I might have had. I found the best way to transmit information that I had was to actually do it. I get them to do it in the hope that they will then share my experience of that thing and so know it in the way that I know it. I have this complete faith that if the players can be made to feel a thing working they will then know the essential part about how to do it.

When I go out to do a workshop, though I've been doing it for a long time, as I approach the place there is no real confidence in me about what is going to happen. I always have the same sort of feeling. I can never take it for granted. And walking into the room I'm always apprehensive. And sometimes I wonder 'What am I doing? I'm still doing this and worrying about it'. And there was one period recently which, because of other problems, was particularly hard. And as I travelled towards the place I would think: 'I'll have to give this up. I just don't have that sort of energy any more'. Then I would get there, walk into the room, and there would be about fifteen people in there all playing their arses off – great! The impact was just beautiful. And they, the 'pupils', got me there during that time. Then it was easy. The energy came from them.

What's interesting, one of the things that I see as important, is this: I've had to try and avoid a situation where they relied on me to come in and set the whole thing up. I made a rule: I said to them 'You're coming here because you're supposed to want to play. This is a room in which you can play, so, as soon as you get in this room you are going to prove you want to play by getting on and playing. If you don't want to do that, none of what I'm doing here makes any sense whatsoever. If there are four or two or even if you are the first to arrive, as soon as you get here – start playing. And if someone comes who's new to the class then it's the responsibility of the people who are experienced in the class to invite the newcomer to play. In a sense, that is what it is about'. Well, that took a long time to initiate but now there are always people playing together. And now it provides me with a great lift.

The thing about workshops, or improvisation classes, is that you will have some people for, say, three weeks on the trot, and there is something developing. It's becoming almost like a group. Then, a couple of new people will come in. Now, you have to be prepared to let go of the development you have and go wherever the addition of those new people takes it. Whether they can play or not. It's got to go back to a common point.

What I have to keep in touch with at the workshop is a feeling of freedom about playing music, and coupled with that, the feeling of wanting other people to have that same freedom.

Most teaching concerns itself with transmitting a type of proficiency, with imparting a skill, technical ability or know-how. The aim of teaching usually is to show people how to do something. What Stevens aims at, it seems to me, is to instil in the people he works with enough confidence to try and attempt what they want to do *before* they know how to do it. Encouraging them to work empirically, and trusting that they will then learn, with some guidance, from the attempted playing experience.

My object is to incorporate all the people in the room in an experience. A free playing experience. (Relatively free because my presence there as a 'teacher' is always a bit weird.) You get them to apply themselves to this joint experience and some point arrives where we are all 'doing it'. When they walk away from there, that's when the other bit comes in. They are going to examine that experience and try to decide how it happened and what they did to help it happen. And they are going to try and work out how to make it happen again. And the teaching comes in when you provide them with the group experience. Which they provide themselves anyway. And even though this is to do with free playing and it is possible to enter into this without being able to play in tune, or to be able to do anything really, if you are going to continue in music – any kind of music – that group activity experience should be useful to any musical situation you might find yourself in. So it has a general usefulness, I think.

We talked about the non-improviser and went through the business dealt with in a previous chapter of how the non-improviser is often a musician who is blocked off from improvising by his training. A training which builds up an attitude towards playing music which prohibits the *attempt* to improvise:

> If somebody says to me 'I can't improvise!' – and they could be somebody with the biggest chunk of classical training imaginable in their background – I would find that very inspiring. Because I know that within a very short time they will be doing it and saying 'Oh, is that it?'. And then they will do it again. You see, it's the most natural thing in the world.

Subsequently, John Stevens collected his experience of teaching in this way into a book, *Search and Reflect*, which is now used as the basis of all teaching carried out by Community Music of London, who also publish it.

***

A musician whose approach to improvising is in many ways totally different to that of John Stevens is the Dutch drummer Han Bennink. For a long time he took, jointly with Misha Mengelberg (his partner in a regular improvising duo), a weekly class in free improvisation. Teaching at a conservatory, the *Muziekschool* in Haarlem, Holland, meant that the people taught by Han Bennink were, unlike those in John Stevens' classes, trained musicians. We had the following discussion about his approach to teaching them free improvisation.

> I do nothing when I go there.
> *Nothing?*
> We play records sometimes – say Korean music. Maybe we talk about jazz – how it was. We get them to talk about themselves.
> *Do you play with them?*
> Yes, we use those little rules we used to use years ago, you know. Split them into groups – get quiet instruments to play very loud – loud instruments very quiet – play staccato passages – long lines – we use those sort of indeterminate scoring instructions. We used to divide the day into three parts, one part theory, one part analysis, one part playing. Now Misha and I go as the duo – as though we were going to play a gig. We play a little, stop and discuss it, maybe Misha analyses it. Maybe we all talk about it. We keep busy. Everything develops from that. We try and give a little energy to the pupils.
> *Give energy to the pupils?*

I do nothing when I go there. I ask them to think of their own ideas. Any person who is busy with music can think of better ideas than I can. So what I try is to get the ideas coming from the pupils. When it comes to the point that they offer nothing then, of course, I've got some tricks.
Tricks?

If they are not producing anything themselves, then I have some simple statements, some ideas, on which we can work to provoke them, to start them off. For instance, last week I took a radio and tuned it to the end of the FM scale where you can hear a sort of code, here in Holland. It repeats but after a couple of seconds it's altering – it's that sort of sign, you know. Well, we take that sign and we analyse it, find the notes, the rhythms and we start to play with it. This week I'll take a kettle with a whistle which, when it boils, produces different pitches in rather an odd, unpredictable way. If it is necessary, we will use that. If it doesn't work out too well you can always say it wasn't your cup of tea.

After a suitable pause, Han returned to the idea.

There you go, it's just the idea – the kettle – certain tones, what's happening with the water and why do you boil water. Is it music and what makes music and what doesn't make music? Examining the idea from every angle – being busy with the idea. That's the whole thing. Looking for each way to come to the middle of it. You can take anything – a piece of paper, a record.

The people Han and Misha teach are either graduates or in their last year at the conservatory, and in addition to being composers and teachers all possess a fairly high level of instrumental ability.

Many of them improvise anyway, you see. Some play the blues or something. Always a borrowed music. Narrow. We try and introduce a broader scale of improvising – as broad as daily life. We are teaching them to make music out of their own background, not someone else's background. Learning what you are. In my eyes that's all you can do. Let people find out what they are and where they are and where their musical influences and preferences come from. Teach them to explore their own background.

It will have become obvious, I hope, that many of the characteristic features of idiomatic improvisation are to be found in free improvisation. In some particulars what can be said about one area of improvisation can be said about all areas. It is true of teaching. The traditional way of learning to improvise – studying with an experienced improviser in a practical way – joining him in his work – is what is offered to their students by John Stevens and Han Bennink.

Chapter 21

Instrumental teaching as music teaching

Keith Swanwick

LEARNING TO LEARN

On the surface, and compared with general music teaching, instrumental instruction appears to be relatively uncomplicated by considerations of knowledge and value. I play an instrument; therefore I can show you or anyone else how to play it. But life is not quite so simple, and there is a great deal involved in any educational transaction. In many ways instrumental teaching seems a very haphazard affair with idiosyncratic extremes, depending on the individual teacher who can be somewhat isolated in the confines of the music room or studio. We may think that the instrumental student simply wants to learn to play an instrument, but what does that mean? There are ways of teaching the trombone or the bass guitar that open up the way into musical playing and musical understanding more effectively than others, that are either a part of an initiation process into musical discourse or are not.

Getting people to play any instrument without musical understanding – not really 'knowing music' – is an offence against human kind. It denies both feeling and cognition and under such conditions the world becomes meaningless. Discourse is stripped of significance, shorn of quality; intuitive understanding is driven out and the knife of technical analysis cuts away to the bare bone. Some of the most disturbing teaching I have witnessed has been in the instrumental studio, where – in a one-to-one relationship giving the teacher considerable power – a student can be confronted simultaneously by a complex page of notation, a bow in one hand and a violin in the other, along with exhortations to play in time, in tune, with a good tone. On the contrary, however, some of the very best teaching has been by instrumentalists. For example, take this case study, a description by Christine Jarvis of children at work as part of the Tower Hamlets project in London primary schools.

> The violins were tuned by the teacher while each child bowed the open-
> strings. This prepares children for the time when they are able to tune

their own instruments, familiarizing them with both the sound and the process, though in most group lessons violins are pre-tuned to save time. The teacher then distributed 'practise sheets' with four tunes written out in note names or Sol-fa.

The lesson proceeded with a revision of the bow-hold, and attention to general posture, followed by a performance of 'Hoe down', which was played once more. 'Cowboy chorus' was then performed several times, the children walking round in a circle as they played, three or four being invited to improvise answering phrases between each performance of the tune. The leader then introduced a sight-reading game, 'spin-a-tune', and a few minutes were spent reading through a piece, examining the rhythm and naming the notes before playing it.

The lesson continued with work on the D-major scale, first singing it to Sol-fa, then playing it using rhythms chosen by the children based on short sentences including colour, animal, action, place. Some amusing sentences were produced, making quite long rhythms. Posture and bow-hold were checked again, and the lesson concluded with 'Ringing bell' played with varied bowings, including tremolo and spiccato.

The pace was fast, with active involvement and lively participation of the children throughout. Teaching was very child-centred and made technical work fun by using a variety of games. The teacher always found things to which they could relate.

Group Lessons: The third and fourth years (ninety-two children in all) are usually divided into two groups for simultaneous lessons in the two school halls. On this occasion, with a Christmas concert looming, the morning began by rehearsing Christmas songs. The teaching team was present, as were all the class teachers involved. Eight songs were practised, some in a less traditional version, the words of one or two being adapted. For example in 'The 12 days of Christmas', five gold rings became five ripe mangoes, and so on. Other songs included two rounds and three other seasonal songs, two of which were sung as a duet. Attention was directed to intonation, and there was some rhythmic practise. The project teacher was helping to prepare all the classes in the school for the Christmas concert and was observed in a lively session with infants and nursery children in the afternoon, all class teachers being present.

Following the morning singing session, they divided into two string groups. The smaller group (seventeen violins and three cellos) were given a lesson centred on bowing technique in two pieces. Some time was spent practising slurred bowing in preparation for one of these pieces. Notation was also revised and fingering sung before playing pieces through. This lesson was more technical than the average large group session.

Meanwhile, the noticeably less-advanced large group (fifty-two children), rehearsed some items for the school Christmas concert. These included 'Hoe down' and open-string versions of both 'Jingle bells' and 'Silent night' with the melody played on the piano. A Bengali teacher learns the violin with the group, and one or two other class teachers were present, including the deputy head. This group do not have back-up lessons. The emphasis in this lesson was essentially on the enjoyment of the musical experience.

(Swanwick and Jarvis 1990: 27–8)

The teaching and learning described in this passage were fairly typical of sessions in the Tower Hamlets String Teaching Project, now unfortunately closed down through a policy of removing education budgets from town halls and putting money directly into schools. This remarkable scheme achieved an international reputation. The essence of the project was to bring a team of musician-teachers into regular contact with unselected classes of children in primary schools – mainly in the East End of London – and to make music a constant feature in the life of the school. The main lessons with whole classes of around twenty-five unselected children were backed up by work in smaller groups where there was a more technical focus. The complexities of playing a stringed instrument were not tackled by narrowing down attention to one way of approaching music or by confining activities to one style of practising or to hacking through a tutor book page by page. Musical learning in these schools took place through multi-faceted engagement: singing; playing; moving; listening to others; performing in different size groups; and integrating the various activities we associate with music. Those teachers responsible for bringing this about saw their job as teaching music through an instrument, not just teaching the instrument. They understood that musical knowledge has several strands, different levels of analysis; and they left space for intuitive engagement – where all knowledge begins and ends.

Even at the level of 'knowing how' – the psycho-motor technical management of an instrument – there are insights to be won into how we actually learn complex skills and sensitivities, gaining control over sound materials. The simple view of what happens would be to assume that a skilled action – say playing 'Hoe down' on a violin – is the result of tying together into one bundle a number of smaller technical bits into a larger whole, rather like making a broom or a peg rug. But do we really build up a technique from individual bristles, from atoms of muscular behaviour? The element of truth in this is rather small and needs a massive correction. Above all the performance of a skill requires a *plan*, a blueprint, a *schema*, an action pattern.

When I run towards a moving tennis ball – hoping to hit it back over the net – I am not just stringing together a number of totally separate physical movements of legs, arms, hand and so on. I am co-ordinating hand, eye and body into a unique variation on a known theme, called 'getting the ball back'. When I play a piece on the piano or trombone I am not only drawing on specific bits of knowledge but will be executing a plan, a blueprint, managing the piece in accordance with a set of requirements 'in my head', which unfolds and to some extent changes as we go along. Once I lose the thread of the plan – perhaps by getting behind in my musical thinking – or perhaps too far in front of the unfolding moment – then things tend to fall apart.

Building up a representation or *schema* seems to be facilitated by varied practices. For instance, I might stand in front of a dart-board or archery target practising hitting the bull's-eye. But if I always stand in exactly the same practice position with the same weight of arrow or dart and then eventually test myself with a fixed number of tries I am likely to be less successful than if I had the same number of practice shots from different distances, perhaps with differing weights of projectile. I am forming a *plan*, an image of how to throw at a dart-board or shoot at a target, not acquiring a set of automated muscular tricks from a fixed position. In any case, it is impossible to perform any action twice in exactly the same way. Seeing the target and feeling the action from differing perspectives helps me to get the plan in better shape; there seems to be more of mind at work. Variable practice has been shown to be important in *schema* formation (Schmidt, 1975). When teaching music, educators have always suspected this to be true and good instrumental teachers have found ways of getting their students to play the same material – perhaps scales or pieces – slowly, quickly, detached, *legato*, in dotted rhythms, with accents falling in different places, using alternative fingerings or hand positions and so on. This variety and depth of approach was characteristic of the Tower Hamlets project, where children clapped, moved, played, sang and listened to music.

We are also helped to form plans by the use of metaphors, mental images, mind pictures of the action. For example, I want to take hold of a cello bow in a way that conforms both to the shape of my hand and the stick and allows me maximum flexibility and control in action. One fairly common approach seems to be to try to sort out the position of each finger in turn, perhaps having a teacher move my hand about or place appropriate fingers at the right angles and in the right places. But that would be the teacher's plan, not *mine* and things are likely to go wrong when I am left on my own. Alternatively, I could put my hand in a 'pretend' bucket of water and shake off the drops – now the hand and arm are free and loose. Then – following an idea of Phyllis Young – I might imagine that I take up a fairly soft strawberry between thumb and second finger, applying this 'plan' to the bow itself (Young, 1978). Through a series of metaphors and drawing on an existing repertoire of movements, I come to be in control of my own bow-hold and will have begun to generate a *schema* or plan of my own – a mental picture which can be refined and further developed. In developing images of action a student is learning how to manage music, becoming autonomous, learning how to learn. How different all this is from a teacher pushing my fingers around – something that is done to me rather than anything that *I* am doing. Unfortunately it seems that much instrumental teaching tends not to be informed by this realization.

Fiona Pacey studied the effect of introducing varied practice over an eight-week period, during which a number of young string players between the ages of eight and twelve were asked to work with their teachers to test out the strength of the hypothesis (Pacey, 1993). In one of a number of experimental projects the particular set of sound materials to be brought further under control concerned loudness levels: the ability to play a passage quietly or loudly, a skill in string playing which depends crucially on the movement and weight of the right arm, the speed and amount of bow and, of course, the monitoring ear. After some weeks of 'normal' teaching, the teachers moved to a more intensive variable practice schedule, where, during three sessions, they had the students use a great variety of bowing actions using several parts of the bow. In organizing practice towards this end the teachers did not limit themselves to practising only the required simple *forte* and *piano* difference. That would be rather like always standing at the same position during target practice. Before and after this intervention, each pupil was recorded on tape playing the tune 'Lightly row', a relatively easy piece marked with required changes of loudness level indicated by *f* and *p*, in basic notation which they all understood.

Example 1 'Lightly row'

Altogether there were forty-seven instrumentalists playing violin, viola or cello and these were taught by nine different teachers in small groups. The project was organized within an overall time schedule that randomized the placing of the intervention of variable practice. So group 'A' began to work in this way after the third observation (recording); group 'B; after the second; and group 'C' after the fourth observation. Thus, although the whole project spanned eight weekly sessions, students from any single group were recorded in only six performances, the 'observations' – 'O'. For example, the schedule for Group 'A' was as follows.

$$O^1 \quad O^2 \quad O^3 \quad \text{INTERVENTION} \quad O^4 \quad O^5 \quad O^6$$

The research design is a time series based on product analysis – judges listening to the playing of the students. Repeated observations over a time series are a more ecologically sensitive way of gathering data than 'one-shot' testing. The situation is quite complex though and, as we might predict, there is a good deal of variance between individual pupils, those playing different instruments and groups with particular teachers. Seven independent observers – all teachers and members of performing groups – were asked to assess on a low to high continuum the level of success in playing *forte* and *piano*. Six performances of every student were presented to them on tape-recordings – in random order of course – with no prior knowledge

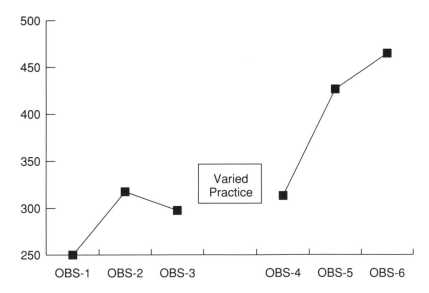

Figure 21.1 Control of loudness on string instruments: Group 'A' – seventeen players

of which student was which. The assessments of these 'judges' were then averaged to help us look for estimated change over time.

As expected, there is a general upward trend over the six occasions of measurement. We always tend to optimistically assume that playing improves over time and with teaching. Taking all three groups together there was a suggestion that the slope of the upward trend increased slightly after the intervention point, though because of the relatively small numbers involved and the complications of pupil, teacher and instrumental variables this cannot be confirmed to a level of statistical significance.

It is worth looking more carefully at one of the larger groups – the seventeen pupils in group 'A'. With this group the introduction of varied practice began at the end of the third session, just following the third observation (recording). The next session included quite a range of varied practice with different bow lengths and this was continued into the fifth session, at the end of which the fourth observation took place. Figure 21.1 shows the pattern of change for students in this group.

Inspection of these data suggests a fairly sharp increase in the upward slope after the intervention with the varied practice programme. Looking a little closer at the data, we can also see a difference between those students whose earlier performances of 'Lightly row' were rated by the expert judges to be on the low side in terms of loudness control and those whose performances from the start were already perceived to demonstrate

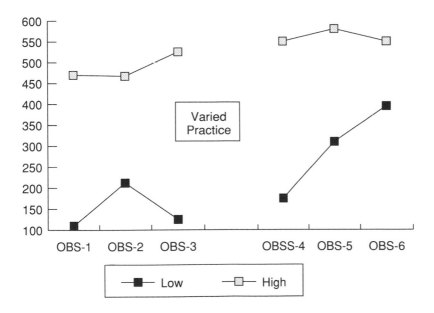

Figure 21.2 Control of loudness on string instruments: high and low starts

control of the bow to produce different loudness levels. Figure 21.2 shows this pattern. It is interesting if not surprising to notice that those students given initial high ratings by the teacher-judges appear to change little over time. There is obviously a limit to the amount of improvement to be expected beyond what is already a good performance. After a time any task gets to be insignificant in its level of challenge. However, the ten students with first-time lower ratings produce a steep climb in managing changes of loudness level following the intervention as can be seen in Figure 20.2.

Variable practice in this case really did seem to pay off, though mostly for those students who initially were not able to manage control of loud and soft playing so very well, while the more advanced students appeared to improve hardly at all. This is not so surprising; we are hardly likely to become more fluent in a skill which is already well under control. Such results are encouraging, an analysis of what we already intuitively suspect to be true, carried out as far as possible under research conditions. Approaching technical control from several different angles facilitates learning. It makes sense. If I can play a piece in only one way – perhaps at one speed with one level of articulation – then things are like to go adrift fairly easily and the whole thing can break down when something untoward happens. But if I have practised altering the expressive character by adjusting speed, accentuation and relative loudness levels, then not only is my technique likely to be improved but the chances of an interesting performance are raised. Musical decisions are being taken.

Giving time to experiment with music in various ways does two things. First it lets in the prospect of intuitive insights, unconsciously coming to new ways of approaching the performance; second, it supplies alternative slices of analysis, bringing to consciousness a broader repertoire of expressive possibilities. Often it seems that instrumental students are confronted with one technical hurdle after another with little musical gratification on the way, no sense of accomplishment and hardly any chance to make performance judgements for themselves. Playing becomes mindless and routine, and musical knowledge is neither gained nor projected to an audience. Two educational settings are especially likely to produce this unhappy state of affairs; one is the individual lesson and the other the very large group with one instructor. In the first there is a tendency to be pushed mainly into technical mastery to the exclusion of musical judgements; in the second it is all too easy to become another cog in a machine.

An account by Kevin Thompson of his study of instrumental teachers at work suggests that attention tends to be focused on aural, manipulative and notational skills and on teaching technical terminology. Figure 21.3 shows the proportion of time spent by four fairly typical teachers in various ways during weekly lessons over one month. These students were aged between nine and twelve years and they were playing wind, brass and string instruments.

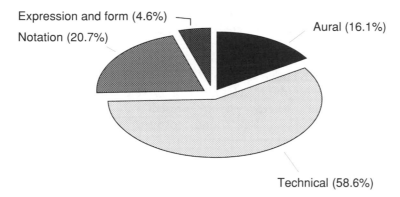

Expression and form (4.6%)

Notation (20.7%)

Aural (16.1%)

Technical (58.6%)

Figure 21.3 Use of time in instrumental lessons: four teachers observed four times

The emphasis within instrumental teaching that we see here is pretty clear. Technical work and technical talk seems to be the order of the day and there may be good reasons for this. Sessions are often short and teachers want to be sure that students are getting into 'good habits'. Without technique nothing is possible. Since technique itself appears to be enhanced by varied practice, we need to be sure that we are not just grinding away within a narrow set of routines. Playing passages in one way may not be the best way to meet even the limited aim of acquiring a manipulative skill. In general, it would be better to have students play more pieces in different ways and at lower levels of manipulative difficulty, than always to press on relentlessly with the next exacting assignment, a strategy which leaves no time for intuition or analysis and keeps the discourse in the studio fixed on the level of mastery of materials.

GROUP INTERACTION

One way of broadening the instrumental teaching agenda is through work in groups. I ought to make it clear that I am not advocating group teaching exclusively, nor am I denigrating the private teacher. I simply want to draw attention to some of the potential benefits of group teaching as just one valuable strategy in instrumental instruction. To begin with, music-making in groups has infinite possibilities for broadening the range of experience, including critical assessment of the playing of others and a sense of performance. Music is not only performed in a social context but is learned and understood in such a context. Music and music learning involves building up plans, images, *schemata*, through ways of thinking, practising, playing and responding; learning by imitation of and comparison with other people. We are strongly motivated by observing others and we strive to emulate our peers, often with a more direct effect than being instructed by those persons designated as 'teachers'. Imitation and emulation are particularly strong between people of similar ages and social groups. The basic requirements for anyone playing an instrument are careful listening and perceptive watching. A group with a good teacher is an ideal circumstance for the development of these attitudes. We might think of 'master-classes' where everyone present can learn something. Giving attention to someone else's sound, posture, style of playing and technical achievement, is all part of group motivation; so is the stimulation of other people's triumphs and the consolation of recognizing their difficulties. There is here scope for intuitive knowledge, learning by osmosis.

Group teaching is not at all the same as teaching individuals who happen to be scheduled in a group, giving attention to each of them, say, on the basis of ten minutes each over half an hour. Working with a group is a totally different form of educational endeavour. To start with, the teacher has to be especially alert. There can be no casual drifting into lessons without previous preparation. There can be no listening with half an ear whilst looking out of the window, consulting the diary of engagements or attending to the length of one's fingernails. There are constant questions to be addressed. What is the next stage of development and where do we go from here? How do we involve all students at all times?

Involvement does not mean only the physical activity of playing the instrument. In a group, an important activity will be listening and diagnosing, discussing and trying-out. One of the most striking things about good group teaching is this degree and range of participation of all group members. Every teacher will remember the kind of experience where we feel, 'If only so-and-so were able to hear this', or 'how much time might be saved if I could get all these people together'. Group-teaching does not exclude individual help and is certainly not 'anti-technique'. Kevin Thompson observed his four teacher-colleagues at work with individual students and also with groups of up to eight people. By systematically observing an individual in each group who was 'matched' as closely as possible with a student having individual lessons, Thompson found that:

> individual and group-taught students received more or less the same spread of time to the various aspects of learning in music, with the exception of notational skills. In spite of group-taught students having received less time in this category, their level of achievement in fluency of notation was disproportionately high. Perhaps teachers made fewer repetitive statements in group settings and saved instructional time. This, coupled with the possibility of learning from others, may account for the alacrity with which the group-taught students acquired notational skills.
> (Thompson, 1984: 168–9)

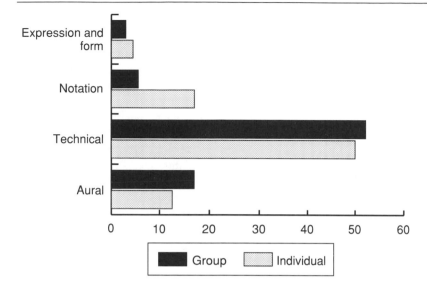

Figure 21.4 Group and individual teaching: focus of attention

No more time was spent 'off task' or setting up equipment in group settings than in individual lessons and Thompson observed that, while students in groups seemed to be acquiring a wider range of skills in more varied musical and social conditions, the teachers behaved very differently when working with groups, with positive changes in levels of preparedness, interaction and personal dynamism. From interviews he conducted with fourteen experienced group instrumental teachers, he concluded that they saw instrumental groups as educationally valuable rather than as an economical necessity and that working with groups was the preferred mode of teaching, though they recognized the necessity at times for individual instruction.

Resistance to instrumental group-teaching most often comes from those who have come through music schools and conservatoires where the one-to-one ratio is jealously preserved and no other alternative seems feasible. Yet we recognize that people can learn a great deal by sitting next to other players in a brass band, guitar class, a rock group, or as a member of a chorus. There is an obvious example here in the school and college bands of North America. In these essentially large-scale teaching groups of mixed instruments, people learn much of their playing technique and stylistic understanding from within the group itself. I would not advocate this necessarily as the best way of organizing instrumental learning but refer to it merely in order to point out that the one-to-one way of working is an extreme at the opposite end of a spectrum.

How much time in lessons is spent on common problems? Is there anything to be learned from regular participation in a small ensemble? Are there not dull lessons when both teacher and pupil feel lethargic, tired, uninspired and might not a group even out the ups and downs of personal temperament and present a constantly stimulating challenge to teachers who are really interested in teaching?

It is unwise to teach individuals on a kind of deficit model; they bring along their mistakes to the lesson and we try to sort them out. This is neither possible nor desirable in a group setting. Good group teachers know how to structure sessions to avoid mistakes and misunderstanding from the outset. A group should be large enough to be a potential music-making ensemble but small enough for any individual to play a distinctive part. A number somewhere between six and fifteen tends to be seen as optimum by those who work with groups. The major requirement is that the teacher has to prepare beforehand; the major benefit is that – under the cover of a group environment – the pupil can be learning on the intuitive side as well as taking part in a range of analytical work that will lead towards student autonomy, freedom from the teacher.

LITERACY OR FLUENCY?

Staff notation seems to have a curious effect on musical behaviour and it certainly has a strong influence on instrumental teaching and playing. The greatest virtue of written signs is their potential for communicating certain details of performance that would easily be lost in aural transmission, just forgotten. Imagine what would happen if the production and preservation of any large-scale classical symphonies had been entirely dependent on the collective memories of composers and performing groups. It is inconceivable that many if any of these works could have been composed at all without the visual maps and designs that constitute the making of a score. But imagine also what happens if these scores are converted either by machine or by mechanical playing into sound, as for example, in the distinctive regularity of fair-ground organs. Without aural performance traditions, most expressive and structural shaping is missing. Worse, imagine the consequences of insisting on notating jazz, rock, a *raga* improvisation or almost any folk music *before* performance. Such a needless exercise would impede fluency and stifle creative thought. Yet in instrumental teaching within the western classical tradition, notational 'literacy' is thought to be essential and thus notation is often central to instruction and is frequently the starting point.

This apparent tension between improvisation and notation has bothered educators for some time. Consider Kodály: 'millions are condemned to musical illiteracy, falling prey to the poorest of music' (Kodály, 1974: 119–204). He thought that every child by the year 2000 should be able to read music and every detail of his *Choral Method* leads towards this goal. On the other hand, for Dalcroze, music reading came second to feeling music in movement. Orff considered notation to be important but his emphasis is on making music rather than reading it. Although Kodály advocated improvisation we hear very little about it in the *Choral Method*. For Dalcroze, improvisation had a very important function, to awaken the 'motor tactile consciousness'. For Orff the central principle of his *Schulwerk* was not the performance of written-out music with ready-made accompaniments but, as he said a 'continuous inventing', though imitation is the 'beginning of improvisation'. Orff is looking for a 'spontaneous art of discovery with a hundred ways and a thousand possible structures' (Thomas in Keetman, 1974: 13).

Music educators and other musicians do seem to agree that one goal of music education should be to help people to develop what is sometimes called the 'inner ear', a 'dynamic library' of musical possibilities which we draw on in performance. Jazz musicians certainly have strong views on improvisation. I made notes at a conference I was chairing in London, where jazz players extolled the virtues and essential nature of improvisation. In brief summary, the collective wisdom of this group appeared to be as follows:

- everyone can improvise from the first day of playing;
- the basic principle is to have something fixed and something free, the fixed including scale, riff, chord, chord sequence and – crucially – beat;
- it is possible to make great music at any technical level;
- use systems but beware of fixed, rigid teaching strategies;
- imitation is necessary for invention and copying by ear is a creative effort;
- improvisation is characterized by problem-solving and a high level of personal interaction;
- there is no consensus as to how people can be helped to practise improvisation – commitment leads to self-tuition and the motivation is 'delight';
- improvisation is self-transcending not self-indulgent and the product matters, we make contact with something beyond our own experience, it makes demands upon the way we listen;
- the secret of playing jazz is the aural building of a 'dynamic library'.

There is no mention of notation here, yet once again we can identify the intuition/analysis dialectic. Improvising is the development and demonstration of a retrieval system and intuition is its essential process. The spotlight of the mind that searches what we already know for what is relevant *at this time* is guided, not by conscious thought, but by intuitive scanning. But as we know, intuitive knowledge can only grow if it is complemented by analytical mapping; and this includes identifying the 'something fixed', both channelling and extending the way we listen. 'Copying', imitating, are themselves acts of analysis where we sift out certain elements for attention – those things we want to emulate. Varied practice is also analytical, a way of consciously extending the dynamic library, cataloguing, classifying, building up a *schema*, an action pattern.

The 'inner ear' is essentially the forming of music images and this faculty is developed through the interaction of intuitive musical expression and analytical sifting. All musical performance is inevitably 'playing by ear' and an astute analysis of this curious term by Philip Priest brings out clearly the diverse educational activities that fall under the common terminology. His definition of 'playing by ear' is comprehensive: 'all playing that takes place without notation being used at the time' (Priest, 1989). The categories below point to some of the various possibilities:

- memorized signs, where the player's memory of the notation from which the music has been learned is used as a visual aid;
- imagined signs, where the player constructs such signs for the first time as an aid to finding pitch notes;
- imitation of a model (seen and heard), where both the physical actions and sounds they produce are observed and copied;
- imitation of a model (heard only), the copying of a pattern or tune based on what is heard – whether live or recorded;
- imitation of imagined sound, where the player attempts to reproduce remembered tunes or patterns;
- improvised variation, altering the original music (read or remembered) by elaboration but keeping to the structure;
- invention within a framework, playing from a sketch (chord symbols or figured bass) in the prevailing rhythm and style;
- invention with no framework, sometimes called extemporization, the player being free to choose every aspect of the music;
- experimental invention, discovering sounds and nuances new to the player and perhaps to music.

(Priest, 1989: 174)

Priest derives a pedagogical model from this – seen in Figure 21.5 – an analysis which greatly assists us to envisage a range and depth of teaching possibilities.

Musical activities often involve more than one of the processes shown in Figure 21.5 at the same time and any player may be more or less conscious of them – more or less intuitive or analytical. Analysis takes place whenever we stop to think, sort out a fingering or choose to separate out a strand or section for practise. Using notation of any kind is always a form of analysis; certain elements of music are abstracted, taken out of the dynamic library for inspection and given special attention, perhaps pitch or rhythm relationships or chord sequences. As Priest says, it has been assumed among music educators that skill with musical notation with its implicit underlying

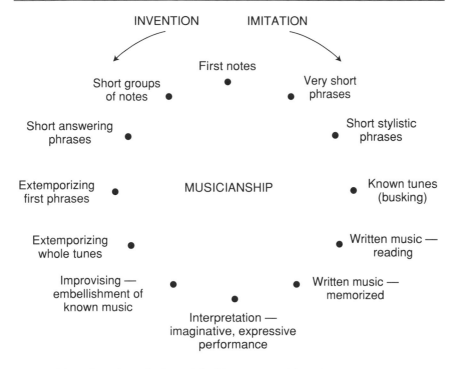

INVENTION   IMITATION

First notes
●

Short groups   Very short
of notes   ●   ●   phrases

Short answering   Short stylistic
phrases   ●   ●   phrases

Extemporizing   ●   MUSICIANSHIP   Known tunes
first phrases   ●   (busking)

Extemporizing   ●   Written music —
whole tunes   ●   reading

Improvising —   ●   Written music —
embellishment of   ●   memorized
known music   ●

Interpretation —
imaginative, expressive
performance

Figure 21.5   A pedagogical model of instrumental learning
Source: Priest (1989)

analysis is essential for an 'understanding' of music. The concept of
'musicianship' in music curricula is often closely tied in with notational
skills and certain limited kinds of aural tests. Yet the value of notation as a
remembering and transmitting device is not always needed and is now more
than ever under question, thanks to micro-technology and especially
sophisticated recording techniques. In much music-making it is no longer
essential. As an analytical performance and compositional tool it can have
value but only if the analysis is in the first place and ultimately aural. Priest
again:

> Naming notes and recognizing signs are *ancillary* skills for a player, not
> essential to performance nor to understanding if by understanding we
> mean *thinking in sounds* and *being able to appreciate and convey artistic expression
> through music.*

(Priest, 1989: 175; italics in original)

The alternative may be that students just 'bark at print' – a phrase used to
refer to reading out aloud without any real sense of meaning. Listening to
some students practising the piano is rather like have me read Mandarin

from a phonetic transcription. I would have no idea what it means and it must sound dreadful. There must be better ways.

THE FOURTH FINGER ON THE A STRING

Daniel is seven. He now has a half-size cello which not only looks wonderful but can – in the right hands – sound well too. Why a cello? Someone came to his school and played one. Thereafter he wanted to play 'a big instrument like the cello'. When taken to the first half of a concert which included Strauss's *First Horn Concerto* and seated on the front row, he resolutely ignored the horn soloist in front of his nose and scrutinized the celli. Why this should be is hard to know. Visual and aural images of instrumentalists playing seem to linger in the memory and perhaps there are ranges of instrumental sonority that seek out particular people as if to say 'Hi! you're on my wavelength, my sound spectrum coincides with your way of taking the world'. Sound materials are wonderfully compelling, even before the music starts. They are the beginning and the end of musical experience.

We have a recommended tutor book but, when getting him started at home, I am puzzled by the titles of the pages: 'fourth finger on the A string', and by the captions within pages: 'the bow-hold', 'ledger lines', 'basic knowledge' (which turns out to be about the notation of the bass clef), 'the minim', 'the semibreve rest'. This particular slice of musical analysis fails to captivate Daniel and it worries me.

I do not even play the cello, beyond the most elementary level, but I have worked intensively with string players and I think I know what matters. They care about the sound they make, they know that string sonorities can be powerfully evocative and that the instruments have all sorts of potential (how near the bow is to the bridge or fingerboard, which part of the bow is appropriate, off or on the string) and they like their playing to be coherent, structured. Just wandering through a piece is no way to play it.

So we begin. 'Pluck each string in turn four times – yes anchor your right thumb lightly against the side of the finger-board'. Now let's get the bow to work. 'Try pulling it across the "C" string and then pushing it back again' (first getting the fresh strawberry hold) and 'feel the sound in your chest'. 'Now the next string'. I am soon becoming a pianist expert in vernacular patterns based on the open strings of the cello, and these figures organize our music-making. They include horn calls, dramatic *tremolo*, flowing divisions of the beat that lead us on to the next change of string and Latin American rhythm patterns (especially the *habanera* or *tango*) that seem to fall under the bow so effectively. We are making music and it is the first lesson. In time we shall explore other sets of sound, including the up and down patterns of left-hand fingers on the A string – especially the difference between C and C# which so strongly affects expressive character.

This personal account – a small case-study description, a thumb-nail sketch of an encounter with music – serves only to press the point that instrumental teaching must be *musical* teaching, not merely technical instruction on the instrument. There is no point in teaching music at all unless we believe that it is a form of human discourse and that the beginning instrumental player is being initiated from 'day one' into this discourse and not into 'the semibreve rest'. Analysis on only a narrow technical level and without intuitive response leads nowhere. Perhaps this is why so many instrumental students give up. In *Music, Mind and Education* I characterized the apparent analysis/intuitive rift as a tension between instruction and encounter.

> this tension between instruction and encounter is both inevitable and fertile. These apparently contradictory aspects of human learning are the positive and negative poles between which the electricity of educational transactions flow. Encounter and instruction correspond with the left and right of the musical spiral, with the natural ebb and flow of musical experience. To some extent, it is possible to proceed by instruction in the acquisition of manipulative skills, vernacular conventions, idiomatic traditions, systematic procedures. Here, learning can be more easily structured and sequenced. But it is encounter that characterizes the left-hand side: sensory impression, personal expression, structural speculation and symbolic veneration. Here, the student needs to be left alone with possibilities, many of which will exist thanks to some instructional framing. Theories and practice of music education that fail to acknowledge a dynamic relationship between left and right, leave us trying to clap with one hand.
>
> (Swanwick, 1988: 135)

Rule number one: no lesson is in order without music and music means delight and control of materials, heightened awareness of expression and whenever possible the delight of good form. A session without music is time wasted and the wrong message is taken away – that it is sometimes in order to play unmusically. It is *never* in order.

Rule number two: always go for intuitive fluency before analytical literacy. In the early days at least, music should be articulated freely before sorting out notation. We do not need the limited analysis of a printed copy in front of our faces *every* time we play. Aural awareness precedes and is the foundation, the real 'rudiments of music'; it is also the end-game of musical knowledge.

Rule number three: by all means push but also pull. Students can be drawn into what they sense to be worthwhile. How well do we and other people play for and with the student? Is music an invitation? Students need to feel that what they do contributes to sustaining human mind, we all do.

Instruction without encounter, analysis without intuition, artistic craft without aesthetic pleasure; these are recipes for educational disaster. Meaningless action is worse than no activity at all and leads to confusion and apathy, whereas meaning generates its own models and motivation and in so doing frees the student from the teacher. Thus we take charge of our own learning; there is no other way.

REFERENCES

Keetman, G. (1974) *Elementaria: First Acquaintance with Orff-Schulwerk*, London. Schott.

Pacey, F. (1993) 'Schema theory and the effect of variable practice in string teaching', *British Journal of Music Education* 10(2).

Priest, P. (1989) 'Playing by ear: its nature and application to instrumental learning', *British Journal of Music Education* 6(2): 173–91.

Schmidt, R. A. (1975) 'A schema theory of discrete motor skill learning', *Psychological Review* 82(4).

Swanwick, K. (1988) *Music, Mind and Education*, London: Routledge.

Swanwick, K. and Jarvis, C. (1990) *The Tower Hamlets String Teaching Project: A Research Report* London: University of London, Institute of Education.

Thompson, K. (1984) 'An analysis of group instrumental music teaching', *British Journal of Music Education* 1(2): 153–71.

Young, P. (1978) *Playing the String Game*, Austin: University of Texas.

Part V

Music education and research

Chapter 22

Some observations on research and music education

Keith Swanwick

THE IMPORTANCE OF RESEARCH

It is generally accepted that research is a 'good' thing to do. Indeed, some of us have research activities written into our terms of employment, as though the fact of engaging in some kind of investigation automatically conferred a distinctive status and *raison d'être* on an academic. Why is this so?

I would suggest that good research has at least three positive outcomes. The first is that a researcher's own teaching and professional practice is illuminated by the activity; the second, that the professional community is strengthened by deeper knowledge and understanding; and the third is that we are better equipped to respond to the challenges of forward-planning and accountability.

This last requirement became very evident in the UK, when at a Gulbenkian Conference, The Arts and Higher Education, we discovered that we just did not know to what extent the arts were being affected by cuts in education, or even what the base-line of provision was from which to estimate any reduction in services being offered to the community in schools and colleges.[1] The same is true of music education in schools. Have we really enough evidence to say that schools are a unique and vital agent in music education and that music opportunities and insights would be denied to young people if programmes were reduced or abolished? The answer is not as obvious as it may appear. Other people may point to massive opportunities outside of schools, to community organizations, to informal music making and especially to the mass-media, bringing all kinds of music within easy reach of all sorts of people. There is little research information with which either to counter such statements or to support them. Such debate therefore becomes ideological rather than intellectual.

RESEARCH DEFINED

I do not subscribe to the idea that all research is worthwhile. There is bad research as well as good research, there is research which is shoddy, misleading or badly focused. For this reason, we need to establish some credentials for research in the field of music education and raise broad criteria by which to evaluate research.

It has been argued that research constitutes a limitless range of activities. For example, I have heard visual artists and composers claim that painting and composing are themselves research, in that the artist/musician explores new territory and creates new ideas, embodied in his or her work. Such activities are indeed exploratory but are they research in any useful sense of the term? Similarly, it is sometimes asserted that teachers are researching as they teach and develop curriculum ideas, just as a scientist is researching as a matter of course just by behaving scientifically.

I would want to say that there is an element of truth in this, to the extent that all professional activity implies a commitment to development. This, however, would not automatically constitute research. Take, for example, a medical doctor carrying out the professional responsibilities of diagnosis and treatment. There is certainly a good deal of professional development here arising out of cumulative clinical experience. The medical profession though, would not count this as research; it is lacking in systematic method among other things. However, many doctors do also undertake research and are often trained to do so in addition to their clinical and scientific training.

There seem to be at least four essential conditions which characterize research.

1 A particular problem or field of enquiry is identified and located in a wider context.
2 It is made explicit that the problem is to be viewed in a particular way: in other words, a conceptual framework is declared.
3 A methodology is articulated which promotes a certain level of objectivity. This involves a certain standing back and viewing our procedures from a critical position.
4 The results of the investigation are shared with others, often though not always formally published. This public sharing makes possible further discussion and sometimes replication of a study to re-examine the credibility of the findings.

In the light of this, it becomes fairly clear as to what research is not. It is not stating deeply held convictions without reasoning them through or presenting relevant evidence; it is not quoting the views of others without critical comment or synthesis; it is not the narration of selected anecdotes; nor is it expression of the obvious in difficult language. (There was once a German professor whose advice to research students was, *es muss etwas dunkel sein*).

A degree of objectivity, careful methodology and clarity of communication are the operational criteria, and the work must be seen to have relevance to the wider concerns of the field – music education in our case – and to stand on a strong conceptual framework. A review of available methodologies will bring out these points and raise other issues.

TRADITIONAL METHODOLOGIES

Conceptual clarification

Strictly speaking, establishing a conceptual framework, by logical analysis and synthesis, is not a discrete methodology. It is vital to all good research. Yet it is possible to conduct an enquiry that goes no further in methodological techniques than reasoned and structured argument based on the process of deduction. A philosopher or mathematician would usually work in this way. So to a certain extent might we when we address ourselves to such problems as 'what does it mean to be musically educated?' or 'is music education asthetic education?'. Work of this kind is very difficult to bring off well and easily drifts off into the mists of metaphysical speculation. Inevitably there is recourse to descriptive analogies, which have to be examined very closely for reliability, and to examples and illustrations, which need scrutiny to see if they are truly representative of the case under discussion. However, much useful work has yet to be done in conceptual 'ground clearing', and any piece of work, no matter how practical or empirical in methodology, has to be founded on and sustained by intelligent and honest deductions. Much confusion arises when concepts remain unexamined; for example, where words are taken at face value as meaning the same thing in spite of very different contexts. (An instance of this would be the unquestioning equation of 'literacy' in the wider sense with 'musical literacy').

Historical scholarship

Hitorical methodologies are closely related to conceptual ones in that deductive processes are brought to bear; this time on documentary evidence. One by-product of sifting older books and papers is the realization that many of our 'new' ideas have roots in the past and may, indeed, have received a better form of expression before we were born. For example, creativity and the development of imagination have been linked together and argued about long before Orff or more recent practitioners. (Not to go too far back, we might instance the brilliant *Essay on the Creative Imagination*, by Ribot.)[2]

The central element of historical scholarship though, is the willingness to go to primary material rather than secondary sources in order to tease out evidence from the documentation of the past. It often seems difficult to base any future action on such evidence. Yet it would be good to have the information required to engage in discussion with a Junior Education Minister who once declared that music education had been 'counter-productive', in that before music education became an accepted part of schooling our northern cities had more bands and choirs than they do today!

Above all, historical investigation lays before us a perspective in which to frame our present activities.

Experimental designs

The experimental tradition in research has become the accepted methodology for research in general, in spite of great difficulties caused by its indiscriminate application to problems in the social sciences. The reasons for the prestige of this, the 'horticultural' model, are easy to detect. We are offered a 'scientific' approach, induction from observed data. We plant cabbage seeds, try fertilizer 'A' on one batch and 'B' on another and measure the differences in growth. There are many statistical tests of significant variance and of correlation that enable us to accept or reject the null hypothesis that plant food 'A' does not bring about more growth than fertilizer 'B'.

Such procedures require us to strive after laboratory conditions where all the subordinate variables (heat, humidity, light) are steadily controlled, allowing us to manipulate the 'independent' variable (the type of fertilizer) and measure the 'dependent' variable (the size of the cabbages). We ought to be able to check for reliability by replicating the experiment and, if the findings are to be useful, to confidently claim that the materials and conditions of the experiment are close enough to life outside of the laboratory to have a general external validity (all or most cabbages would benefit from preparation 'A' even if planted in other soils).

It seems important to re-state the obvious here in order to notice difficulties about this model for education in general and music education in particular. Research in education is not usually carried out under laboratory conditions. We cannot talk about 'the learner' as we talk about 'the cabbage'. The student is much more than a learner, whereas the vegetable is no more than a cabbage. Any attempt therefore to specify an experimental model for, say, curriculum development, is problematic from the start.

Furthermore, the measurement of organic growth, while easy with a rule calibrated in centimetres, is not easily transferred to a setting where there is no accepted index of measurement. With what rule do we measure liking for music, technical efficiency, aesthetic understanding, or grasp of style? Small wonder that of all the investigative possibilities opened up by Seashore in his seminal book, the testing of aural discriminations has received perhaps more than its fair share of research attention.[3] This plethora of music 'ability' tests springs from the possibility of estimating where discrimination gives out in tasks of increasing refinement. In other words, measurement looks to be possible. Unfortunately, it is the task which is calibrated in more of these cases, not an independent objective instrument of measurement, and this gives rise to all sorts of anomalies in interpreting results. For instance, is it true with tests of pitch discrimination, where the subject is to indicate which of two tones is lower or higher, that more errors are made when the intervals are smaller? In many cases, probably not: the element of guessing is too strong in such a design. Or again, can we really deduce from test results that rhythmic ability develops before melodic memory and both before harmonic awareness? Certainly not, since we do not know whether the 'rule' we use for rhythm is marked out in the same intervals as the one used for melody or for harmony. All we can say is that subjects score higher grades on one of our tests than on another. The separate tests may be on totally different scales of difficulty. We have no way of knowing.

These remarks are intended only to draw attention to some of the difficulties of experimental procedure in the social sciences. There is indeed ample scope for developing and modifying these methodologies for our own use, but we shall need to train ourselves to use them well and retain a clear vision of what music education is about if we are not to focus on small, even trivial events, clumsily demonstrating the obvious and often missing important variables that pass unnoticed. (There is a classic story of the experimenter who took two groups of grasshoppers and applied glue to the undersides of one group. When he thumped the table he noticed that only the other group jumped. He concluded that glue makes grasshoppers deaf!) We certainly are required to find the right questions before attempting any answers.

Survey techniques

A good deal of research in education is of the survey kind, intended to tease out the level of various forms of provision, the conditions under which people work and attitudes towards other people, subjects, schools and so on. We are all familiar with the ubiquitous questionnaire which may have small questions cunningly designed to camouflage the large question. From a series of short statements of point of view it is possible to determine where a teacher 'fits' into a spectrum, from, let us say, 'progressive' to 'traditional' teaching styles.[4]

Survey techniques do uncover certain kinds of information and they offer the possibility of examining a large statistical sample across a representative population. However, the same tendency to triviality and inconsequentiality can be observed as with experimental methodologies. Furthermore, we are one step removed from experiment or observation, in that we do not ourselves chronicle the behaviour of the subjects but ask them to describe their own attitudes and possible actions. In so doing we run the risk of losing or distorting evidence, since people tend to give answers that reinforce their self-image and will generally claim to be more liberal, to be more positive, to care more and to work harder than is often the case.[5] Imagine the difference between a written description of what takes place in a school music programme, compared with what actually happens. Now imagine that the written description is structured by a series of short items on a questionnaire. We are obviously likely to lose verisimilitude in this process, unless the questionnaire is very carefully designed indeed.

ETHNOGRAPHIC METHODOLOGIES

In order to ease some of the difficulties and doubts relating to traditional research methodologies, and to try to capture the complex richness of the educational transaction, many researchers have turned to ethnographic methodologies. These are characterized by fieldwork, a degree of immersion in the total life-situation and correspondingly less 'distance' between researchers and subjects. To some degree the researcher 'lives with the tribe', or at least examines the artefacts of a group of people (*ethnos* = people or race; *graphy* = description). Several techniques are available within this style of research and they are frequently used in combination to refine observation in a 'natural' setting.

Product evaluation

Here we look at or listen to what is made, said or played; transcripts of conversations, tape-recorded musical excerpts and verbal impressions of particular events. In order to preserve some degree of objectivity it is essential to follow certain procedures in the evaluation of the 'products'. One of these is that the impression of the event, or product, should be neutrally recorded. Interpretation may follow, but must never be intertwined with description. Another safeguard is that, whenever possible, more than one observer or 'judge' should register an impression. We have found that the use of a small number of expert judges can be seen to yield inter-observer reliability in a number of music education settings. Recently, one of the writer's research students found that teachers experienced in music and with young children could determine with a high degree of statistical reliability the ages of children by year from age three to nine, by listening to randomized tapes of their musical creations. This allows us to assume that there is a recognizable sequence of development and to press on with an analysis of what kind of stages may be involved and what kind of activities may further the developmental process.

Systematic observation

It is often preferable to look at what we wish to investigate through a systematic filter rather than to register a general impression. A classic case of such a framework is Flander's Interaction Analysis, where the amount and type of classroom talk is qualified and quantified by use of time-sampling and ten pre-determined categories of communication.[6] Such methods have much to offer in illuminating the musical classroom transaction. One of the writer's students time-sampled the degree to which composition, performance, audition, skill development and literature studies seemed to be emphasized over several sessions of observation in middle schools. (The conceptual model for this can be found in *A Basis for Music Education*.)[7] He found that the greatest proportion of time was spent in the development of skills *per se*, much more, in fact, than the teachers themselves predicted would be the case.

There are, of course, many variations and degrees of systematized observation, including critical event sampling and the subversive monitoring of the behaviour of two or three people in a group who remain unaware of their special 'target' role. Both of these devices reduce the observational task to manageable proportions. A combination of time-sampling and pupil-sampling (within a group) along with a systematically evolved model of musical behaviours has helped another of our students to compare outcomes between individual and group instrumental instruction.

Case studies

Case studies have been described as 'strong in reality but difficult to organize'.[8] A case may be an individual or even an institution. The study of several cases makes it possible to make provisional and tentative comparisons, though never to look for statistical 'trends'. It is also possible to examine a case or two in depth in preparation for more systematic research with larger numbers. However, such studies do have validity without further development of this kind, though it is often difficult to interpret the information or get beyond the merely descriptive, and this is essential for good quality research.

A great deal of valuable pioneering work has been undertaken on the basis of case observation. Freud and Piaget, for instance, generated extremely important theoretical frameworks from a limited number of cases; patients and children respectively. Under these conditions, case studies not only stimulate the development of a conceptual framework, but also provide us with a large supply of 'for instances'; we may experience a 'shock of recognition' as we hear them described —the illustration lights up the concept for us.

The preservation of an objective distance with case studies becomes problematic at times. The adoption of what has been called a triangulation procedure can help, when the perceptions of teacher, pupils and a neutral observer are all taken into account in analysing an event, a lesson, rehearsal, or whatever. In my own department, valuable work has been done on a case study basis, where, for example, professional musicians who began their musical activities in the Salvation Army describe the various processes involved, or when a small number of 'music lovers' describe why and how they came to value music. There are things to be learned here, about motivation, self-instruction and value-systems, that inform music educators working in whatever field.

Participant observation

The careful reader may notice that we have moved from the most detached form of research – conceptual analysis – through the rigours of experimental design and structured observation, becoming more and more involved with the people we seek to study. Participant observation is almost the final degree of involvement before our criteria – identifying a field, declaring a conceptual framework, articulating a methodology and publication of results – cease to be met. To be an active participant, for example a teacher in a school or college, and at the same time to unobtrusively structure and evaluate descriptions of what is taking place around us, is the most difficult and sensitive of tasks. We may even set out to study and evaluate our own practice, though we would be wise to use some independent witness(es). If we ourselves become so involved as part of the assessment field, then we might properly describe this as action research. Here the information is certainly rich but most probably unmanageable.

Many attempted participant or action schemes have failed to deliver, simply because objective reporting is almost impossible and the external validity of the 'findings' – the way they may be transposed to other times and places – is almost nil. It is all too easy to end up with data chasing a hypothesis, or with data highly selected to fit a hypothesis. If this turns out to be so, we ought to forget the idea of research and get on with teaching and music!

It may seem strange to have spent time on this brief resumé of methodologies, well known as they are to many workers in psychology and the other social sciences. However, I am persuaded that music educators may not be quite so aware of the range of possibilities and of the debate about methodologies which is evident elsewhere.

In London we have been able to develop an eclectic view which serves us well in a field as complex and potentially rich as music education. We have also identified the need for research training, which is one essential purpose behind our MA degree in Music Education. Life is too short to encourage attempts at Ph.D. level work without preliminary research experience.

Not all research is for academic honours and a great deal of helpful data has been brought together by other groups and individuals. 'The teacher as researcher' has become something of a catchphrase in the UK. In many instances this seems to mean the teacher as curriculum developer, and this is indeed an essential professional element of teaching, though not research in any helpful way of defining the term. In other cases there has been a real contribution to our understanding of why things are, how things 'work' and how to do things better. In other words, the teacher can be a researcher, but only if certain criteria are met, otherwise the word research becomes meaningless by abuse.

In conclusion I should draw attention to general areas where research is needed. There are probably only three that are central to music education.

The first is to do with people, our students. How do they 'tick' musically speaking? What are their attitudes to music? How do children musically develop? What counts as achievement in music?

The second area is to do with music. What kind of experiences constitute musical experience? Is there a deep structure to this experience that transcends local and historical differences of style and form? What are the keys that unlock the doors to particular idioms?

The third area is to do with the social or institutional context, where music and students meet. Are schools appropriate places for what kinds of musical activities? How can different ethnic and cultural groups relate together to different kinds of music? What sized groupings are optimum for special purposes?

In an article of this kind the level of generality has had to be fairly high. It is hoped that the reader will feel that this is appropriate for the first issue of a new journal. Included in subsequent issues we presumably may see a focus on specific research issues and illuminating findings. I hope too that such work is discussed, rather than merely noted; for the strength of a profession is indicated by a willingness to test each other's assumptions.

Francis Bacon said, 'we are more likely to reach the truth through error than through confusion'. Even error can be expressed in a clear and lively way and is more easily recognized for what it is when stripped of unnecessary jargon.

NOTES

1 *The Arts and Higher Education*, edited by K. Robinson, Gulbenkian Foundation, UK, 1982.
2 Th. Ribot, *Essay on the Creative Imagination*, trans. A. H. N. Baron, Chicago, 1906.
3 C. E. Seashore, *Psychology of Music*, 1938, Dover edn, NY, 1967.
4 N. Bennett, *Teaching Styles and Pupil Progress*, Open Books, London, 1976.
5 A. A. M. Oppenheim, *Questionnaire Design and Attitude Measurement*, Heinemann, London, 1966.

6 N. A. Flanders, *Analysing Teacher Behaviour*, Addison-Wesley, Reading, MA, 1970.
7 K. Swanwick, *A Basis for Music Education*, NFER, UK, 1979.
8 Adelman *et al.*, 'Re-thinking case studies: notes from the second Cambridge Conference', *Cambridge Journal of Education* 6(3), 1976.

Acknowledgements

Chapter 1 *Onward from Butler*, by Bernarr Rainbow (1985), reproduced by permission of the author and The Curwen Institute.

Chapter 2 'Music education and the National Curriculum', by Keith Swanwick (1992), from *The London File*, Papers from the Institute of Education, published by the Tufnell Press, reproduced by permission of the author.

Chapter 3 'Developmental psychology and music education' by David Hargreaves (1986), reproduced by permission of the author, the Society for Research in Psychology of Music and Music Education and the editor of *Psychology of Music*.

Chapter 4 'Music education and the natural learning model' by Margaret Barrett (1992), from *International Journal of Music Education*, 20. This article is reproduced by permission of the International Society for Music Education. For further information about membership of ISME, its Conferences and Publications, please contact ICRME, University of Reading, Bulmershe Court, Reading, RG6 1HY.

Chapter 5 'In search of a child's musical imagination', by Robert Walker (1988), from *Imagination and Education*, reproduced by permission of the Teachers' College Press.

Chapter 6 'Creativity as creative thinking', by Peter R. Webster, in *Music Educators' Journal*, May 1990. © Copyright 1990 by Music Educators National Conference. Reprinted with permission.

Chapter 7 'Creativity and special needs: a suggested framework for technology applications', by David Collins (1992), from *British Journal of Music Education*, 9, reproduced by permission from Cambridge University Press.

Chapter 8 'Musical development in the primary years', by Janet Mills (1992), in *Music in the Primary Years*, reproduced by permission of Cambridge University Press.

Chapter 9 'Gender, musical meaning and education', by Lucy Green (1994), from *Philosophy of Education Review* 2 (2), reproduced by permission of the author and first presented at the International Symposium II, Philosophy of Music Education, Toronto, 12–16 June, 1994.

Chapter 10 'Music with emotionally disturbed children', by Yvonne Packer (1989), in *British Journal of Music Education* 6(9), reproduced by permission of Cambridge University Press.

Chapter 11 'Music education and a European dimension', by Janet Hoskyns (1992), in *British Journal of Music Education*, 9, reproduced by permission of Cambridge University Press.

Chapter 12 'Concepts of world music and their integration within western secondary music education', by Jonathan Stock (1994), in *International Journal of*

Music Education 23. This article is reproduced by permission of the International Society for Music Education. For further information about membership of ISME, its Conferences and Publications, please contact ICRME, University of Reading, Bulmershe Court, Reading, RG6 1HY.

Chapter 14 'Music as I see it', by George Odam (1987), in *International Journal of Music Education* 10 (3). This article is reproduced by permission of the International Society for Music Education. For further information about membership of ISME, its Conferences and Publications, please contact ICRME, University of Reading, Bulmershe Court, Reading, RG6 1HY.

Chapter 15 'Classroom management for beginning music educators', by Margaret Merrion (1991), in *Music Educators' Journal*, October 1991. © Copyright 1990 by Music Educators National Conference. Reprinted with permission.

Chapter 16 'RX for technophobia', by Kirk Kassner (1990), in *Music Educators' Journal*, November 1988. © Copyright 1990 by Music Educators National Conference. Reprinted with permission.

Chapter 17 'MIDI-assisted composing in your classroom', by Sam Reese (1995), in *Music Educators' Journal*, January 1995. © Copyright 1990 by Music Educators National Conference. Reprinted with permission.

Chapter 18 'Putting listening first: a case of priorities', by Philip Priest (1993), in *British Journal of Music Education*, 10, reproduced by permission of Cambridge University Press.

Chapter 19 'Designing a teaching model for popular music', by Peter Dunbar-Hall (1993), in *International Journal of Music Education* 21. This article is reproduced by permission of the International Society for Music Education. For further information about membership of ISME, its Conferences and Publications, please contact ICRME, University of Reading, Bulmershe Court, Reading, RG6 1HY.

Chapter 20 'Classroom improvisation', by Derek Bailey, in *Improvisation: Its Nature and Practice in Music* (2nd edition) (1992), reproduced by permission of The British Library Board.

Chapter 21 'Instrumental teaching as music teaching', by Keith Swanwick, in *Musical Knowledge* (1994), reproduced by permission of Routledge.

Chapter 22 'Some observations on research and music education', by Keith Swanwick (1983), in *International Journal of Music Education* 1. This article is reproduced by permission of the International Society for Music Education. For further information about membership of ISME, its Conferences and Publications, please contact ICRME, University of Reading, Bulmershe Court, Reading, RG6 1HY.

Notes on sources

Chapter 1   B. Rainbow (1985) *Onward from Butler*, Coventry, Curwen Publications.

Chapter 2   K. Swanwick (1992) 'Music education before the National Curriculum', *The London File*, London, University of London, Institute of Education and Tufnell Press.

Chapter 3   D. Hargreaves (1986) 'The developmental psychology of music education: scopes and aims', *Psychology of Music* 14 (2).

Chapter 4   M. Barrett (1992) 'Music education and the natural learning model', *International Journal of Music Education* 20.

Chapter 5   R. Walker (1988), Milton Keynes, Open University Press.

Chapter 6   P. Webster (1990) 'Creativity as creative thinking', *Music Educators' Journal*, May 1990.

Chapter 7   D. Collins (1992) 'Creativity and special needs: a suggested framework for technology applications', *British Journal of Music Education* 9.

Chapter 8   J. Mills (1992) 'Musical development in the primary years', in *Music in the Primary Years*, Cambridge, Cambridge University Press.

Chapter 9   L. Green (1994) 'Gender, musical meaning and education', *Philosophy of Education Review* 2 (2).

Chapter 10   Y. Packer (1989) 'Music with emotionally disturbed children', *British Journal of Music Education* 6 (9).

Chapter 11   J. Hoskins (1992) 'Music education and a European dimension', *British Journal of Music Education* 9.

Chapter 12   J. Stock (1994) 'Concepts of world music and their integration within western secondary music education', *International Journal of Music Education* 23.

Chapter 13   Commissioned for this volume.

Chapter 14   G. Odam (1987) 'Music education as I see it: a report of an interview with a seventeen-year-old student concerning his music education', *International Journal of Music Education* 10 (3).

Chapter 15   M. Merrion (1991) 'Classroom management for beginning music educators', *Music Educators' Journal*, October 1991.

Chapter 16   K. Kassner (1988) 'RX for technophobia', *Music Educators' Journal*, November 1988.

Chapter 17   S. Reese (1995) 'MIDI-assisted composing in your classroom', *Music Educators' Journal*, January 1995.

Chapter 18   P. Priest (1993) 'Putting listening first: a case of priorities', *British Journal of Music Education* 10.

Chapter 19   P. Dunbar-Hall (1993) 'Designing a teaching model for popular music', *International Journal of Music Education* 21.

Chapter 20   D. Bailey (1992) 'Classroom improvisation', in *Improvisation: Its Nature and Practice in Music* (2nd edition), London, British Library National Sound Archive.

Chapter 21   K. Swanwick (1994) 'Instrumental teaching as music teaching', in *Musical Knowledge*, London, Routledge.

Chapter 22   K. Swanwick (1983) 'Some observations on research and music education', *International Journal of Music Education* 1.

Index